Harper's
Grammar of French

Harper's Grammar of French

Samuel N. Rosenberg
Mona Tobin Houston
Richard A. Carr
John K. Hyde
Marvin Dale Moody
Edward W. Najam
Indiana University, Bloomington

1817

HARPER & ROW, PUBLISHERS, New York
Cambridge, Philadelphia, San Francisco,
London, Mexico City, São Paulo, Sydney

Sponsoring Editor: Alan McClare
Project Editor: Brigitte Pelner
Designer: Madalyn Hart
Production Manager: Marion A. Palen
Compositor: Waldman Graphics, Inc.
Printer and Binder: R. R. Donnelley & Sons Co.

Harper's Grammar of French

Library of Congress Cataloging in Publication Data

Main entry under title:

Harper's grammar of French.

Includes index.
1. French language—Grammar—1950-   . I. Rosenberg, Samuel N.
PC2112.H32   1983   448.2'421   82-21281
ISBN 0-06-045581-0

Contents

Preface

This book arose out of a lack we perceived in teaching our third-year under-graduate course in advanced grammar and composition. We needed a work that would combine the detail of a comprehensive reference grammar with readings and exercises developing proficiency in the written language. After several versions, in both French and English, all tested in the classroom, the book has emerged not only as a text but also as a reference work whose use-fulness goes well beyond the confines of any particular course. English, speaking directly to a public of Anglophones, has proved to be the appropriate and reasonable vehicle of presentation.

Our twofold purpose is reflected in the organization of the book, which presents first a complete, autonomous grammar of French and then a *Work-book* channeling the grammar into classroom use. The chapters of the grammar are defined, rather traditionally, by forms and syntax. The pedagogical mate-rials, presented in the *Workbook*, consist of twentieth-century readings in light literature with exercises focusing on vocabulary and including *thèmes d'imita-tion*. Intertwined with these ten readings are twenty lessons, which comprise both phrasal and sentence-long exercises on particular points of grammar. For the exercises accompanying the readings and the lessons in the *Workbook*, authoritative monolingual and bilingual dictionaries are indispensable.

The grammar is presented in pragmatic, rather than theoretical, terms. We have done our best to avoid excessively abstract or complicated, jargon-filled explanations and have tried to make the illustrative examples carry much of the expository burden. Except for those instances where schematic examples seemed fitting, the examples are more full than is customary, lexi-cally richer, and stylistically more varied. They express a real world of com-munication, in which the literature and high culture of France are not viewed as the inevitable central interest of all people studying French. They take for granted that French is used globally and that it is used to speak of a vast spectrum of human concerns. The translations—and all the example sentences are translated—offer the same naturalness of idiom. They are not meant to reflect the construction of the French sentences but rather their meaning and tone, and they may thus also serve to introduce users of the book to prob-lems of translation. Obviously, both examples and translations, as well as the grammatical exposition, will reward careful attention.

The book is intended for a year-long course at the advanced level, fol-lowing our order of presentation of readings and lessons. The *Workbook* con-tains ten pedagogical units, each consisting of one reading and two lessons.

We recommend that the *thème d'imitation* found at the end of each reading be assigned as a review after the two lessons of that unit.

Please note that, in the text, lists of examples are representative rather than exhaustive, unless specified otherwise.

The collaborators—Richard A. Carr, Mona T. Houston, John K. Hyde, Marvin D. Moody, Edward W. Najam, and Samuel N. Rosenberg—express their thanks to Thomas Vessely and to their colleague Roy E. Leake, Jr., for very useful assistance.

1

Verbs

The verb in French has an infinitive, one or more stems, and two participles, from which all verb tenses are derived.

I. TENSES OF THE INDICATIVE*

A. The present

1. **Forms.** The present indicative is formed by adding to the verb stem an ending which indicates person and number.

   a. In the singular, there are two sets of endings; in the plural, all verbs take the same set of endings.

      i. **-er** verbs, as well as **ouvrir, couvrir, offrir, souffrir, assaillir, défaillir, tressaillir, cueillir,** and their compounds.

Singular	*Plural*
-e	-ons
-es	-ez
-e	-ent

Note that there is one exception: **aller—je vais, tu vas, elle va, ils vont.**

      ii. All other verbs.

Singular	*Plural*
-s	-ons
-s	-ez
-t	-ent

---

*The discussion of tenses in this section will focus on the active voice and will treat pronominal verbs only tangentially, although what is said here about the uses of the tenses of the indicative is equally applicable to the passive and to pronominals. For comprehensive treatment of the passive voice, see Section IV; for pronominal verbs, see Section III.

Note that there are several exceptions.

avoir—j'ai, il a, elles ont
(re)dire—vous (re)dites
être—nous sommes, vous êtes, ils sont
faire (and compounds)—vous faites, ils font
pouvoir—je peux, tu peux
(con)vaincre—il (con)vainc
valoir—je vaux, tu vaux
vouloir—je veux, tu veux

Note, too, that the **-t** of the singular is not added if the stem ends in **-t** or **-d: elle met, on vend.**

    b. Verbs may be classified according to the number of present stems which they have.

        i. *One-stem verbs.* Most verbs have one present stem, formed by dropping the infinitive ending.

        (a) all **-er** verbs (except **aller**—see Section iii. below): **montrer → montr-.**
        (b) **-ir** verbs like **ouvrir** (see Section 1.a.i. above): **ouvrir → ouvr-.**
        (c) **-re** verbs like **attendre: attendre → attend-;** these include the following verbs and their compounds: **fondre, correspondre, répondre, fendre, descendre, entendre, prétendre, rendre, pendre, répandre, perdre, mordre, tordre, rompre**
        (d) **vêtir** and its compounds: **vêtir vêt-.**

        See also Appendix 2 for orthographical changes in the stems of some of the above verbs.

        ii. *Two-stem verbs.* Some verbs have two stems, a long stem for the plural and a short stem for the singular. Such verbs fall into one of the following categories:

        (a) long stem based on infinitive: **mettre → mett-/met-, dormir → dorm-/dor-.**
        All verbs in **-ttre** are conjugated like **mettre;** the following **-ir** verbs and their compounds are conjugated like **dormir: partir, sortir, mentir, sentir, servir, (se) repentir**
        (b) long stem in **-ss-: finir → finiss-/fini-, connaître → connaiss-/connai-.**
        Most **-ir** verbs are conjugated like **finir** (except **vêtir** and those listed in Section 1.a.i.); all verbs in **-ître** are conjugated like **connaître** (see, however, Appendix 2 for the placement of the circumflex in such verbs).
        (c) long stem in **-s-: conduire → conduis-/condui-.**
        The following verbs and their compounds are conjugated like **conduire: construire, cuire, déduire, instruire, nuire, introduire, produire, réduire, séduire, traduire, lire, dire** (except: **vous (re)dites), suffire, plaire, (se) taire**

(d) long stem in **-gn-: rejoindre** → **rejoign-/rejoin-**.

All verbs in **-indre** are conjugated like **rejoindre**.

iii.   *Verbs with three or more stems*

vou l oir		**pou v oir**		**de v oir**	
nous vou	l ons	nous pou	v ons	nous de	v ons
vous vou	l ez	vous pou	v ez	vous de	v ez
ils veu	l ent	elles peu	v ent	elles doi	v ent
je veu	x	je peu	x*	je doi	s
tu veu	x	tu peu	x	tu doi	s
il veu	t	elle peu	t	elle doi	t

ve n ir		**pren d re**		**fai re**	
nous ve	n ons	nous pren	ons	nous fai	s ons
vous ve	n ez	vous pren	ez	vous fai	t es
ils vien	n ent	ils pren	n ent	elles font	
je vien	s	je pren	d s	je fai	s
tu vien	s	tu pren	d s	tu fai	s
il vien	t	il pren	d	elle fai	t

av oir		**être**		**all er**	
nous av	ons	nous sommes		nous all	ons
vous av	ez	vous êt	es	vous all	ez
ils ont		elles sont		ils vont	
j' ai		je sui	s	je vai	s
tu a	s	tu e	s	tu va	s
il a		elle es	t	il va	

Compounds of the above verbs are conjugated in the same way; **tenir** and its compounds are conjugated like **venir**. For other irregular verbs, see Appendix 3.

2.   **General uses of the present.** French has only one present indicative whereas English has three (two in negative sentences).

Elle parle italien.   *She is speaking Italian.*
     She does speak Italian.
     She speaks Italian.

Elle parle italien?   *Is she speaking Italian?*
     Does she speak Italian?
     She speaks Italian?

*****Pouvoir** has another first person singular form, **puis,** which may be used in place of **je peux** and which is required in inverted forms: **Puis-je vous dire un mot?** (*May I have a word with you?*)

Elle ne parle pas italien.   *She isn't speaking Italian.*
                                She doesn't speak Italian.

The present indicative in French, as in English, has a strict meaning as well as a broad or figurative sense.

a. In the strict sense, the present may express an action or a state occurring at the moment of speaking.

Qu'est-ce que vous faites? —Je range mes affaires.
What are you doing? —I'm putting my things away.

En ce moment, son père regarde la télévision.
Right now his father is watching television.

Voici l'autobus qui arrive.
Here comes the bus.

La porte est ouverte.
The door is open.

Je ne me sens pas très bien.
I don't feel very well.

Tu aimes faire la cuisine?
Do you like to cook?

To emphasize that an action is in progress, **être en train de** + infinitive is used. This expression occurs only in the present and imperfect tenses and is far less frequent than the present progressive in English, as in *I'm doing, he is watching.*

Je suis en train de ranger mes affaires.
I'm [in the process of] putting my things away.

Son père est en train de regarder la télévision.
His father is [busy] watching television.

b. In a broader sense, the present may indicate the habitual or permanent aspect of an occurrence, without reference to a specific time. In addition, it may refer to the future.

   i. *Habit or permanence*

Ces ouvriers ne travaillent pas le week-end.
These workers don't work on weekends.

Avant de se coucher, elle prend une infusion.
Before going to bed, she always has a cup of tea.

Chez qui allez-vous pour acheter une robe?
Where do you go to buy a dress?

Le français est plus facile que l'espagnol, selon certains.
French is easier than Spanish, according to some people.

Elle préfère le vin rouge à la bière.
She prefers red wine to beer.

La terre tourne autour du soleil.
The earth revolves around the sun.

Deux et deux font quatre.
Two and two are four.

Qui ne risque rien n'a rien.
Nothing ventured, nothing gained.

La grammaire, c'est l'ensemble des règles à suivre pour parler
et écrire correctement une langue.
Grammar is the set of rules to be followed in order to speak and
write a language correctly.

ii. *Imminent futurity*

Mon train part à six heures.
My train is leaving (leaves) at six o'clock.

Elle se marie dans trois jours.
She's getting married in three days.

L'été prochain nous allons en Grèce.
Next summer we're going to Greece.

Je suis à vous dans un moment.
I'll be with you in a moment.

iii. *Future reference in si-clauses.* In **si**-clauses that express conditions, the present tense is used when the main clause is in the
future. English uses the present, the future, or the conditional
should in such cases.

Si vous acceptez, je serai bien content.
If you accept, I'll be very happy.

Nous viendrons de bonne heure demain si cela vous convient.
We'll come early tomorrow if that is (will be) all right with you.

S'il vient, je lui demanderai de vous attendre.
If he comes (should come), I'll ask him to wait for you.

Note that the future of the main clause may be replaced by the present to express the
direct and imminent consequence of a condition or occurrence.

Je crois que la petite a de la fièvre. —Eh bien, si elle a de la fièvre, j'appelle le
médecin.
I think she has a fever. —Well, if she has a fever, I'll call the doctor.

For the use of other tenses in sentences which express conditions, see Section VI.

3.   Special uses of the present. The French present tense, unlike the English, is sometimes used to express past time.

   a.   Common verbs of motion may be used in the present to refer to a recent past event. There is often an adverbial expression which situates the event in the past.

   Je viens vous dire que nous sommes prêts.
   I've come to tell you that we're ready.

   Marc sort justement de chez le coiffeur.
   Mark has just come out of the barber's.

Note that a recent past is most often expressed by **venir de** + infinitive; it is used only in the present and imperfect.

   Elle vient d'apprendre la mort de son chat et est tout à fait inconsolable.
   She has just learned of the death of her cat and is utterly inconsolable.

   b.   In literary style, the present is often used to express past events. This is called the historical present (**présent historique**) and is frequently used to make the account more lively, to involve the reader more directly in the events.

   Une foule de cavaliers français . . . s'étaient tirés de la bataille et rendus aux Anglais. En ce moment on vint dire au roi qu'un corps français pille ses bagages, et d'autre part il voit dans l'arrière-garde des Bretons ou Gascons qui faisaient mine de revenir sur lui. Il eut un moment de crainte. (Michelet)
   A crowd of French horsemen. . . .had withdrawn from the battle and surrendered to the English. At this moment, someone came to tell the king that a French unit was pillaging his baggage; at the same time, he saw some Bretons or Gascons in the rear-guard who looked as if they were going to come at him. He had a moment of fear.

   c.   For the use of the present with **depuis, il y a,** etc., see Section J.2.

B.   The future tense

 1.   Forms

   a.   *The simple future.* The simple future is formed by adding to the future stem an ending which indicates person and number.

i.   All verbs, regular and irregular, take the same endings.

Singular	*Plural*
-ai	-ons
-as	-ez
-a	-ont

ii.   The future stem of all verbs is constant through all persons and numbers.

(a) *Regular verbs.* The future stem of regular **-er** and **-ir** verbs is the infinitive; that of **-re** verbs is found by dropping **-e**: **montrer** → **montrer-, finir** → **finir-, attendre** → **attendr-, conduire** → **conduir-.**

See Appendix 2 for orthographic changes in the future stem of some **-er** verbs.

(b) *Irregular verbs.* The future stem of these verbs is unpredictable.

aller	ir-	pleuvoir	pleuvr-
avoir	aur-	pouvoir	pourr-
courir	courr-	recevoir	recevr-
cueillir	cueiller-	savoir	saur-
devoir	devr-	tenir	tiendr-
envoyer	enverr-	valoir	vaudr-
être	ser-	venir	viendr-
faire	fer-	voir	verr-
falloir	faudr-	vouloir	voudr-
mourir	mourr-		

b. *The immediate future:* present tense of **aller** + infinitive.

D'après toutes les indications, l'industrie du textile va traverser une période difficile.

According to all indications, the textile industry is going to go through a difficult time.

2. **General uses of the future.** The difference between the simple future and the immediate future is essentially like that between *will* and *be going to* in English.

a. *The immediate future*

i.   The immediate future often emphasizes the intent of the speaker at the present moment, implying that the event in question is somehow already in progress, at least in the mind of the speaker.

Je viens d'entendre un morceau de musique étonnant; je vais en chercher la partition demain.

I have just heard an astonishing piece of music; I am going to look for a score tomorrow.

ii.   Unlike English, if the event is going to occur immediately after the time of speaking, French uses the immediate future.

Vous ne comprenez pas? Eh bien, je vais vous l'expliquer.
You don't understand? Okay, I'll explain it to you.

See also Section A.2.b.ii. for the use of the present as an immediate future.

Note that the expression **être sur le point de** + infinitive may stress the imminence of an action.

Le train va partir bientôt.
The train is going to leave soon.

Le train est sur le point de partir.
The train is about to leave.

b. *The simple future** *

i.   While the immediate future emphasizes continuity with the present moment, the simple future merely indicates the occurrence of an event subsequent to the moment of speaking.

Je toucherai mon chèque à la fin du mois et je réglerai la facture à ce moment-là.
I will cash my check at the end of the month and I'll settle the bill then.

Un jour nous visiterons la lune, nous aussi.
Someday we too will travel to the moon.

ii.   **Ce que, ce qui, quand, lorsque, dès que, aussitôt que, comme, à peine, après que, tant que,** and **pendant que** are always followed by the future when the main clause is in the future or imperative and future time is implied.

Il agira comme il a toujours agi, c'est-à-dire, comme il lui plaira.
He will act as he has always acted, that is to say, as he pleases.

Appelez l'infirmier quand vous aurez besoin de lui.
Call the nurse when you need him.

---

*Care must be taken in translating English *will* to distinguish its use as an auxiliary to indicate the future and its uses as an equivalent to the French **vouloir.**

Will that help me understand the problem?
Est-ce que cela m'aidera à comprendre le problème?

This problem is very difficult, will you (are you willing to) explain it to me?
Ce problème est très difficile, voulez-vous me l'expliquer?

3. Special uses of the future

a. The future may be used as an imperative.

Pour la prochaine fois, vous lirez le deuxième chapitre.
For next time, read the second chapter.

b. The future is used after **si** (*whether*) if the context indicates a future and the main verb is one of indirect discourse, such as **savoir, ignorer, se demander.**

On ne saurait prévoir s'ils accepteront notre proposition.
We cannot predict whether they will accept our proposal.

Je ne sais pas s'il viendra ou non.
I don't know whether he's coming or not.

Nous vous demandons si elle pourra finir à temps.
We're wondering whether she can finish on time.

Note that, in other cases, *whether* may be expressed by **si** + present or **que** + subjunctive.

Il se portera candidat si cela convient (que cela convienne) au parti ou non.
He will be a candidate whether or not the party likes it.

c. The future (particularly of the verb **être**) is sometimes used to express probability.

Si elle n'est pas venue, c'est qu'elle sera souffrante.
If she hasn't come, she's probably ill.

Note that probability may be expressed by **devoir** + infinitive or by **sans doute.**

Elle doit être souffrante.
Elle est sans doute souffrante.
She is probably (must be) ill.

For the future in the past, see Section VI.B.1.

C. The future perfect

1. Forms. The future perfect is formed by combining the future of the auxiliary (**avoir** or **être**) with the past participle of the verb in question. The agreement of the past participle is made in the future perfect as in other compound tenses.

j'aurai donné	*I will have given*
tu te seras dépêché(e)	*you will have hurried*
elles seront allées	*they will have gone*

For the choice of auxiliary, formation of past participles, and agreement of past participles, see Section II.

2.   **General uses of the future perfect**

a.   The future perfect is used to refer to an event that will be over and done with at a given moment in the future.

Ne venez pas me chercher tout de suite; je n'aurai pas fini de faire mes valises avant midi.
Don't come for me right away; I won't have finished packing before noon.

Il n'a que 17 ans et bientôt, il aura écrit son premier roman!
He's only 17 and soon he'll have written his first novel!

En l'an 2000, tout aura changé.
By the year 2000, everything will have changed.

b.   The future perfect is used for the first of a sequence of events in the future, where the first must be completed before the second can take place. Most often, the future perfect is preceded by one of the following conjunctions:
quand, lorsque, dès que, aussitôt que, à peine, après que.

Quand j'aurai reçu de vos nouvelles, je serai tranquille.
I'll be relieved when I've heard from you.

Elle partira dès qu'elle aura mangé.
She'll leave as soon as she has eaten.

Note that, with certain verbs implying the attainment of a state, this strict sequence may not necessarily be observed.

Quand je trouverai une place, je vous ferai signe de la main.
When I find a seat, I'll wave to you.

Quand j'aurai trouvé une place, je vous ferai signe de la main.
When I've found a seat, I'll wave to you.

Après que tu auras ton diplôme, tu pourras chercher un appartement.
After you get your degree, you can look for your own apartment.

3.   **Special uses of the future perfect.** The future perfect is used to express probability with respect to a past event.

J'aurai laissé mes lunettes en haut. Cours vite me les chercher.
I must have left my glasses upstairs. Run up and get them for me.

Mon fils n'est pas venu dîner. Il sera sans doute rentré trop tard.
My son didn't come to dinner. He probably got back too late.

Note that the same meaning is conveyed by the **passé composé** of **devoir** followed by an infinitive, or by the use of **sans doute**.

J'ai dû laisser mes lunettes en haut.
I must have left my glasses upstairs.

Il est sans doute rentré trop tard.
He probably got back too late.

D. The *passé simple*

1. **Forms.** The **passé simple** (*simple past* or *past definite*) is formed by adding to the past stem of the verb an ending which indicates person and number.

    a. There are several sets of endings.

        i. **-er** verbs.

-ai	-âmes
-as	-âtes
-a	-èrent

        ii. **-ir** and most **-re** verbs.

-is	-îmes
-is	-îtes
-it	-irent

Note the following exceptions: **courir** and its compounds and **mourir,** for which see Section iii; **venir, tenir,** and their compounds take the following endings.

-ins	-înmes
-ins	-întes
-int	-inrent

      iii. **-oir** and some **-re** verbs (as well as **courir** and its compounds and **mourir**).

-us	-ûmes
-us	-ûtes
-ut	-urent

Note the following exceptions: **(s')asseoir** and **seoir, voir** and its compounds take the endings in Section ii. Note, however, that **pourvoir** takes the endings in **-u-.**

    b. The past stem of all verbs is constant throughout all persons and numbers.

        i. For **-er** and most **-ir** verbs, the stem to which the endings are added is the same as the stem of the infinitive: **aller → all-, mener → men-, finir → fin-, partir → part-.**

        ii. For other verbs, the past stem may be the same as the stem of the infinitive or may be different and sometimes unpredictable.

           (a) **-re** verbs like **attendre** (see Section A.1.b.i.): **attend-.**

(b) **-indre** verbs, such as **rejoindre** (see Section A.1.b.ii.): **rejoign-**.

(c) **-uire** verbs, such as **conduire** (see Section A.1.b.ii.): **conduis-**.

(d) **-cevoir** verbs: **recevoir → reç-**.

(e) **-loir** verbs: **vouloir → voul-**.

(f) **-aire** verbs: **faire → f-**.

(g) **-érir** verbs: **conquérir → conqu-**.

(h) **-ure** verbs: **conclure → concl-**.

(i) Other verbs, including:

avoir	e-	connaître	conn-
boire	b-	coudre	cous-
croire	cr-	écrire	écriv-
devoir	d-	naître	naqu-
dire	d-	résoudre	résol-
être	f-	suffire	suff-
lire	l-	vaincre	vainqu-
mettre	m-	vivre	véc-
pleuvoir	pl-		
pouvoir	p-		
prendre	pr-		
rire	r-		
savoir	s-		
voir	v-		

2. **Use of the *passé simple*.** The **passé simple** expresses a state or an event which is seen as localized in past time and as having no necessary relation to the present. The phenomenon is viewed as fully accomplished, whether at a given moment, at its beginning, at its end, or, globally, in a series of moments.

Le lendemain matin, le roi signa le décret.
The next morning, the king signed the decree.

Après leur expulsion, les exilés cherchèrent à construire une nouvelle société.
After their expulsion, the exiles sought to build a new society.

Jusqu'à leur mort, ils poursuivirent cet idéal.
Until their death, they pursued that ideal.

L'ambassadeur de France resta cinq ans en Suède.
The French ambassador remained in Sweden for five years.

Pendant ces cinq ans, il fit beaucoup de voyages dans les autres pays scandinaves.
During those five years, he made many trips to the other Scandinavian countries.

For further discussion of the **passé simple,** see Section E.3.

E.   The *passé composé*

1.   **Forms.** The **passé composé** (*past indefinite*) is formed by combining the present tense of the auxiliary (**avoir** or **être**) with the past participle of the verb in question.

j'ai donné   *I gave, I did give, I have given*
tu t'es dépêché(e)   *you hurried, you did hurry, you have hurried*
elles sont allées   *they went, they did go, they have gone*

For the choice of auxiliary, formation of past participles, and agreement of past participles, see Section II.

2.   **General uses of the *passé composé*.** The **passé composé** may express, just like the **passé simple,** an event or a state localized in past time and having no necessary relation to the present, or it may express a past event or state which has some bearing on the present.

a.   In the first of these functions, the **passé composé,** like the **passé simple,** is equivalent to the English simple past.

Le lendemain matin, le roi a signé le décret.
The next morning, the king signed the decree.

Après leur expulsion, les exilés ont cherché à construire une nouvelle société.
After their expulsion, the exiles sought to build a new society.

Jusqu'à leur mort, ils ont poursuivi cet idéal.
Until their death, they pursued that ideal.

L'ambassadeur de France est resté cinq ans en Suède.
The French ambassador remained in Sweden for five years.

Pendant ces cinq ans, il a fait beaucoup de voyages dans les autres pays scandinaves.
During those five years, he made many trips to the other Scandinavian countries.

b.   In the second of its functions, the **passé composé** cannot be replaced by the **passé simple;** It is equivalent to the English present perfect.

Depuis la semaine passée, elle a lu trois longs romans.
Since last week, she has read three long novels.

Il est temps de partir. N'as-tu pas terminé ton travail?
It is time to leave. Haven't you finished your work?

3.   **Contrast between the *passé composé* and the *passé simple*.** As indicated in Section 2.a., the **passé composé,** when it expresses the idea of a simple past, is synonymous with the **passé simple.** The

choice of one rather than the other is a matter of style and depends on context. In general, the **passé composé** belongs to conversation and informal written communication, while the **passé simple** is literary in tone and is used in sustained narration. In either case, there is no conflict with the imperfect, which expresses past time from a very different point of view; for the imperfect, see Section F.2.

4. **Special use of the *passé composé*.** The **passé composé** is sometimes used as the equivalent of the future perfect (see Section C.2.b.) and expresses an act about to be fully accomplished.

Ayez patience; j'ai fini (= j'aurai fini) dans un instant.
Be patient; I'll be done in a moment.

F. The imperfect

1. **Forms.** The imperfect is formed by adding to the present stem an ending which indicates person and number.

   a. All verbs take the same endings.

-ais	-ions
-ais	-iez
-ait	-aient

   b. The stem to which the endings are added is constant throughout all persons and numbers. It is always the same as the stem of the first-person plural of the present indicative (see Section A.1.b.): **montrer → montrons → montr-, finir → finissons → finiss-, dormir → dormons → dorm-, prendre → prenons → pren-, pouvoir → pouvons → pouv-.** There is one exception: **être → sommes → ét-.**

2. **General uses of the imperfect.** The imperfect, unlike the **passé simple** and **passé composé,** expresses a past state or event which is seen as nonlocalized in time. The phenomenon is viewed as being in progress rather than fully accomplished or as being indefinitely repeated. The imperfect is thus used to present the framework within which localized events or states (**passé simple** or **passé composé**) may be expressed. French tenses are such that the distinction between localized and nonlocalized past phenomena is necessarily expressed. This is unlike English, which often implies the distinction instead of making it explicit. The possible English equivalents of the French imperfect, the choice of which always depends upon a particular context, are—to use the verb *play* as an example—*played, did play, was playing, used to play, would play.*

   a. The imperfect may describe an entity in the past.

La maison de mon enfance, qui se trouvait à la campagne, était grande et confortable.
My childhood home, which was in the country, was large and comfortable.

b. The imperfect may denote an action or a state in progress when another event took place.

Il pleuvait. Elle se sentait triste. Qu'est-ce qu'elle pouvait faire? Elle a téléphoné à son ami.
It was raining. She felt (was feeling) sad. What could she do? She phoned her friend.

Il jouait du piano quand il a entendu frapper à la porte. C'était le facteur, qui portait une lettre recommandée. Il la lui a tendue.
He was playing the piano when he heard a knock at the door. It was the mailman, who had a registered letter. He handed it to him.

Quand j'avais cinq ans, ma famille a quitté la campagne pour la ville. Puisque nous n'avions pas beaucoup d'argent, il nous a fallu nous habituer à un tout petit appartement.
When I was five, my family left the country for the city. Since we did not have much money, we had to get accustomed to a very small apartment.

c. The imperfect may express habitual action or state in the past.

Quand j'étais étudiant, j'allais souvent au cinéma.
When I was a student, I often went (would often go) to the movies.

J'attendais avec impatience l'annonce de chaque nouveau film.
I used to wait (would wait) impatiently for the announcement of each new film.

Les westerns me plaisaient particulièrement, et j'étais toujours parmi les premiers spectateurs.
I liked westerns particularly, and I was always among the first to see them.

3. Special uses of the imperfect

a. Like an English past tense, the French imperfect may express an event seen as an imminent future with respect to a past occurrence. For a parallel use of the present for an immediate future, see Section A.2.b.ii.

Je me suis levé de bonne heure; mon train partait à six heures.
I got up early; my train was leaving at six a.m.

Elle avait beaucoup à faire puisqu'elle se faisait opérer dans trois jours.
She had a lot to do since she was having an operation in three days.

b. The imperfect is used after **si** to express a suggestion or a wish in an exclamation.

Si nous allions à la pêche!
Suppose we go (How about going) fishing!

Si je pouvais manger de la glace sans grossir!
If only I could eat ice cream without putting on weight!

c. For the use of the imperfect with **depuis, il y a,** etc., see Section J.2.b.

d. For the use of the imperfect in hypothetical statements with **si,** see Section VI.B.5.a.

e. For the difference in meaning between the imperfect and the **passé composé** or **passé simple** with such verbs as **devoir, pouvoir, vouloir, savoir,** see Section VII.

G.   The pluperfect

1.   Forms. The pluperfect is formed by combining the imperfect tense of the auxiliary (**avoir** or **être**) with the past participle of the verb in question.

j'avais donné   *I had given*
tu t'étais dépêché(e)   *you had hurried*
elles étaient allées   *they had gone*

For the choice of auxiliary, formation of the past participles, and agreement of past participles, see Section II.

2.   Uses of the pluperfect

a. The pluperfect expresses an event or state which took place before another event or state in the past. In combination with the imperfect, it may denote habitual prior action.

Bien avant son départ, elle avait terminé tout son travail.
Well before her departure, she had finished all her work.

Une fois qu'ils avaient retrouvé la bonne route, il n'était plus difficile de rentrer chez eux.
Once they had got back on the right road, it was not hard to return home.

Il avait plu toute la nuit, de sorte que le lendemain la ville était inondée.
It had rained all night, so that the next morning the town was flooded.

Après que la famille avait dîné, les enfants regardaient souvent une émission de télévision.
After the family had had dinner, the children would often watch a television program.

b. For the use of the pluperfect in hypothetical statements with **si,** see Section VI.B.5.a.

H.   The *passé antérieur*

1. **Forms.** The **passé antérieur** is formed by combining the **passé simple** of the auxiliary (**avoir** or **être**) with the past participle of the verb in question.

j'eus donné	*I had given*
tu te fus dépêché(e)	*you had hurried*
elles furent allées	*they had gone*

For the choice of auxiliary, formation of the past participles, and agreement of past participles, see Section II.

2. **Use.** Like the pluperfect, the **passé antérieur** denotes a past action or state prior to another past occurrence and is the equivalent of the English past perfect. However, it serves exclusively as a literary tense and is used only in conjunction with the **passé simple.** Moreover, it is used only in clauses introduced by the conjunctions **quand, lorsque, dès que, aussitôt que, après que, une fois que,** or the expression **à peine.**

Dès qu'elle eut parlé, elle s'assit.
As soon as she had spoken, she sat down.

A peine furent-ils arrivés que leur premier petit-fils naquit.
No sooner (Hardly) had they arrived than (when) their first grandson was born.

I.   The *passé surcomposé*

1. **Forms.** The **passé surcomposé** is formed by combining the **passé composé** of the auxiliary **avoir** with the past participle of the verb in question. Intransitive verbs taking the auxiliary **être** are generally not used in this construction; pronominal verbs are even rarer.

j'ai eu donné	*I had given*
(elles ont été allées)	*(they had gone)*

2. **Use.** The **passé surcomposé** occurs only in conversational use, where its function is the same as that of the **passé antérieur** in literary language. Just as the **passé antérieur** is used in conjunction with the **passé simple,** the **passé surcomposé** is used in conjunction with the **passé composé.**

Dès qu'elle a eu parlé, elle s'est assise.
As soon as she had spoken, she sat down.

J.   Special problems in tense selection

There are several instances where French regularly uses the present tense while English uses the present perfect (or present perfect progressive). There are parallel instances where French uses the imperfect while English uses the past perfect (or past perfect progressive).

1. Idiomatic expressions using only present and imperfect

    a. venir de + infinitive

        Nous venons de faire un travail énorme.
        We have just finished a huge job.

        Nous venions de finir un travail énorme.
        We had just finished a huge job.

    b. C'est (C'était) la . . . fois que

        C'est la première fois qu'on me pose une question pareille.
        It's the first time I have been asked such a question.

        C'était la dixième fois que le Président recevait le corps diploma-
        tique.
        It was the tenth time the President had received the diplomatic corps.

2. *Depuis, il y a,* etc.* Tense selection with these and related expressions of time depends upon the continuing or noncontinuing nature of the action or state to be expressed. In the case of continuing action or state, there is an important difference between French and English usage.

    a. In expressing an action or state begun in the past and continuing into the present, French uses the present tense.

    depuis

        Elle croit aux revenants depuis son enfance.
        She has believed in ghosts since her childhood.

        Je suis ici depuis ce matin.
        I have been here since this morning.

        Il dort depuis l'aube.
        He has been sleeping since dawn.

        Depuis qu'il se trouve à l'hôpital, sa santé fait de constants
        progrès.
        Since he has been in the hospital, his health has been making steady
        progress.

---

*For tenses with **pendant, pour,** and other expressions of time, see Chapter 15.

Depuis qu'il est entré à l'hôpital, sa santé fait de constants progrès.
Since he entered the hospital, his health has been making steady progress.

Depuis quand vend-on du bétail sur ce marché? —On en vend depuis 1957.
Since when have they been selling cattle at this market? —They've been selling them since 1957.

Depuis combien de temps étudiez-vous le français? —J'étudie le français depuis quelques mois.
How long have you been studying French? —I have been studying French for a few months.

Note that **depuis quand** (*since when*) asks for the starting point of an action or state, while **depuis combien de temps** (*how long*) asks for the duration of the action or state.

il y a . . . que

Il y a quelques mois seulement que j'étudie le français.
I have been studying French for only a few months. (It's been only a few months that I've been studying French.)

Combien de temps y a-t-il que vous êtes professeur à cette université?
How long have you been a professor at this university?

cela (ça) fait . . . que

Cela fait quelques mois seulement que j'étudie le français.
I have been studying French for only a few months. (It's been only a few months that I've been studying French.)

Ça fait combien de temps que vous êtes professeur à cette université?
How long have you been a professor at this university?

voilà . . . que

Voilà quelques mois seulement que j'étudie le français.
I have been studying French for only a few months. (It's been only a few months that I've been studying French.)

Note that the phrase appearing between **il y a/cela fait/voilà** and **que** necessarily denotes a block of time. Note, too, that **voilà** is not used interrogatively.

b. In expressing an action or state begun in the past and continuing up to a later past moment, which may or may not be specified, French uses the imperfect tense.

depuis

Il ne revoyait plus sa femme depuis leur rupture.
He had not been seeing his wife anymore since their breakup.

Depuis le retour de son mari, elle semblait contente d'une vie
passive, et puis un jour elle se révolta.
*Since her husband's return, she had seemed satisfied with a passive
life, and then one day she rebelled.*

Depuis quand travaillait-il à l'usine? Depuis l'âge de seize ans?
*Since when had he been working at the factory? Since the age of six-
teen?*

Depuis combien de temps dormait-il quand le réveil-matin a
sonné?
How long had he been sleeping when the alarm clock went off?

il y avait . . . que

Il y avait des heures qu'il lisait.
He had been reading for hours.

Combien de temps y avait-il qu'elle jouait de la flûte lorsqu'elle a
donné son premier récital?
*How long had she been playing the flute when she gave her first re-
cital?*

cela (ça) faisait . . . que

Cela faisait des heures qu'il lisait.
He had been reading for hours.

Ça faisait combien de temps qu'elle jouait de la flûte lorsqu'elle a
donné son premier récital?
*How long had she been playing the flute when she gave her first re-
cital?*

c. In the case of a noncontinuing past action or state, French uses
the **passé composé** or the pluperfect, as appropriate. There is
thus no difference between French and English tense usage.

Il n'a pas revu sa famille depuis la guerre.
He has not seen his family since the war.

Depuis quelques jours, j'ai lu trois romans et un poème épique.
*In the past few days (Since a few days ago), I have read three novels
and an epic poem.*

Combien de temps y a-t-il depuis que l'homme a mis pied pour la
première fois sur la lune?
How long has it been since man first stepped onto the moon?

Note that the negative in clauses following **il y a, il y avait, cela fait, cela faisait,** and **voilà** may be expressed by **ne** alone.

Voilà six mois qu'elle ne m'a [pas] écrit.
She has not written to me in six months. (It has been six months since she last wrote to me.)

Il y a longtemps que nous ne nous sommes [pas] revus.
We have not seen each other in a long time. (It has been a long time since we last saw each other.)

Cela faisait un bon moment qu'il n'était [pas] venu nous voir.
He had not come to see us in quite some time. (It had been quite some time since he had last come to see us.)

II. PAST PARTICIPLES

A. Forms

The past participle is normally formed by adding an ending to the infinitive stem. The forms below are all given in the masculine singular; the feminine singular is marked by the addition of **-e** and the plural by the addition of **-s,** except where otherwise noted.

(1) **-er** verbs take **-é: chanter** → **chanté.**
(2) **-ir** verbs take **-i: finir** → **fini, partir** → **parti.**
(3) **-re** verbs take **-u: rendre** → **rendu.**

Many verbs, however, particularly those ending in **-oir** and **-re,** have a past participle whose form is less predictable.

avoir	eu
devoir	dû (Note absence of circumflex in **dus, due, dues.**)
pleuvoir	plu
pouvoir	pu
recevoir	reçu
savoir	su
voir	vu
falloir	fallu
valoir	valu
vouloir	voulu
tenir	tenu
venir	venu
couvrir	couvert
offrir	offert
ouvrir	ouvert
souffrir	souffert

boire	bu
croire	cru
acquérir	acquis
conquérir	conquis
conduire	conduit
déduire	déduit
dire	dit
écrire	écrit
nuire	nui
rire	ri
suffire	suffi
conclure	conclu
inclure	inclu
plaire	plu
taire	tu
mettre	mis
prendre	pris
craindre	craint
feindre	feint
joindre	joint
peindre	peint
teindre	teint
absoudre	absous (Note feminine **absoute, absoutes.**)
moudre	moulu
résoudre	résolu
coudre	cousu
asseoir	assis
connaître	connu
courir	couru
être	été
faire	fait
lire	lu
mourir	mort
naître	né
vivre	vécu

B.   Uses of the past participle

In addition to its use in compound tenses (see Sections I.C., E., G., H., and I.), the past participle may function as an adjective, preposition, or adverb.

1. As an adjective, the past participle agrees in number and gender with the noun it modifies.

   un homme connu
   a well-known man

   une chaise recouverte de velours
   a chair covered in velvet (a velvet-covered chair)

   Les murs étaient peints en blanc.
   The walls were painted white.

   Elles revenaient du marché, chargées de bonnes choses à manger.
   They were coming back from the market, laden with good things to eat.

   Ses dettes payées, il a pu se remettre à son roman.
   *Once his debts had been paid (His debts paid), he could get back to his
       novel.*

   Une fois l'autoroute terminée, nous trouverons plus facile de nous
       rendre en ville.
   When the highway is finished, it will be easier for us to get to town.

2. Certain past participles function as prepositions when used before a noun. Their form is invariable.

attendu	*considering*
excepté	*except [for]*
passé	*past, beyond*
vu	*given, in view of*
y compris	*including*
étant donné	*given*

   Vu les circonstances, on peut l'excuser.
   In view of (Considering) the circumstances, we can excuse him (her).

   Passé la date, ce billet n'est plus valable.
   Past the date, this ticket is no longer valid.

Note that when these participles follow the noun, they show agreement in number and gender.

   Tous les périodiques, les quotidiens exceptés, se trouvent dans la salle de lecture
       au fond du couloir.
   All periodicals, except dailies, are in the reading room at the end of the corridor.

3. **Ci-annexé, ci-inclus,** and **ci-joint** may function as adverbs, in which case they are invariable. When they are used as adjectives, they show agreement with the noun they modify.

   Veuillez trouver ci-joint les documents que vous avez demandés.
   Please find attached the papers that you requested.

Les documents ci-joints sont ceux que vous avez demandés.
The documents attached (The attached documents) are those that you requested.

C. Agreement of the past participle in compound tenses

In certain instances, the past participle shows agreement in number and gender.

1. With the following intransitive verbs conjugated with **être,** the past participle agrees with the subject.

naître	*be born*	sortir	*go (come) out*
mourir	*die*	monter	*go (come) up*
décéder	*die*	descendre	*go (come) down*
arriver	*arrive, happen*	rentrer	*return*
partir	*leave*	retourner	*return, go back*
aller	*go*	entrer	*enter*
venir	*come*	tomber	*fall*
revenir	*come back*		
parvenir	*arrive*		
devenir	*become*		
rester	*stay, remain*		

Elle est partie.
She left.

Ils seraient descendus.
They would have gone (come) down.

Note that the verbs in the right-hand column may be used transitively, in which case the auxiliary is **avoir** and there is no agreement with the subject.

Ils auraient descendu l'escalier.
They would have come (gone) down the stairs.

Ils ont monté la malle.
They took (brought) up the trunk.

2. Certain intransitive verbs, such as the ones below, are conjugated with **avoir** or with **être.** When the auxiliary used is **être,** the past participle agrees with the subject.

accourir	*run up (to)*
apparaître	*appear*
atterrir	*land*
convenir	*agree*
demeurer	*remain, reside*
passer	*pass*
ressusciter	*revive*

En promenant son chien, elle a passé devant le chantier.
Walking her dog, she passed by the construction site.

Elle est passée me voir.
She stopped by to see me.
Nous avons demeuré dans cet immeuble pendant un an.
We lived in that building for a year.

Nous sommes demeurés dans la rue un bon moment à attendre un taxi.
We remained in the street a good while waiting for a taxi.

3. In the passive voice, the past participle agrees with the subject.

Toutes ces difficultés seront bientôt résolues.
All these difficulties will soon be resolved.

Les contrats ont été signés la semaine dernière.
The contracts were signed last week.

For detailed treatment of the passive, see Section IV.

4. With pronominal verbs, the past participle agrees with the reflexive pronoun, except when the pronoun represents an indirect object.

Les nageurs se sont enduits de graisse pour se protéger du froid.
The swimmers covered themselves with grease to protect themselves from the cold.

S'étant intéressée à l'informatique, elle a fait un stage de dix semaines.
Having become interested in computer science, she attended a ten-week training session.

Les conservateurs se sont aperçus de la perte d'un tableau.
The curators noticed the loss of a painting.

Au bout de sa première année de travail, elle s'est offert une voiture.
At the end of her first year of work, she treated herself to a car.

Nous nous sommes creusé la tête à chercher un cadeau convenable.
We racked our brains looking for a suitable present.

For detailed treatment of pronominal verbs, see Section III.

5. With all transitive verbs, including transitive pronominals (see Section 4.), the past participle agrees with a preceding direct object.

Quels journaux as-tu lus pendant ton séjour en France?
Which newspapers did you read while you were in France?

Je les ai déjà vus, ces films-là.
I've already seen those films.

La chambre qu'il avait louée donnait sur la cour.
The room he had rented looked out on the courtyard.

On comprend souvent mal les pénitences que se sont imposées les saints.
We often have trouble understanding the penances that the saints imposed upon themselves.

Certain verbs conjugated with **avoir** may take an adverbial complement of time, measure, or distance instead of a direct object. They are intransitive, and their past participles show no agreement.

courir	*run*
coûter	*cost*
dormir	*sleep*
durer	*last*
marcher	*walk*
mesurer	*measure*
peser	*weigh*
régner	*reign*
valoir	*be worth*
vivre	*live*

Les trois heures que j'ai dormi m'ont fait beaucoup de bien.
The three hours I slept did me a lot of good.

Les années qu'il a vécu dans le Midi ont beaucoup contribué à sa peinture.*
The years he lived in the south of France contributed a great deal to his painting.

When **courir, coûter, peser, valoir,** and **vivre** are used with nouns that do not express measurement, they function as transitives and their past participles show agreement as with other preceding direct objects.

La course qu'il a courue l'a épuisé.
The race he ran exhausted him.

Les vingt kilomètres qu'il a couru l'ont épuisé.
The twenty kilometers he ran exhausted him.

---

*Compare, with agreement:

Les années qu'il a passées . . .
The years he spent . . .

Les résultats compensent les peines que m'a coûtées ce tableau.
The results make up for the trouble that this painting cost me.

Les 25 francs qu'a coûté ce médicament seront remboursés par la Sécurité Sociale.
The 25 francs that this medicine cost will be reimbursed by the national health insurance.

Elle a toujours des cauchemars à cause des horreurs qu'elle a vécues pendant la guerre.
She still has nightmares because of the horrors she lived through during the war.

6. The past participles of impersonal verbs are invariable.

Quels efforts il a fallu pour maintenir la paix!
What efforts it took to keep the peace!

Les chaleurs qu'il a fait cet été ont été insupportables.
This summer's heat has been unbearable.

7. In the causative **faire** construction (see Section IX.), the past participle is invariable.

Il nous a fait bien rire.
He really made us laugh.

8. Certain verbs are frequently accompanied by a direct object and an infinitive complement. When the direct object precedes and is also the subject of the infinitive, the past participle shows agreement. If it is not also the subject, there is no agreement.

apercevoir	*notice*
écouter	*listen to*
entendre	*hear*
regarder	*look at*
sentir	*feel*
voir	*see*
envoyer	*send*
laisser	*allow*
mener	*lead, take*

La chorale que j'ai entendue chanter venait de Strasbourg.
The chorus that I heard sing came from Strasbourg.

Les mélodies que j'ai entendu chanter étaient de Fauré.
The songs that I heard sung were by Fauré.

La neige que nous avons regardée tomber hier soir sera déjà fondue demain.
The snow we watched falling last night will be melted by tomorrow.

Les feuilles mortes que nous avons regardé balayer hier seront remplacées par d'autres demain.
The dead leaves we watched being swept up yesterday will be replaced by others tomorrow.

Les ouvriers que j'ai envoyés chercher les planches ne sont pas encore revenus.
The workers I sent to get the boards have not yet returned.

Les ouvriers que j'ai envoyé chercher ne sont pas encore venus.
The workers I sent for have not yet come.

9. When the preceding direct object is governed by an implied infinitive or clause, past participles do not show agreement. The following past participles are often found in such constructions.

cru   (croire) *believe*
dit   (dire) *say*
dû   (devoir) *must, have*
pensé   (penser) *think*
permis   (permettre) *permit*
prévu   (prévoir) *foresee*
pu   (pouvoir) *be able*
su   (savoir) *know*
voulu   (vouloir) *want*

Elle n'a lu que les histoires que sa mère lui a permis [de lire].
She read only the stories that her mother let her [read].

Ils ont fait toutes les courses que j'aurais voulu [qu'ils fassent].
They did all the errands I'd have wanted [them to do].

L'entreprise s'est révélée moins difficile que nous n'avions prévu [qu'elle serait].★
The undertaking turned out less difficult than we had expected [it to be].

III. PRONOMINAL VERBS

Pronominal verbs are those accompanied by an object pronoun (the *reflexive pronoun*) which denotes the same entity as the subject. In the compound tenses, they are conjugated with the auxiliary **être**.

★Or: . . . **que nous ne l'avions prévu,** in which the neuter **l'** (**le**) represents the understood clause **qu'elle serait.**

A. The reflexive pronouns

The reflexive pronouns are the same as the direct/indirect object pronouns except in the third person, where **se** is used in both singular and plural.

(je)	me	(nous)	nous
(tu)	te	(vous)	vous
(il)	se	(ils)	se
(elle)	se	(elles)	se

A reflexive pronoun may function as a direct or indirect object, depending upon the verb and its context.

Pourquoi te regardes-tu dans toutes les devantures?
Why do you look at yourself in all the store windows?

Depuis leur brouille, ils ne se disent même plus bonjour.
Since their quarrel, they no longer even say hello to each other.

Elle s'est lavée.†
She got washed.

Elle s'est lavé les mains.†
She washed her hands.

Note that the reflexive pronoun agrees with the subject of an infinitive or present participle just as it does with the subject of an inflected verb.

Vous avez tort de vous moquer de lui.
You are wrong to make fun of him.

M'étant couché(e) très tard, j'ai manqué mon premier rendez-vous du matin.
Having gone to bed very late, I missed my first appointment of the morning.

B. Uses of the pronominal verbs

From the point of view of meaning, there are four types of pronominal verbs: reflexive, reciprocal, purely pronominal, and passive.

1. Reflexive verbs express an action directed back to the subject. Most verbs that take an object, whether direct or indirect, can be used reflexively.

   Il s'estime le plus grand écrivain du monde.
   He considers himself the world's greatest writer.

   Nous nous habillons pour sortir ce soir.
   We are getting dressed (are dressing) to go out this evening.

---

†For the question of the agreement of past participles, see Section II.C.4.

Les enfants ne se sont pas encore brossé les dents.
The children have not yet brushed their teeth.

Note that the English equivalent of a French reflexive construction most often does not contain a reflexive pronoun. In English, many verbs are used both transitively and intransitively; the intransitive sense is generally expressed in French by a reflexive verb.

He stopped a passerby to ask the right way..
Il a arrêté un passant pour lui demander la bonne route.

He stopped to ask a passerby the right way.
Il s'est arrêté pour demander la bonne route à un passant.

He had to hasten his departure.
Il a dû hâter son départ.

He had to hasten.
Il a dû se hâter.

2. Reciprocal verbs express an action directed back to the separate constituents of a plural subject.

    Ces trois amis se voient une fois par an.
    These three friends see one another once a year.

    Vous étiez-vous écrit souvent?
    Had you written to each other often?

The reciprocal sense may be underscored by the addition of **l'un(e) l'autre, les un(e)s les autres, l'un(e) à l'autre, les un(e)s aux autres, mutuellement, réciproquement, entre eux/elles.**

Elles se louent l'une l'autre.
They praise each other.

Dans ma famille, nous sommes toujours prêts à nous rendre des services les uns aux autres.
In my family, we are always ready to help one another out.

Malgré leur politesse, ils se détestent mutuellement.
Despite their politeness, they hate each other.

3. Purely pronominal verbs fall into two groups: those which occur exclusively in combination with a reflexive object and those which may take some other object but which with a reflexive express a quite distinct meaning. In either case, these verbs are not readily analyzed into their component parts, and the role of the reflexive pronoun is often unclear.

a. Verbs occurring only in pronominal form.

s'abstenir de	*abstain from*
s'adonner à	*devote oneself to*
s'agenouiller	*kneel (down)*
s'arroger qqch.★	*lay claim to sth.*
se blottir	*crouch, huddle*
s'écrier	*cry out, exclaim*
s'écrouler	*collapse*
s'efforcer de	*endeavor, strive*
s'emparer de	*seize, take hold of*
s'empresser de	*hasten to*
s'en aller	*go away*
s'enfuir	*flee*
s'évader	*escape, run away*
s'évanouir	*faint*
se fier à	*trust*
se méfier de	*mistrust*
se méprendre sur	*be mistaken about*
se moquer de	*make fun of*
se repentir de	*repent of*
se révolter	*rebel, revolt*
se soucier de	*trouble about, concern oneself about*
se souvenir de	*remember*
se suicider	*commit suicide*

b. Common verbs with a special meaning in the pronominal form.

apercevoir	*see, notice*
s'apercevoir de	*become aware of*
attendre	*wait (for)*
s'attendre à	*expect*
battre	*beat*
se battre	*fight*
conduire	*lead, drive*
se conduire	*behave*
coucher	*put to bed, spend the night*
se coucher	*go to bed*
demander	*ask (for)*
se demander★	*wonder*
douter de	*doubt*
se douter de	*suspect*
endormir	*put to sleep*
s'endormir	*go to sleep*
ennuyer	*bore, annoy*

★The reflexive pronoun functions as an indirect object; in compound tenses, the past participle shows no agreement.

s'ennuyer	*get bored*
occuper	*occupy*
s'occuper de	*take care of, be concerned with*
plaindre	*pity*
se plaindre de	*complain about*
plaire à	*please*
se plaire à★	*enjoy, be fond of*
promener	*take for a walk*
se promener	*go for a walk*
rappeler	*call back*
se rappeler	*remember, recall*
sauver	*save*
se sauver	*run away*
servir	*serve*
se servir de	*use*
taire	*not reveal*
se taire	*be/become silent*
tromper	*deceive*
se tromper	*be mistaken*
trouver	*find*
se trouver	*be, happen to be*

4. The pronominal form may be used with transitive verbs to convey a passive meaning. In this construction, the subject is of the third person and is usually inanimate; no agent is ever specified. Utterances of this type often express an habitual action or state or a general truth.

Une maison ne se construit pas en un jour.
A house is not built in a day.

Porter une cravate pour aller en classe? Mais ça ne se fait presque plus.
Wear a tie to class? But that's hardly done anymore.

Les voitures se vendent bien cette année.
Cars are selling well this year.

Sa réponse paraît un peu étrange mais en fait s'explique facilement.
His answer appears a bit strange but in fact is easily explained.

La clé perdue s'est enfin retrouvée.
The lost key was finally found.

J'ai très chaud. Ça se voit, n'est-ce pas?
I'm very hot. It shows, doesn't it?

★The reflexive pronoun functions as an indirect object; in compound tenses, the past participle shows no agreement.

Un homme s'est rencontré qui allait tout changer.*
A man came along who was going to change everything.

IV. THE PASSIVE VOICE

A. Forms

The passive forms of a verb are composed of the auxiliary **être** and the past participle.

nous sommes assiégé(e)s	*we are (are being) besieged*
tu as été interrogé(e)	*you were questioned*
ils auraient été entendus	*they would have been heard*
qu'il soit nommé	*let him be named*
être assiégé	*to be besieged*
avoir été interrogé	*to have been questioned*
étant entendu	*being heard*
ayant été nommé	*having been named*

Note that the past participle agrees in number and gender with the subject of the verb.

B. Use of the passive

The only verbs used passively are those which are both transitive and nonpronominal. Thus, the passive is not possible for **se rappeler (qqch.)**, which is transitive but is also pronominal; nor is it possible for verbs like **marcher** and **venir**, which are not pronominal but are also not transitive.

1. The passive construction may express either a real action or a state.

    La porte a été ouverte par mon fils.
    The door was opened by my son.

    La porte est ouverte de midi à 15 heures.
    The door is open from noon to 3 P.M.

    Ce plat est vite préparé.
    This dish is quickly prepared.

    Ce plat est préparé depuis trois heures déjà.
    This dish has been ready for three hours.

---

*The use of the passive pronominal for persons is restricted by the demands of clarity. **Le criminel s'est pendu** can mean only *The criminal hanged himself* and not *The criminal was hanged*, which is **Le criminel a été pendu** or **On a pendu le criminel.**

Toutes ces roses viennent d'être cueillies.
All these roses have just been picked.

La pelouse est belle maintenant; elle est tondue.
The lawn is lovely now; it is mowed.

2. Whereas in English any object—direct or indirect or even the object of a preposition—may become the subject of a passive construction, in French only a direct object may assume that function.

They were awarded a prize.
Un prix leur a été décerné.
On leur a décerné un prix.

She is very well spoken of.
On dit beaucoup de bien d'elle.

A letter will be sent to you in three days.
You will be sent a letter in three days.
Une lettre vous sera envoyée dans trois jours.
On vous enverra une lettre dans trois jours.

Note that in the case of just a few verbs, the indirect object of the active construction may be used as the subject of a passive.

Il obéit à sa mère. Elle est obéie.
He obeys his mother. She is obeyed.

Il a désobéi aux prières de la reine. Elles ont été désobéies.
He did not heed the supplications of the queen. They were not heeded.

Pardonnez aux autres et vous serez pardonné.
Forgive others and you shall be forgiven.

Note that there are common English passive phrases of the following type, which, for the reason given above, cannot be construed passively in French.

I have been told that . . .
On m'a dit que . . .

She was permitted to . . .
On lui a permis de . . .

We were promised that . . .
On nous a promis que . . .

There is another area in which English, but not French, allows the use of the passive: before an infinitive complement.

They will be made to wait.
On les fera attendre.

He was seen to leave.
On l'a vu partir.

She has been known to lie.
Il lui arrive de mentir.
On sait qu'elle ment parfois.

3. The passive may be used in impersonal constructions with transitive verbs.

Il leur a été décerné des prix.
There were prizes awarded to them.
They were awarded prizes.

Elle peut faire sa demande, mais il lui sera sûrement répondu que la chose est impossible.
She can make her request, but she will surely be told that it's impossible. *★*

4. When the agent of the passive is expressed, it is introduced by **par** or **de.**

   a. Generally speaking, **par** is used when the passive construction denotes a real action.

Il a été interpellé par deux policiers.
He was stopped by two policemen.

Il sera étonné par cette nouvelle.
He will be astonished by this news.

Le pauvre cheval a dû être accablé par sa charge.
The poor horse must have been overwhelmed by his load.

Cette montre m'a été offerte par mes grands-parents.
This watch was given me by my grandparents.

Le fromage a été dévoré par les souris.
The cheese was devoured by the mice.

La ville fut vite entourée par les troupes ennemies.
The city was quickly surrounded by the enemy troops.

   b. Generally speaking, **de** is used when the passive construction denotes a state, when the verb is used figuratively, or when the speaker envisages the noun in question less as the agent than as the instrument of the passive action.

Elle est aimée de toutes ses camarades.
She is loved by all her friends.

Ils étaient dévorés de doute.
They were overcome with doubt.

---

*★The impersonal passive construction is occasionally used in administrative language even with intransitive verbs.

Il a été procédé au vote.
The vote was then taken.

La ville était toujours entourée de troupes ennemies.
The city was still surrounded by enemy troops.

Soudain, le ciel a été couvert de nuages.
Suddenly, the sky was covered with clouds.

Ils étaient souvent menacés d'une invasion.
They were often threatened with invasion.

C.   Rendering the English passive into French

The idea of a passive action, which English regularly expresses by a
passive verb, is very often expressed in French, not by a passive, but
by some other construction.

1.   *on* with the active voice

You're wanted on the phone.
On vous demande au téléphone.

I have been told that she'll be back soon.
On m'a dit qu'elle sera bientôt de retour.

They were given two hours to complete the work.
On leur a donné deux heures pour achever le travail.

We will no doubt be asked to accompany them to the airport.
On nous demandera sans doute de les accompagner à l'aéroport.

They were shown in immediately upon their arrival.
On les a fait entrer dès leur arrivée.

2.   The pronominal construction

These roses are sold by the piece.
Ces roses se vendent à la pièce.

His love was based on esteem.
Son amour se fondait sur l'estime.

That's not done.
Cela ne se fait pas.

This use of the pronominal construction is generally limited to inanimate subjects. See Section III.B.4. footnote.

3.   *se voir* with an infinitive

She was awarded the first prize.
Elle s'est vu décerner le premier prix.

He does not like to be approached by those people.
Il n'aime pas se voir aborder par ces gens-là.

V. THE IMPERATIVE MOOD

The imperative is used to command, request, exhort, persuade. Strictly speaking, it occurs in the first person plural and in the second person singular and plural; it has two tenses; it is marked by the absence of the subject pronoun. The intent of the imperative may also be conveyed by the use of the third person in the subjunctive mood and by the infinitive.

A. The present imperative

1. Second person singular

a. For **-er** verbs and those **-ir** verbs which have present indicative forms in **-e**, for example, **assaillir, cueillir, offrir, ouvrir, souffrir,** the form of the imperative is the second person singular of the present indicative without the final **-s**.

Parle plus bas!
Speak more softly!

N'ouvre pas la porte!
Don't open the door!

Va chez la voisine!
Go to the neighbor's.

The **-s** is restored when the imperative form is followed by the pronoun **y** or **en**.

Parles-en plus bas!
Speak of it more softly!

Vas-y!
Go there!
Go to it!

b. For all other verbs, with the exception of **avoir, être, savoir,** and **vouloir** (see Section 3.), the form of the imperative is the second person singular of the present indicative.

Remplis le vase!
Fill the vase!

Cours les accueillir!
Run and greet them!

Reçois les visiteurs!
Receive the visitors!

Ne suspends pas les négotiations!
Don't suspend negotiations!

2. **First and second persons plural.** The forms of the imperative for
   all verbs except **avoir, être, savoir,** and **vouloir** (see Section 3.) are
   the same as those of the present indicative.

Parlons plus bas!   Parlez plus bas!
Let's speak more softly!   *Speak more softly!*

Ouvrons la porte!   N'ouvrez jamais cette porte!
Let's open the door!   *Never open this door!*

Ne remplissons pas le vase!   Remplissez le vase!
Let's not fill the vase!   *Fill the vase!*

Courons les accueillir!   Courez les accueillir!
Let's run and greet them!   *Run and greet them!*

Recevons les visiteurs!   Recevez les visiteurs!
Let's receive the visitors!   *Receive the visitors!*

Suspendons les négotiations!   Suspendez les négotiations!
Let's suspend negotiations!   *Suspend negotiations!*

Note that the English speaker must be careful to distinguish between the first-person
plural imperative and constructions with **laisser.**

Sortons d'ici!
Let's get out of here!

Laissez-nous sortir d'ici!
Let us (permit, allow us to) leave this place.

Laissons les choses comme elles sont.
Let's leave things as they are.

3. **Irregular imperative forms**

avoir	aie	ayez	ayons
être	sois	soyez	soyons
savoir	sache	sachez	sachons
vouloir	—	veuillez*	—

Note that the forms **aies** and **saches,** with **-s,** are used if **y** or **en**
follows immediately.

Saches-en la vérité!
Learn the truth about it!

---

*Essentially, **vouloir** has no imperative. For the use of **veuillez,** see Section E. Note, however, **en vouloir à** (*be angry with*) in the negative: **ne m'en veux pas, ne lui en voulez pas,
ne leur en voulons pas.**

B.   The past imperative

The past imperative presents the desired action as an obligation to be accomplished by a given time. It conveys a greater sense of urgency than the present imperative.

Soyez parti demain!
Be gone by tomorrow!

Aie fini ce travail avant midi!
Get this work done by noon!

Aie rangé tes livres avant que ton père [ne] les voie.
Get your books put away before your father sees them.

C.   Indirect imperatives

1.   Third person singular and plural of the present subjunctive

Qu'il parle plus bas!
Let him speak more softly!

Qu'elle n'ouvre la porte à personne!
Let her open the door to no one!
Let her not open the door to anyone!

Qu'on remplisse le vase!
Let the vase be filled!

Qu'ils courent les accueillir!
Let them run and greet them!

Qu'elles suspendent les négotiations!
Let them suspend negotiations!

Que chacun dise sa pensée!
Let each one say what he thinks!

Que personne ne sorte!
Let no one leave!

Note that the intent of the past imperative may be expressed by the past subjunctive.

Qu'il soit parti demain!
Let him be gone by tomorrow!

Qu'elles aient fini ce travail avant midi!
Let them have this work done by noon!

Note, as in Section A.2., that the indirect imperative should not be confused with constructions with **laisser.**

Qu'il ne sorte pas!
Let him not leave!
He must not leave!

Ne le laissez pas sortir!
Don't let him leave!

2. **The administrative imperative.** The infinitive is often used with an imperative sense on signs, official forms, directions for use, and the like.

Ne rien jeter par la fenêtre.
Do not throw objects out of window.

Ecrire en lettres d'imprimerie.
Print.

Tenir au frais.
Keep in a cool place.

D.   **The imperative with object pronouns**

Placement of object pronouns varies accordingly as the imperative is affirmative or negative.*

1. **Affirmative imperative.** Pronouns follow the verb and are joined to it and to each other with hyphens; in stressed position, **me** and **te** are replaced by **moi** and **toi.**

Raconte l'histoire! Raconte-la!
Tell the story! Tell it!

Raconte-la-lui!
Tell it to her (him)!

Parlez-moi de cette histoire! Parlez-en!
Tell me about this business! Tell (speak) about it!

Parlez-m'en!
Tell me about it!

Parlons-lui-en!
Let's speak to him (her) about it!

Parles-en!
Speak (tell) about it!

Repose-toi!
Take a rest!

Lave-toi les mains! Lave-toi-les!
Wash your hands! Wash them!

---

*For detailed treatment of the placement of object pronouns, see Chapter 8.

2. **Negative imperative.** Pronouns precede the verb as in nonimperative utterances.

Ne raconte pas cette histoire! Ne la raconte pas!
Don't tell that story! Don't tell it.

Ne la leur raconte pas!
Don't tell it to them!

Ne me parlez pas de cette histoire! N'en parlez pas!
Don't speak to me about that affair! Don't speak of it!

Ne m'en parlez pas!
Don't speak to me about it!

Ne lui en parlons pas!
Let's not speak to him (her) about it!

N'en parle plus!
Don't speak about it anymore!

Ne te repose pas!
Don't rest!

Ne vous dépêchez pas!
Don't rush!

Ne te lave pas les mains! Ne te les lave pas!
Don't wash your hands! Don't wash them!

E. **The imperative and formulas of politeness**

1. To attenuate the brusqueness of the simple imperative, French, like English, has recourse to certain formulaic constructions. Some of these make use of imperative forms, while others do not. The following list is not exhaustive.

   a. Imperative + **donc**

      Reprenez donc du vin!
      Do have some more wine!

   b. **Veuillez** + infinitive

      Veuillez vous asseoir.
      Please sit down.
      Do sit down.

   c. **Ayez la bonté / la gentillesse / l'amabilité / l'obligeance de** + infinitive

      Ayez la bonté de faire suivre cette lettre.
      Please be so good as to forward this letter.
      Would you be so kind as to forward this letter?

   d. **Faites (Fais) le plaisir / l'honneur à qqn. de faire qqch.**

      Faites-nous l'honneur de venir dîner vendredi soir.
      Please do us the honor of coming to dinner Friday evening.
      Won't you please come to dinner Friday evening?

Fais-moi le plaisir de m'accompagner au concert.
Please come to the concert with me.

e.   Interrogative **vouloir [bien]** + infinitive

Voulez-vous vous mettre à table?
Will you come to the table?

Veux-tu bien nous apporter le café?
Will you please bring us the coffee?

Voudriez-vous me retéléphoner demain?
Would you mind calling me back tomorrow?

Tu ne voudrais pas emmener les petits au cirque?
Wouldn't you like to take the children to the circus?

f.   Future or conditional of **être** + **[bien] gentil** / **aimable** / **bon de** + infinitive

Vous serez gentil de lui envoyer ces documents.
I would appreciate your sending him these papers.

Tu serais bien bon d'aller reprendre le linge.
Would you please go pick up the laundry?

2.   **Closing formulas of letters.** The imperative is used to close almost all letters in French, from the most perfunctory commercial or formal letters to all but the most intimate. These closings are followed immediately by the signature.

Recevez, Monsieur, mes salutations distinguées.
Veuillez agréer, Monsieur, l'expression de mes sentiments distingués.
Veuillez croire, chère Madame, à l'expression de ma sincère reconnaissance.
Recevez, Madame, mes hommages respectueux.

These formulas—and numerous others—express serious nuances of relationship between persons. However quaint they may seem to the speaker of English, recalling as they may *I remain, Sir, your obedient servant*, they are indeed used and used with care, being far more subtly distinguished than such English phrases as *Very truly yours, Sincerely yours,* and *Cordially*.

VI. THE CONDITIONAL

The conditional has two main functions: to express futurity with regard to the past and to express the consequence of a nonrealized condition. It has two tenses, present and past.

A.   Forms

1.   **Present.** The present conditional is formed by adding the endings of the imperfect indicative (see Section I.F.1.) to the future stem (see Section I.B.1.).

je parlerais	*I would (should) speak*
tu réfléchirais	*you would reflect*
il suspendrait	*he would suspend*
nous saurions	*we would (should) know*
vous auriez	*you would have*
elles feraient	*they would do (make)*

2. **Past (conditional perfect).** The past conditional is formed by combining the present conditional of the auxiliary **avoir** or **être** with the past participle of the verb in question.

j'aurais donné	*I would have given*
tu te serais dépêché(e)	*you would have hurried*
elles seraient allées	*they would have gone*

B. Uses of the conditional

1. **Conditional as future in the past.** When the main verb is in the past, the conditional is used to express futurity in the subordinate clause.

Le metteur en scène a toujours cru que la pièce serait un énorme succès.
The director always believed that the play would be a huge success.

En 1940 beaucoup de gens pensaient que la guerre aurait pris fin avant six mois tout au plus.
In 1940 many people thought that the war would be over in six months at most.

L'oracle avait prédit qu'Oedipe tuerait son père.
The oracle had predicted that Oedipus would kill his father.

César se fia à celui qui le trahirait.
Caesar trusted the man who was to (would) betray him.

The same futurity is expressed in indirect discourse.

Il m'a dit qu'ils viendraient au concert.
He told me they would come to the concert.

Elle avait promis que son frère serait là aussi.
She had promised that her brother would be there too.

Elle a promis qu'elles viendraient chez nous aussitôt qu'elle aurait fini sa lettre.
She promised that they would come to our house as soon as she [had] finished her letter.

2. **The conditional of reporting.** The conditional is used to state a reported, but perhaps not verified, fact; this use is frequent in journalism.

Le Président des Etats-Unis rencontrerait la reine Elisabeth.
U.S. President to Meet with Queen Elizabeth.
It is reported (It appears) that the President of the United States will
*   meet with Queen Elizabeth.*

Les ouvriers de Ford seraient entrés en grève.
Ford Workers Out on Strike.
Ford workers are reported to have gone out on strike.

Selon les chercheurs, les troubles cardiaques chez ces bûcherons
    s'expliqueraient plutôt par leur régime lourd en graisse animale
    que par le stress de leur métier.
According to researchers, heart disease in these loggers is due to their diet
*   heavy in animal fat rather than the stress of their work.*

3. **The attenuative conditional.** For politeness, as in English, the con-
    ditional often replaces the indicative.

Je voudrais vous parler dans mon bureau.
I should like to speak to you in my office.

Puis-je vous servir du thé? —J'en prendrais volontiers, merci.
May I serve you some tea? —I'd gladly have some, thank you.

Pourquoi a-t-il démissionné? —Nous aimerions mieux ne pas le
    dire.
Why did he resign? —We'd rather not say.

Seriez-vous le candidat dont on m'a tant parlé?
Are you perhaps the candidate I've heard so much about?

4. The conditional is used in relative clauses which form part of a gen-
    eralizing simile.

Il agit comme quelqu'un qui se serait égaré.
He is behaving like someone who has got lost.

Elle nous fixait comme une femme qui aurait perdu la raison.
She was staring at us like a woman who had taken leave of her senses.

The same idea may be conveyed by **on dirait** + noun.

On dirait un égaré.
He looks like someone lost.

On dirait des picotements sous la peau.
It feels like a prickling under the skin.

Note that **on dirait** and **on jurerait** are frequently used in elliptical comparisons, often
expressing some degree of irony or surprise.

A le voir agir de la sorte, on dirait que c'est lui le patron.
Seeing him act that way, you'd think he was the boss.

Ce n'est pas possible! C'est de la dinde! Mais on dirait du veau!
Why, that's impossible! You say it's turkey! But it tastes like veal!

Les rues sont désertes; on dirait une station de ski à la morte saison.
The streets are deserted; you'd think it was a ski resort in off-season.

On jurerait que la bébé parle chinois!
You'd swear the baby was speaking Chinese!

On aurait juré qu'il parlait latin!
You'd have sworn he was speaking Latin!

5.   The conditional is used to express an event or a state dependent
     upon the prior realization of a condition which is either contrary to
     fact or unlikely to be fulfilled.

Si j'étais roi, tu serais reine.
If I were king, you would be queen.

a.   Condition clauses introduced by **si**. In reference to present or fu-
     ture time, the verb in the **si**-clause occurs in the imperfect indica-
     tive; in reference to past time, it occurs in the pluperfect indica-
     tive. The verb in the result clause is given in the present
     conditional if it refers to present or future time; it is given in the
     past conditional if it refers to past time. In no case is the condi-
     tional (or the future) ever used in a **si**-clause.★

Si j'étais [de] toi, je lui écrirais tout de suite.
If I were you, I would write to her immediately.

Si nous avions ce livre, nous te le prêterions volontiers.
If we had that book, we would gladly lend it to you.

S'il avait trouvé le livre, il l'aurait lu avant l'examen.
If he had found the book, he would have read it before the exam.

Je le ferais encore si je devais le faire.
I would do it again if I had to do it.

Ils seraient ici ce soir s'ils avaient reçu l'invitation à temps.
*They would be here this evening if they had received the invitation on
    time.*

Note that, in formal literary style, a pluperfect indicative in the **si**-clause may be replaced by the pluperfect subjunctive, and a past conditional in the result clause may
also be replaced by the pluperfect subjunctive.

★When **si** means *whether*, it may be followed by the conditional or the future.

Je ne savais pas s'il viendrait avec moi.
I did not know whether (if) he would come with me.

Je ne sais pas s'il viendra avec moi.
I do not know whether (if) he will come with me.

Il eût sauvé son peuple si son peuple avait pu être sauvé.
Il aurait sauvé son peuple si son peuple eût pu être sauvé.
Il eût sauvé son peuple si son peuple eût pu être sauvé.
He would have saved his people if his people could have been saved.

In colloquial use, the condition itself may be rendered by the conditional, but in that case **si** is omitted. The result clause may be introduced by **que**.

Nous aurions ce livre, [que] nous te le prêterions volontiers.
If we had that book, we would gladly lend it to you.

Il aurait trouvé le livre, [qu']il l'aurait lu avant l'examen.
If he had found the book, he would have read it before the exam.

    b. A **si**-clause expressing the condition necessary for the realization of an event or state may be replaced by an elliptical expression or may simply remain implicit in the context.

        A ta place, je lui écrirais tout de suite.
        If I were you, I would write to her immediately.

        Plutôt que de pleurer, tu devrais essuyer le lait.
        Rather than cry, you ought to wipe up the milk.

        Il est parti? Quel dommage! Nous aurions tant aimé le voir!
        He's left? What a pity! It would have been so nice to see him!

        Tu ferais mieux de te taire.
        You'd do better to keep quiet.
        No back talk!

    c. The conditional may be used in a relative clause to express a hypothesis.

        Toute femme qui serait l'objet de sollicitations abusives de la part de son patron ferait bien de porter plainte.
        Any woman whose employer made improper advances to her would do well to lodge a complaint.

        Tout autre homme qui se serait égaré dans cette forêt aurait agi de la même façon.
        Any other man who had got lost in this forest would have acted the same way.

    d. The conditional may be used after **quand, quand même, quand bien même,** and **au cas où** to convey approximately the same idea as a **si**-clause.

        Quand vous n'auriez jamais laissé seuls les petits, à quoi cela aurait-il servi?
        Supposing you had never left the children alone, what good would that have done?

Quand même il l'aurait dit, il ne serait pas nécessaire de le croire.
Even if he had said it, you wouldn't have to believe it.

Au cas où la secrétaire ne serait pas là, adressez-vous au concierge.
In case the secretary isn't there, see the concierge.

6. Note that **si** may well introduce a condition which is likely to be fulfilled; the result clause does NOT then contain a verb in the conditional.

   a. When the **si**-clause has a verb in the present tense, the consequence is expressed by the present, future, or imperative.

   Si je prends le train de 17 heures, je suis sûr d'être chez ma sœur pour le dîner.
   If I take the 5 P.M. train, I'm sure to be at my sister's in time for dinner.

   Si tu prends le train de 17 heures, tu y arriveras pour le dîner.
   If you take the 5 P.M. train, you'll get there in time for dinner.

   Si tu manques le train de 17 heures, téléphone-nous.
   If you miss the 5 P.M. train, phone us.

   b. When the **si**-clause has a verb in the **passé composé** or the simple past, the consequence is expressed by the present or future.

   Si l'avion est parti à l'heure, mon frère est maintenant au-dessus des Montagnes Rocheuses.
   If the plane left on time, my brother is now over the Rocky Mountains.

   S'il est parti hier comme prévu, il sera ici tout à l'heure.
   If he left yesterday as planned, he will be here shortly.

   S'il a réussi, c'est qu'il a tout sacrifié à son ambition.
   If he has succeeded, it's because he has sacrificed everything to his ambition.

   Si Jeanne d'Arc refusa de nier ses voix, c'est qu'elle y croyait fermement.
   If Joan of Arc refused to deny her voices, it is because she firmly believed in them.

VII. DEVOIR, POUVOIR, VOULOIR, SAVOIR

These verbs are noteworthy for the semantic changes which they undergo in the various tenses.

A. *Devoir*

When used with a direct object or equivalent infinitive phrase, **devoir** means *to owe.*

Elle me devait cent mille francs.
She owed me one hundred thousand francs.

Le succès de cette pièce est dû★ au talent des comédiens.
The success of this play is due to the talent of the actors.

Vous vous devez de prendre des vacances cet été.
You owe it to yourself to take a vacation this summer.

Il doit à ses parents de leur épargner cet effort.
He owes it to his parents to spare them that effort.

When used with a following infinitive, **devoir** changes meaning somewhat according to text and context. Principally, it expresses obligation, necessity, intention, or probability.

1.   *Devoir* **in the present**

Nous devons tous payer les impôts, c'est la loi.
We all have to (must) pay taxes; it's the law.

Mon fils a eu un accident; je dois rentrer tout de suite.
My son has had an accident; I've got to go home right away.

Elle doit partir aujourd'hui, mais il est fort possible que les conditions météorologiques l'obligent à rester encore un jour.
She is supposed to leave today, but it is very likely that weather conditions will force her to remain another day.

Ils doivent être très contents; ils viennent d'hériter d'une somme immense.
They must be very happy; they've just inherited a huge sum of money.

Vous devez vous tromper dans vos calculs.
You must be making a mistake in your figures.

Ne partez pas! Elles doivent arriver à l'instant.
Don't leave! They'll surely be here in a minute.

Il doit y avoir des maisons à louer dans cette ville, mais je n'arrive pas à en trouver une.
There must (have to) be houses for rent in this town, but I haven't been able to find one.

★For the forms of the past participle, see Section II.A.

Vous devez vous être trompé dans l'addition.★
You must have made a mistake in the check.

Vous ne devez pas courir dans les couloirs, mes enfants.
You mustn't run in the halls, children.†

Sa mission est si délicate qu'il ne doit en parler à personne.
His mission is so delicate that he may (must) not speak of it to anyone.

2. *Devoir* in the imperfect

A l'époque des pionniers, même les femmes devaient savoir se servir d'une arme à feu.
In pioneer days, even women had to know how to use firearms.

Mon fils avait eu un accident; je devais rentrer tout de suite mais j'étais trop bouleversé pour conduire.
My son had had an accident; I had to get home right away but I was too upset to drive.

La guerre a éclaté; je devais partir pour le front, mais il n'y avait plus de transports.
War broke out; I was supposed to leave for the front, but there was no transportation.

Il devait être minuit passé quand ils sont rentrés.
It must have been past midnight when they came home.

Ils devaient être très contents; ils venaient d'hériter d'une somme immense.
They must have been very happy; they had just inherited a huge sum of money.

En 1789, Louis XVI ignorait qu'il devait mourir décapité.
In 1789, Louis XVI was unaware that he was to (would) be beheaded.

Jusqu'à une époque récente, les femmes ne devaient pas fumer en public.
Until recently, women were not supposed to smoke in public.

★The same thought may be expressed by putting the inflected verb, rather than the infinitive, into the past.

Vous avez dû vous tromper dans l'addition.
You must have made a mistake in the check.

†Note that **devoir** continues to express obligation even in the negative. To convey the absence of obligation, French makes use of other constructions.

Take it easy! You don't have to run. There is plenty of time.
Doucement! Il n'est pas nécessaire de courir. Tu as tout le temps.
Doucement! Tu n'es pas obligé de courir. Tu as tout le temps.
Doucement! Tu n'as pas besoin de courir. Tu as tout le temps.

3. ***Devoir* in the *passé composé* and simple past**

La guerre a éclaté; j'ai dû partir pour le front le jour même.
War broke out; I had to leave for the front the very same day.

Elle a dû manquer l'avion; je ne la vois pas parmi les passagers.*
She must have missed the plane; I don't see her among the passengers.

Henri IV dut se convertir pour accéder au trône.
Henry IV had to convert in order to accede to the throne.

Le comte Joachim de Metz dut mourir de la peste, mais personne
ne le sait avec certitude.
*Count Joachim de Metz must have died of bubonic plague, but no one
really knows.*

Tu n'as pas dû aimer ton dîner; tu n'as presque pas mangé.
You must not have liked your dinner; you've eaten almost nothing.

4. ***Devoir* in the future and future perfect**

Si la neige continue, ils devront remettre leur départ à lundi.
*If the snow continues, they will have to postpone their departure until
Monday.*

Une fois ce projet adopté, on devra penser aux détails de sa réalisa-
tion.
*Once this project has been adopted, we shall have to think about the
details of its implementation.*

Si vous lui refusez sa demande aujourd'hui, vous ne devrez sûrement pas changer d'avis demain.
*If you deny him his request today, you certainly mustn't change your
mind tomorrow.*

Ce n'est sûrement pas ma belle-sœur! Il est neuf heures; elle aura
dû partir pour l'aéroport.
*It's surely not my sister-in-law. It's nine o'clock; she has no doubt had to
leave for the airport.*

5. ***Devoir* in the present and past conditional**

Au lieu de te laisser influencer par tous ces soi-disant amis, tu devrais résoudre le problème toi-même.
*Instead of letting yourself be influenced by all those so-called friends, you
should (ought to) resolve the problem yourself.*

---

*The same thought may be expressed by putting the inflected verb into the present and
using the perfect infinitive.

Elle doit avoir manqué l'avion.
She must have missed the plane.

J'aurais dû rentrer tout de suite, mais je n'en avais franchement pas envie.
I should (ought to) have gone home right away, but frankly I didn't feel like it.

C'était une confidence. Vous n'auriez pas dû en parler.
It was a confidential matter. You should not have spoken of it.

B. *Pouvoir*

Pouvoir may have a pronoun complement.

Les électeurs de ce sénateur croyaient qu'il pouvait tout.
This senator's constituents thought he could do anything.

Je regrette, mais même dans ce cas-là je ne pourrais rien pour toi.
I'm sorry, but even in that case I couldn't (wouldn't be able to) do a thing for you.

On n'y peut rien; la décision est déjà prise.
We're helpless; the decision has been made.

Voilà cinq heures que nous attendons ce coup de fil; nous n'en pouvons plus.
We've been waiting for that phone call for five hours; we can't take it any more.

When used with a following infinitive, **pouvoir** changes meaning somewhat according to tense and context. Principally, it expresses ability, permission, or possibility.

1. *Pouvoir* in the present

Leur meilleur coureur peut faire les 100 mètres en moins de 11 secondes.
Their best runner can do the 100-meter dash in less than 11 seconds.

Tu peux t'asseoir, si tu veux.
You may (can) sit down, if you like.

Il me semble vous l'avoir dit, mais je peux me tromper.
I think I told you, but I may be wrong.

Examinez bien la marchandise; il peut y avoir des défauts.
Inspect the goods well; there may be some flaws.

2. *Pouvoir* in the imperfect

Tu pouvais résoudre ce problème de plusieurs façons. Quelle solution as-tu choisie?
You could have resolved (were able to resolve) this problem in several ways. Which solution did you choose?

Autrefois, quand on ne pouvait pas payer ses dettes, on risquait la prison.
It used to be that, if you couldn't pay your debts, you risked going to prison.

Il était accompagné d'une femme qui pouvait avoir trente ou quarante ans.
He was accompanied by a woman who might (could) have been thirty or forty years old.

3. ***Pouvoir*** in the *passé composé* **and simple past**

En revenant sur ses pas, elle a pu retrouver ses clés.
By retracing her steps, she was able to find (succeeded in finding, found) her keys.

Ils exposaient tous leurs arguments, mais ils n'ont pas pu nous faire changer d'avis.
They presented all their arguments, but they couldn't (were not able to, failed to) make us change our minds.

Où est-ce que j'ai bien pu les mettre, ces ciseaux?
Where could I have (did I) put those scissors?

Après avoir salué leurs grands-parents, les enfants purent sortir jouer.
After having greeted their grandparents, the children could go out and play.

Tu as bien pu le fâcher en perdant ses disques.
You might (may) very well have made him angry by losing his records.

4. ***Pouvoir*** in the future and future perfect

Si vous lui donnez un préavis aujourd'hui, vous pourrez déménager dans un mois.
If you give her notice today, you can (may, will be able to) move out in a month.

On t'enlèvera le plâtre après-demain, mais tu ne pourras toujours pas jouer dans le match de lundi prochain.
Your cast will come off the day after tomorrow, but you still won't be able to (can't) play in next Monday's game.

Veux-tu dire à ton frère qu'il me rende mon magnétophone? Je pourrai en avoir besoin cette semaine.
Will you tell your brother to return my tape recorder? I may need it this week.

Je leur communiquerai le texte du manuscrit dès que j'aurai pu le
déchiffrer.
*I will send them the text of the manuscript as soon as I've been able to
decipher it.*

5. **Pouvoir in the present and past conditional**

Pourriez-vous me dire où se trouvent les encyclopédies?
Could you tell me where the encyclopedias are?

Les Pelletier doivent venir dîner dimanche. Je pourrais faire un rôti
de veau ou bien un gigot. Lequel préfères-tu?
*The Pelletiers are to come to dinner on Sunday. I could make a veal
roast or a leg of lamb. Which do you prefer?*

Les Pelletier doivent venir dîner dimanche. Je pourrais faire un rôti
de veau. Je déciderai demain.
*The Pelletiers are to come to dinner on Sunday. I might make a veal
roast. I'll decide tomorrow.*

Certains exilés croyaient qu'ils pourraient un jour regagner leur patrie. La nouvelle loi les désabusa.
*Certain exiles thought that one day they could (would be able to) return
to their homeland. The new law set them straight.*

Vous avez eu de la chance. Vous auriez pu vous faire mal en utili-
sant cette vieille échelle.
*You were lucky. You could (might) have hurt yourself using that old
ladder.*

Nous sommes contents qu'il ait remis sa visite à mercredi. On n'aurait pas pu le voir autrement.
*We were glad he postponed his visit until Wednesday. We would not
have been able to see (could not have seen) him otherwise.*

C. *Vouloir*

Vouloir, which expresses volition, may take various complements.
Nuances sometimes change according to tense.

1. **Vouloir in the present**

Il veut une voiture neuve.
He wants a new car.

Voulez-vous bien le recevoir maintenant, monsieur? —Je veux bien.
Will you see him now, sir? —All right.

Je veux bien admettre la logique de vos arguments, mais je ne saurais accepter votre conclusion.
I am willing to grant the logic of your arguments, but I cannot accept your conclusion.

L'honneur veut que vous obteniez une réparation.
Honor demands (requires) that you seek satisfaction.

Nous sommes déjà en retard, et le moteur ne veut pas démarrer!
We're already late, and the engine won't (refuses to) start!

Elles se veulent conservatrices, mais en fait elles sont réactionnaires.
They claim to be conservative, but in fact they are reactionaries.

2. ***Vouloir* in the imperfect**

Elle voulait une voiture neuve, mais elle n'a pas pu s'en offrir une.
She wanted a new car, but she couldn't afford one.

Depuis très longtemps, il voulait arrêter de fumer.
For a very long time, he had been wanting to stop smoking.

Nous ne voulions pas que l'architecte construise un édifice prétentieux.
We did not want the architect to construct a pretentious building.

Je sais que vous vouliez bien le recevoir mais que les circonstances vous en ont empêché.
I know that you were willing to see him but that circumstances prevented you.

3. ***Vouloir* in the *passé composé* and simple past**

On lui avait conseillé de rester dans la salle d'attente, mais il a voulu absolument voir sa femme avant l'opération.
He had been advised to stay in the waiting room, but he absolutely insisted on seeing his wife before the operation.

Je lui ai demandé les raisons de son refus, mais elle n'a pas voulu me les dire.
I asked her the grounds for her refusal, but she refused to (would not) tell me.

Il voulait qu'elle l'accompagne au théâtre, mais elle n'a pas voulu et il a dû y aller tout seul.
He wanted her to accompany him to the theater, but she wouldn't (refused) and he had to go alone.

La police enfonça la porte; le terroriste voulut s'échapper par la fenêtre, mais l'accès en était déjà bloqué.
The police broke down the door; the terrorist tried to escape through the window, but the way was already blocked.

D. *Savoir*

In addition to meaning *to know* or *to know how*, **savoir** takes on special senses in the **passé composé**, simple past, and present conditional.

1. *Savoir* in the *passé composé* and simple past★

    J'ignorais alors ce qui était arrivé, mais je l'ai su depuis.
    I didn't know at the time what had happened, but I found out later.

    Comment saviez-vous que j'allais être limogé? Moi, je ne l'ai su que
     ce matin.
    *How did you know I was going to be fired? I only found out this morn-
     ing.*

    Napoléon ne sut que trop tard que les Alliés se massaient contre lui.
    Napoleon learned only too late that the Allies were massing against him.

    Malgré une surveillance permanente, l'ôtage a su faire passer une
     lettre aux journalistes.
    *Despite round-the-clock surveillance, the hostage succeeded in getting
     (was able to get) a letter to the reporters.*

2. **Savoir** in the present conditional has a special sense only in the
    negative (without **pas**).

    Une société ne saurait subsister sans gouvernement.
    A society cannot survive without a government.

    Quelle heure est-il? —Je ne saurais vous le dire.
    What time is it? —I couldn't tell you.

VIII. THE INFINITIVE

The infinitive is a nominal form of the verb, which expresses the idea of
an action or state without an indication of person or number.

★Just as **savoir** in these tenses denotes the beginning of knowledge, **connaître** in the same
tenses denotes the beginning of acquaintance.

Nous nous sommes connus il y a quinze ans.
We met fifteen years ago.

Ils l'ont connue à Paris.
They met her (made her acquaintance) in Paris.

A. Forms

1. **The present infinitive.** All forms end in **-er, -ir, -re,** or **-oir.** The time of the present infinitive is the same as that of the main verb or is subsequent to it.

Je les entends crier.
I hear them shout (shouting).

Je les ai entendus crier.
I heard them shout (shouting).

Il rêvait d'être un jour président.
He dreamed of being president one day.

2. **The past infinitive.** The past, or perfect, infinitive is formed by combining **avoir** or **être** with the past participle of the verb in question. The time of the past infinitive is prior to that of the main verb.

Elle croit avoir signé ces contrats avant-hier.
She thinks she signed those contracts the day before yesterday.

Elle croyait les avoir signés deux jours auparavant.
She thought she had signed them two days earlier.

Après nous être dépêchés, nous avons vu que c'était inutile.
After hurrying (having hurried), we saw that it was useless.

For the passive infinitive, see Section IV.A.

B. Uses of the infinitive

The infinitive, which is a verbal noun, may be used in any regular noun function: subject or object of a verb, object of a preposition, and so forth. At the same time, it may take its own complements as any finite verb might: objects, adverbial phrases, and so forth. In a limited number of constructions, the infinitive occurs in place of a finite verb.

1. **Infinitive as subject.** When used as the subject of a verb, the infinitive is often followed by the reprise pronoun **ce** or **cela** (**ça**). This always occurs when the inflected verb is a form of **être** in the affirmative and the predicate is another infinitive; otherwise, it is optional.

Voir c'est croire.
Seeing is believing.

Parler n'est pas faire.
Talking is not the same thing as doing.

Assister à une scène pareille [ça] ferait pleurer le moins sensible d'entre nous.
To witness (Witnessing) such a scene would make the least sensitive among us weep.

Le voir encore une fois avant sa mort, c'est tout ce que je peux espérer.
To see him again before his death is all I can hope for.

For the infinitive subject in impersonal construction, see Section X.B.3., 4., and 5.

2. **Infinitive as object of a preposition.** The infinitive may be used after any preposition that makes sense with a verbal object except **en** (which must be followed by the **-ant** form of the verb).

sans manger	*without eating*
sans avoir mangé	*without having eaten*
au lieu de se promener	*instead of taking a walk*

a. **Après** must be followed by the past infinitive.

Après être sortie, elle a dû rentrer chercher son parapluie.
After going (having gone) out, she had to go back in for her umbrella.

b. **Avant** becomes **avant de** (or, in formal literary style, **avant que de**) before an infinitive.

Avant [que] de décrire le suicide de Mme Bovary, Flaubert a étudié plusieurs traités médicaux.
Before describing the suicide of Madame Bovary, Flaubert studied several medical treatises.

c. **Pour** followed by an infinitive may have various senses, depending upon sentence construction or lexical choice. Generally, when followed by a present infinitive, it denotes purpose and, when followed by a past infinitive, denotes cause.

Il faut manger pour vivre.
You have to eat to live.

La dactylo s'est fait renvoyer pour avoir passé le plus clair de son temps au téléphone.
The typist was fired for spending (because she spent) most of her time on the telephone.

3. **Infinitive as object of a verb.** As the object of a verb, the infinitive may or may not be introduced by a preposition. It is the main verb which determines whether there is a preposition and, if so, whether it is **à, de,** or another.

Nous voulons voyager en Chine.
We want to travel to China.

Où choisiriez-vous d'aller?
Where would you choose to go?

Je songe à me rendre en Inde.
I am thinking of going to India.

For a list of essential verbs showing their construction with infinitive complements, see Chapter 15, Section VI.

4. **Infinitive as complement of a verbal expression.** A number of common expressions consisting of a verb and its object (introduced by no article or an indefinite or partitive article) take an infinitive complement. The linking preposition may be either **à** or **de**, depending upon the expression.

avoir avantage à	*do well to*
avoir intérêt à	*do well to*
avoir [de la] peine à	*find it hard to*
avoir [une] tendance à	*have a tendency to*
avoir des difficultés à	*have trouble -ing*
avoir de la facilité à	*find it easy to*
avoir de la joie à	*be delighted to*
avoir du mal à	*find it hard to*
avoir du plaisir à	*find it a pleasure to*
donner matière à	*give cause for -ing*
éprouver de la (une) joie à	*feel joy in -ing*
éprouver du plaisir à	*find pleasure in -ing*
prendre plaisir à	*take pleasure in -ing*
trouver une joie à	*find joy in -ing*
trouver du plaisir à	*find pleasure in -ing*

Etant donné la difficulté du cours, vous auriez intérêt à vous procurer ce livre le plus tôt possible.
Given the difficulty of the course, you would do well to obtain this book as soon as possible.

Au dix-huitième siècle, les gens trouvaient du plaisir à assister à des exécutions publiques.
In the eighteenth century, people took pleasure in attending public executions.

avoir coutume de	*be accustomed to*
avoir hâte de	*be in a hurry to*
avoir honte de	*be ashamed to*
avoir de la chance de	*be lucky to*
se faire une joie de	*be delighted to*
se faire un plaisir de	*be pleased to*

Les ouvriers se sont fait un plaisir de montrer aux visiteurs leur
usine modèle.
The workers took real pleasure in showing the visitors their model plant.

5. **Infinitive as complement of a noun.** In this use, the infinitive is
introduced by a preposition, usually **de** or **à**.

   a. When the infinitive serves to delimit the scope of an abstract
   noun, it is normally introduced by **de**.

      Il a la politesse de répondre tout de suite aux lettres qu'il reçoit.
      He has the courtesy to answer his letters immediately.

      J'ai raccourci mon voyage pour le plaisir de vous revoir.
      I shortened my trip for the pleasure of seeing you again.

   b. The infinitive of a transitive verb may be linked to a direct object
   by **à** to express intention or obligation.

      J'avais tant de choses à vous dire!
      I had so many things to tell you!

      Il y a beaucoup de formulaires à remplir pour obtenir sa carte
      d'identité.
      There are so many forms to fill out to get your identity card.

      Cette maison n'est pas à vendre.
      This house is not for sale.

      Après la guerre, il était difficile de trouver un appartement à
      louer.
      After the war, it was hard to find an apartment to rent.

   c. The infinitive preceded by **à** may function as an adjective of purpose in the formation of a compound noun.

      | la machine à écrire | *typewriter* |
      | le fer à repasser | *iron* |
      | la salle à manger | *dining room* |

      For detailed treatment of prepositions in compound nouns, see
      Chapter 15, Section III.A.

6. **Infinitive as complement of an adjective.** The two parts of the
phrase are always linked by a preposition, usually **à** or **de**.

   a. The adjective may determine the choice of preposition.

      Avec Grand-mère, il faut être attentif à prononcer distinctement;
      elle est un peu dure d'oreille.
      *With Grandmother, you have to take care to articulate distinctly; she
      is a bit hard of hearing.*

J'ai été stupéfait de voir de si belles roses en janvier.
I was astonished to see such beautiful roses in January.

For a list of common adjectives showing their construction with infinitive complements, see Chapter 15, Section V.

b. *Adjective + à + infinitive of a transitive verb.* In this construction, the infinitive phrase specifies the area to which the adjective applies.

Ces bottes ne sont pas difficiles à mettre, mais bien difficiles à enlever.
These boots are not hard to put on, but very hard to take off.

Son français est agréable à entendre et facile à comprendre.
His French is a pleasure to hear and easy to understand.

Note that the same sense can be conveyed by an impersonal construction.

Il est agréable d'entendre son français et facile de le comprendre.
It is a pleasure to hear his French and easy to understand it.

For detailed treatment of this impersonal construction, see Section X.B.3.c.

c. *Adjective + à + infinitive.* In this construction, the infinitive functions as an intensifier of the adjective.

Je ne veux pas monter dans cet autobus, il est plein à craquer.
I don't want to get on this bus; it's full to bursting.

Note some other expressions of this type.*

bête (triste) à pleurer	*stupid (sad) enough to make one weep*
triste à faire pleurer	*sad enough to make one weep*
joli (mignon) à croquer	*pretty (cute) as a picture*
laid (maigre) à faire peur	*frighteningly ugly (thin)*

7. Infinitive as imperative. See Section VI.C.2.

8. Infinitive in interrogative or exclamatory phrases

Les sinistrés regardaient hébétés les décombres: Que faire maintenant? Comment rebâtir? Pourquoi ne pas tout abandonner?
The disaster victims, stunned, looked at the ruins: What should they do now? How could they rebuild? Why not give everything up?

---

*Note that there are a few intensifying infinitive phrases which are attached not to adjectives but to **ce** denoting a situation.

Tu l'as entendu injurier son collègue? C'était à mourir de honte!
Did you hear him insult his colleague? I could have died of shame!

Le voir s'empêtrer dans ses explications, c'est à se tordre de rire.
To see him get tangled up in his explanations just makes you die laughing.

Nous, répéter des commérages! Jamais de la vie!
We, repeat gossip! Never!

9. **Historical infinitive.** The infinitive may be used to replace, for vividness, a past tense in a narrative. It is preceded by **de**, accompanied by a subject, and usually introduced by **et**.

L'idole, guitare en main, chemise ouverte jusqu'au nombril, surgit
sur scène, et la foule d'exploser.
The rock star, guitar in hand, shirt open down to the navel, sprang onto
the stage, and the crowd went wild.

IX. THE CAUSATIVE AND SIMILAR CONSTRUCTIONS

Faire is often used as an auxiliary with a following verb to indicate that the subject, instead of performing the action, causes it to be performed by another agent, which may be merely implied. This is called the causative construction. It is considerably more common than its literal equivalent, *to have (make) someone do something*, is in English and it often serves as the idiomatic equivalent of a simple English transitive verb. Following are some common examples of such correspondence.

faire bouillir qqch.	*boil sth.*
faire circuler qqch.	*circulate sth.*
faire cuire qqch.	*cook sth.*
faire construire qqch.	*build sth.*
faire dire à qqn. que . . .	*send word to s.o. that . . .*
faire entrer qqn.	*introduce s.o., usher s.o. in, show s.o. in*
faire fondre qqch.	*melt sth. down, dissolve sth.*
faire passer qqch.	*pass sth., pass sth. around*
faire publier qqch.	*publish sth.*
faire remarquer à qqn. que . . . /qqch. à qqn.	*point out to s.o. that . . ./sth. to s.o.*
faire sauter qqch.	*blow sth. up, burst sth., break sth.*
faire savoir à qqn. que . . .	*inform s.o. that . . .*
faire sortir qqn.	*show s.o. out*
faire suivre qqch.	*forward sth., e.g., the mail*
faire taire qqn.	*silence s.o.*
faire venir qqn.	*summon s.o., send for s.o.*
faire voir qqch. à qqn.	*reveal sth. to s.o., point sth. out to s.o., show sth. to s.o.*

A. Infinitive + its subject

The infinitive may be accompanied by a noun which is the subject of the infinitive and which is placed after it.

Elle a fait entrer les candidats.
She showed in the candidates.

When the noun subject of the infinitive is replaced by a personal pronoun, it has the form of a direct object and is placed before **faire** or, in the case of the affirmative imperative, immediately afterward.

Le professeur fait lire ses étudiants. Il les fait lire.
The professor has his students read. He has them read.

Nous ne savons pas faire marcher cet appareil. Nous ne savons pas le faire marcher.
We do not know how to operate this machine. We do not know how to operate it.

Veux-tu faire bouillir les pommes de terre? Veux-tu les faire bouillir?
Will you boil the potatoes? Will you boil them?

Faites venir le médecin. Faites-le venir.
Send for the doctor. Send for him.

B. Infinitive + its direct object

The infinitive may be accompanied by a noun which is the direct object of the infinitive and which is placed after it.

Avez-vous fait publier votre livre?
Have you published your book?
(Have you had your book published?)

When the direct object of the infinitive is a pronoun, it is placed before **faire** or, in the case of the affirmative imperative, immediately afterward. Note that the past participle **fait** remains invariable in the causative construction. Note, too, that the direct object may be a reflexive pronoun.

Le professeur fait lire les revues. Il les fait lire.
The professor has the magazines read. He has them read.

Je ferai vérifier les freins de ma voiture. Je les ferai vérifier.
I'll have the brakes on my car checked. I'll have them checked.

En parlant lentement, l'étrangère s'est fait comprendre.
By speaking slowly, the foreigner made herself understood.

Ne fais pas voir cette photo. Ne la fais pas voir.
Don't show that photo. Don't show it.

Faites copier leur lettre. Faites-la copier.
Have their letter copied. Have it copied.

C. Infinitive + its indirect object

The infinitive may be accompanied by a noun or pronoun which is the indirect object of the infinitive.

Le candidat a fait téléphoner aux électeurs de son arrondissement. Il
  leur a fait téléphoner.
*The candidate had phone calls made to the voters in his district. He had
  them phoned.*

Par son seul regard, elle se fait obéir.
With her glance alone, she commands obedience.

D. Infinitive + indirect and direct object

J'ai fait renvoyer le paquet à l'expéditeur. Je l'ai fait renvoyer à l'expéditeur. Je lui ai fait renvoyer le paquet. Je le lui ai fait renvoyer.
*I had the package returned to the sender. I had it returned to the sender. I
  had the package returned to him. I had it returned to him.*

Elle s'est fait couper les cheveux. Elle se les est fait couper.
She had her hair cut. She had it cut.

Fais-toi faire une robe de soie, c'est à la mode. Fais-toi en faire une de
  soie, c'est à la mode.
Have a silk dress made; silk is in. Have a silk one made; silk is in.

E. Infinitive + subject and indirect object

Je fais répondre les étudiants à chacune des questions. Je les y fais
  répondre.
I have the students answer each of the questions. I have them answer them.

Faites obéir les enfants au maître-nageur. Faites-les-lui obéir.
Make the children obey the lifeguard. Make them obey him.

F. Infinitive + subject + direct object

The infinitive may be accompanied by both a subject and a direct object. In this case, the subject is introduced by a preposition, usually à
or **par.** The distinction is quite complex, but, in general, à serves to
present the subject as a kind of goal or beneficiary of the action,
whereas **par** serves to stress the instrumentality of the subject. **Par** is
thus always used with an agent fulfilling his or her normal professional
function.

L'entraîneur a fait étudier à ses coureurs le film de leur dernière rencontre. Il l'a fait étudier à ses coureurs. Il leur a fait étudier le film de leur dernière rencontre. Il le leur a fait étudier.
The coach had his runners study the film of their last meet. He had his runners study it. He had them study the film of their last meet. He had them study it.

Le metteur en scène fera jouer le rôle principal à sa femme. Il le fera jouer à sa femme. Il lui fera jouer le rôle principal. Il le lui fera jouer.
The director will have his wife play the main role. He will have his wife play it. He will have her play the main role. He will have her play it.

On a fait entendre à Paul qu'il ne devait pas agir de la sorte. On lui a fait entendre qu'il ne devait pas agir de la sorte. On le lui a fait entendre.
Paul was made to understand that he was not to behave like that. He was made to understand that he was not to behave like that. He was made to understand it.

Le président du tribunal a fait arrêter le manifestant par la police. Il l'a fait arrêter par la police.
The judge had the demonstrator arrested by the police. He had him arrested by the police.

Nous avons fait vacciner notre fille par le médicin du quartier. Nous l'avons fait vacciner par le médecin du quartier.
We had our daughter vaccinated by the neighborhood doctor. We had her vaccinated by the neighborhood doctor.

G.   Infinitive + subject, direct object, and indirect object

When the infinitive is accompanied by a subject and both kinds of object, the subject is necessarily introduced by **par.** This construction normally entails a combination of nouns and pronouns rather than the accumulation of three nouns or three pronouns.

Les clients de l'hôtel se font apporter le petit déjeuner par le garçon de l'étage. Ils se le font apporter par le garçon de l'étage.
The hotel guests have their breakfast brought up by room service. They have it brought up by room service.

Son père lui a fait aménager le nouvel appartement par un décorateur très connu. Il le lui a fait aménager par un décorateur très connu.
His father had the new apartment done for him by a well-known designer. He had it done for him by a well-known designer.

Je leur ferai rendre les livres par Jean (lui). Je les ferai rendre aux enfants par Jean (lui). Je les leur ferai rendre par Jean.
I'll have John (him) give them the books. I'll have John (him) give them to the children. I'll have John give them to them.

H. Special observations

1. *Se faire* + **infinitive.** While the reflexive causative may imply volition or intentionality, it is commonly used as a mere equivalent of the passive.

Pour assurer son succès aux élections, il se fait photographier avec toutes les personnalités locales.
To ensure his success in the elections, he gets himself photographed with all the local dignitaries.

En dépit de toutes ses précautions, le truand s'est fait prendre par la police.
Despite all his precautions, the hoodlum got (was) caught by the police.

In the case of **se faire** + infinitive, whether the reflexive pronoun is functioning as a direct object or as an indirect object, the subject of the infinitive is always introduced by **par** or **de** rather than **à**.

a. **Par** is used with most verbs.

Elle s'est fait soigner par un guérisseur.
She had herself treated by a faith-healer.

Pourquoi ne te fais-tu pas répondre par le président lui-même?
Why don't you get an answer from the president himself?

b. **De** tends to be used with certain verbs when they express a state; compare the passive voice (Section IV.B.4.). Among the most common are the following.

admirer	*admire*	accompagner	*accompany*
aimer	*like, love*	encadrer	*frame, flank*
craindre	*fear*	entourer	*surround*
détester	*hate*	précéder	*precede*
estimer	*esteem*	suivre	*follow*
mépriser	*scorn*		
respecter	*respect*		

La nouvelle présidente de la banque a vite su se faire respecter de ses collègues.
The new bank president quickly succeeded in gaining the respect of her colleagues.

Le dictateur se faisait toujours accompagner d'une dizaine de gardes du corps.
The dictator was always accompanied by ten or so bodyguards.

Note that the above verbs need not be reflexive to entail the use of **de.**

Son tempérament explosif le fait craindre de ses subordonnés.
His volatile temper makes his subordinates fear him.

Ce cinéaste a fait suivre son grand succès d'un court métrage peu apprécié.
That filmmaker followed his great success with a lukewarmly received short feature.

2. *Faire* + **pronominal verb.** When the infinitive is a pronominal verb, the reflexive pronoun is placed between **faire** and the infinitive.

Qu'est-ce qui l'a fait se charger de cette responsabilité?
What made him assume that responsibility?

L'explosion nous a fait nous regarder avec étonnement.
The explosion made us look at each other with surprise.

Note that, with verbs such as **s'asseoir, se repentir,** and **se taire,** the reflexive pronoun may be omitted.

L'ouvreuse fera [s']asseoir les spectateurs.
The usher will seat the audience.

Faites-le [se] taire!
Make him keep quiet!

I.   Constructions similar to the causative

There are several verbs which, like **faire,** may be followed by an infinitive whose subject is different from that of the main verb. These are **laisser, voir, regarder, entendre, écouter, sentir, envoyer, mener,** and **emmener.** Their construction differs from that of **faire** + infinitive in the following ways.

1. **Position of the subject of the infinitive.** A noun, unlike a personal pronoun, may be placed either after the infinitive or between the two verbs.

Le criminel laissa paraître sa culpabilité dans son témoignage.
Le criminel laissa sa culpabilité paraître dans son témoignage.
The criminal let his guilt show in his testimony.

J'entends entrer ma fille par la porte du jardin.
J'entends ma fille entrer par la porte du jardin.
I hear my daughter coming in by the garden gate.

Le criminel la laissa paraître dans son témoignage.
The criminal let it show in his testimony.

Je l'entends entrer par la porte du jardin.
I hear her coming in by the garden gate.

2. **Agreement of past participles.** The past participles **laissé, vu,** etc., agree in number and gender with the subject of the infinitive if that subject precedes the main verb.

Le criminel l'a laissée paraître dans son témoignage.
The criminal let it show in his testimony.

Je l'ai entendue entrer par la porte du jardin.
I heard her come in by the garden gate.

La femme que tu as vue sortir de chez moi est mon avocate.
The woman whom you saw leaving my house is my lawyer.

Note that there is no agreement if the pronoun is the direct object of the infinitive rather than its subject. (See Section II.C.8.)

J'ai entendu chanter la première mélodie de Debussy. Je l'ai entendu chanter.
I have heard Debussy's first song sung. I have heard it sung.

3. **Infinitive accompanied by both subject and direct object**

   a. A noun subject of the infinitive may be placed either before the infinitive or, preceded by **à** or **par,** after it.

   Le règlement avait laissé les prisonniers prendre chaque jour de l'exercice.
   Le règlement avait laissé prendre aux prisonniers chaque jour de l'exercice.
   The rules had let the prisoners take some exercise every day.

   Le musicien n'a pas laissé l'hôtesse de l'air emporter son violon.
   Le musicien n'a pas laissé emporter son violon par l'hôtesse de l'air.
   The musician did not let the stewardess take his violon.

   On entendait la musique du village jouer des marches militaires le samedi soir.
   On entendait jouer des marches militaires par la musique du village le samedi soir.
   Saturday evenings you could hear the village band play military marches.

   b. A pronoun subject of the infinitive occurs as either a direct or an indirect object and is placed before the main verb.

On le vit signer la lettre.
On lui vit signer la lettre.
He was seen signing (to sign) the letter.

Note that, when the first verb is in a compound tense, the past participle agrees with the preceding subject if the latter is given the form of a direct object, but not if it is given the form of an indirect object.

Le règlement les avait laissés prendre chaque jour de l'exercice.
Le règlement leur avait laissé prendre chaque jour de l'exercice.
The rules had let them take some exercise every day.

   c. If both the direct object and the subject of the infinitive are pronouns, the following constructions are all possible.

On le vit la signer.
On lui vit la signer.
On la lui vit signer.
He was seen signing (to sign) it.

Ces paroles, je l'entends les prononcer.
Ces paroles, je lui entends les prononcer.
Ces paroles, je les lui entends prononcer.
I hear him pronounce these words.

X. IMPERSONAL CONSTRUCTIONS

Impersonal constructions are of two types, those impersonal by nature and those impersonal only by construction. These expressions are always in the third person singular, introduced by the neuter subject **il** (sometimes **ce**). The verbs and verbal locutions found in the first category occur only as impersonals, while those in the second are normally personal verbs here constructed impersonally.

A. Impersonals by nature

These include **falloir, s'agir, se pouvoir,** and several verbs denoting meteorological phenomena.

  1. **Falloir** expresses necessity or obligation.

    a. **Falloir** may govern a noun or pronoun.

Cet enfant ne cesse de grandir; il lui faut encore de nouvelles chaussures.
This child doesn't stop growing; he needs new shoes again.

Autrefois il fallait dix heures de train pour aller de Paris à Nice; maintenant, en avion, il n'en faut que deux.
It used to take ten hours by train to go from Paris to Nice; now, by plane, it takes only two.

b. **Falloir** may govern an infinitive.

On n'a plus de temps à perdre, il [nous] faut partir tout de suite. —Tu as raison, il le faut.
We have no time to waste; we've got to leave right away. —You're right; we do.

Note that the subject of the infinitive, if it is general or of the first or second person, is often understood from context, but may for clarity be expressed by the appropriate indirect object pronoun. When the subject is a particular third person, the pronoun must be used.

Il faut honorer ses parents, selon le Décalogue.
One (You, We) must honor one's (your, our) parents, according to the Ten Commandments.

Pourquoi ne l'as-tu pas prévenu de notre réunion? Il aurait fallu lui téléphoner hier matin.
Why didn't you tell him about our meeting? You should have phoned him yesterday morning.

On va démolir son immeuble. Il lui faudra déménager dans un mois.
Her (His) building is going to be demolished. She (He) will have to move in a month.

c. **Falloir** may govern a clause in the subjunctive.

Si elle veut se présenter aux municipales, il faudra qu'elle obtienne encore quelques signatures d'électeurs.
If she wants to run in the city elections, she will have to obtain a few more voters' signatures.

d. When negated, **falloir** continues to express necessity or obligation.

Il ne faut pas courir dans les couloirs, mes enfants.
You mustn't run in the halls, children.

Note that to convey the absence of necessity or obligation, French makes use of other constructions.

You don't have to run. There's plenty of time.
Il n'est pas nécessaire de courir. Vous avez tout le temps.
Vous n'avez pas besoin de courir. Vous avez tout le temps.
Vous n'êtes pas obligés de courir. Vous avez tout le temps.

e. In the **passé composé** and simple past, **falloir** expresses not only the necessity of a given action but also its accomplishment. With other tenses, accomplishment or nonaccomplishment is determined by context.

Si j'arrive en retard, c'est qu'il m'a fallu attendre longtemps chez le médecin.
If I'm late, it's because I had to wait a long time at the doctor's.

Comme il fallait attendre une heure ou deux pour voir le médecin, j'ai décidé de revenir le lendemain.
Since it was necessary to wait an hour or two to see the doctor, I decided to come back the next day.

Comme il fallait attendre une heure ou deux pour voir le médicin, j'ai pu lire un tas de vieilles revues.
Since I had to wait an hour or two to see the doctor, I was able to read a stack of old magazines.

f.   Some fixed locutions with **falloir.**

comme il faut

Il n'a sûrement pas dit une telle grossièreté. C'est un garçon très comme il faut.
He surely didn't say such a coarse thing. He is a very proper boy.

Et pour la réception du maire, où vais-je trouver une robe comme il faut?
Speaking of the mayor's reception, where am I going to find an appropriate dress?

Tout va comme il faut dans nos préparatifs de départ.
Everything is going smoothly in our arrangements to leave.

s'en falloir

Nous sommes perdus, ou peu s'en faut.
We're lost, or just about.

Il s'en fallait de peu que je [ne] lui dise ses quatre vérités.
I almost told him (her) off.

Il s'en faut de beaucoup qu'elle soit disposée à accepter ce contrat.
She is far from being inclined to accept that contract.

2.   **S'agir de** may take a noun, pronoun, or infinitive complement.

Un délégué des ouvriers me demande? De quoi s'agit-il?
There's a representative of the workers asking for me? What's it about?

Dans ce conte sud-américain, il s'agit d'un homme qui se trouve transformé en poisson.
This South American story is about a man who finds himself changed into a fish.

Pour certains, le devoir civique était bien simple; il s'agissait d'être prêt à mourir pour la patrie.
For some people, a citizen's duty was very simple; it was a matter of being ready to die for one's country.

3. **Se pouvoir** is followed by a subjunctive clause.

Il se peut que le garagiste n'ait pas bien réglé les freins.
It may be that the mechanic didn't adjust the brakes properly.

Une fois nettoyé les décombres, il se pourra que le nombre des victimes atteigne des centaines.
Once the ruins are cleaned up, it may be that the number of victims will reach the hundreds.

4. **Meteorological phenomena**

bruiner	*drizzle*
grêler	*hail*
grésiller	*sleet*
neiger	*snow*
pleuvoir	*rain*
tonner	*thunder*

L'avion n'a pas pu décoller parce qu'il avait beaucoup neigé dans la nuit.
The airplane could not take off because it had snowed a lot during the night.

Note that **geler** (*freeze, be freezing*) [also **dégeler** (*thaw*)] is not impersonal by nature.

Selon la météo, il va geler ce soir.
According to the weather report, it is going to freeze this evening.

On gèle ici. Allume le feu, veux-tu?
We're freezing here. Light the fire, will you?

B. **Impersonals by construction**

1. **Verb phrases denoting meteorological phenomena**

faire du brouillard	*be foggy*
faire de la brume	*be misty*
faire des éclairs	*lightning*
faire des nuages	*be cloudy*
faire de l'orage	*storm*
faire du soleil	*be sunny*
faire du vent	*be windy, blow*
faire du verglas	*be icy*
faire beau	*be nice, pleasant*

faire chaud	*be warm, hot*
faire clair	*be bright*
faire doux	*be mild*
faire frais	*be cool, brisk*
faire froid	*be cold*
faire gris	*be cloudy*
faire humide	*be damp, humid*
faire lourd	*be oppressive*
faire mauvais	*be nasty*
faire noir	*be dark*
faire sec	*be dry*

Il faisait tant de brouillard que nous avons évité de justesse un accident.
There was so much fog that we barely avoided an accident.

Quel sale temps! Il fait gris et lourd, et j'ai mal à la tête.
What rotten weather! It's cloudy and oppressive, and I have a headache.

Note too the expressions **il fait jour** (*it is day, it is light*) and **il fait nuit** (*it is night, night is falling*), which may occur, of course, in any tense.*

2.   **Y avoir** expresses existence or occurrence.†

Il y a des corps célestes qui s'appellent astéroïdes.
There are heavenly bodies called asteroids.

Il n'y avait rien à faire, elle avait déjà pris sa décision.
There was nothing to be done; she had already made up her mind.

Combien d'accidents de route y a-t-il eu pendant le week-end?
How many automobile accidents occurred (were there) over the weekend?

Qu'est-ce qu'il y avait dans les bagages perdus?
What was there in the lost baggage?

Note that (**qu'est-**)**ce qu'il y a,** in any tense, also has an idiomatic meaning.

Elles ne répondent plus à mes lettres. Je me demande ce qu'il y a.
They no longer answer my letters. I wonder what's the matter.

Tu as bien mauvaise mine. Qu'est-ce qu'il y a?
You look awful. What's the matter?

---

*Note the idiomatic expression **Demain il fera jour** (*Tomorrow is another day*).
†For **y avoir** expressing time, see Section I.J.2.

3. *Etre*

    a. **Etre** may be used as a synonym of **y avoir** on a somewhat more elevated level of discourse.

Il est, mes chers collègues, des cas où il faut agir avec fermeté.
There are cases, my dear colleagues, in which firm action is necessary.

Le conte des fées traditionnel commence par la formule «Il était une fois . . .».
The traditional fairy tale begins with the formula "Once upon a time there was . . .".

    b. **Etre** is used in statements of time.

Il sera onze heures avant que nous ayons fini ce travail.
It will be eleven o'clock before we've finished this work.

Il était déjà tard quand la séance a été levée.
It was already late when the meeting was adjourned.

    c. **Etre** + adjective serves as an impersonal characterization of a following **de** + infinitive phrase or **que** + clause.

Il est toujours agréable de partir en vacances.
It is always pleasant to go away on vacation.

Il est indispensable que nous soyons là à l'heure indiquée.
It is absolutely necessary for us to be (that we be) there at the appointed hour.

Il est bien évident que la scolarisation n'est plus un privilège mais un droit.
It is quite obvious that schooling is no longer a privilege but a right.

    d. **Etre** + noun serves as an impersonal characterization of a following **de** + infinitive phrase. Note that **que** is optionally used before **de**. The subject of **être** in this construction is **ce**.

Ils sont très forts. Ce serait une folie [que] de résister.
They are very strong. It would be folly to resist.

Pour encourager la production, les Soviétiques ont trouvé que c'était une bonne idée [que] de laisser à chaque paysan un lopin de terre en propre.
To encourage production, the Soviets found that it was a good idea to leave each peasant a patch of ground all his own.

4. The passive voice of many transitive verbs may be used in impersonal construction. This is particularly frequent in legal or other formal language. Following are some examples.

Il est rappelé aux locataires que le ramonage annuel des cheminées est prescrit par la loi.
Tenants are reminded that annual chimney sweeping is required by law.

Il a été décidé (convenu) à la réunion du comité de soumettre cette
question au vote de tous les membres de la société.
*It was decided (agreed) at the meeting of the committee to submit this
question to the vote of the entire membership of the society.*

Il est écrit dans la Bible que l'homme gagnera son pain à la sueur
de son front.
*It is written in the Bible that man will earn his bread by the sweat of
his brow.*

5. Many intransitive verbs may be used in impersonal construction.
    Among the most useful are the following.

advenir	*occur*
arriver	*happen*
convenir	*be fitting*
courir	*run*
entrer	*enter*
exister	*exist*
importer	*be important*
manquer	*be lacking*
paraître	*appear*
plaire	*be pleasing*
rester	*remain*
(en) résulter	*result*
sembler	*seem*
souvenir	*remember*
suffire	*suffice*
tarder	*be eager*
tomber	*fall*
valoir	*be worth*
venir	*come*

Il m'est arrivé quelque chose de très amusant. (Quelque chose de
très amusant m'est arrivé.)
Something very amusing happened to me.

Il convient que notre comité soumette un rapport annuel au Ministère.
*It is appropriate that our committee submit an annual report to the Min-
istry.*

Il a couru des bruits inquiétants sur la situation financière.
(Des bruits inquiétants ont couru sur la situation financière.)
There were some disturbing rumors about the financial situation.

Il importe de vérifier l'authenticité de ces tableaux.
It is important to verify the authenticity of these paintings.

J'ai acheté un bon piano d'occasion, mais il y manque l'ivoire de
quelques touches.
(J'ai acheté un bon piano d'occasion, mais l'ivoire de quelques
touches y manque.)
I bought a good used piano, but it is missing the ivory of a few keys.

Il ne vous reste que trois jours de vacances. Profitez-en!
You have only three days of vacation left. Enjoy them!

Il suffirait d'une seule goutte d'eau pour faire déborder le vase.
(Une seule goutte d'eau suffirait pour faire déborder le vase.)
It would take only one drop of water to make the vase overflow.
(Only one drop of water would suffice to make the vase overflow.)

　　　Note that there are some fixed expressions using these verbs
without **il.**

reste à savoir

Nous venons de leur soumettre le rapport. Reste à savoir s'il sera
lu.
We have just submitted our report to them. It remains to be seen whether
it will be read.

comme bon me (te, lui, etc.) semble

Malgré la désapprobation de leurs collègues, ils agissent comme bon
leur semble.
Despite the disapproval of their colleagues, they act as it suits them.

mieux vaut

Mieux vaudrait attendre devant les portes du théâtre que d'arriver
en retard.
It would be better to wait for the theater doors to open than to arrive
late.

6.　Certain pronominal verbs may be used in impersonal construction.

Il s'est passé hier au stade une chose très curieuse.
(Une chose très curieuse s'est passée hier au stade.)
A very curious thing happened yesterday at the stadium.

Dépêchons-nous! Il se fait tard.
Let's hurry! It's getting late.

Pendant les fêtes, il se vend beaucoup de livres illustrés.
(Pendant les fêtes, beaucoup de livres illustrés se vendent.)
During the holidays, there are lots of illustrated books sold.
(During the holidays, many illustrated books are sold.)

XI. THE -ANT FORM OF THE VERB

Every verb has a form ending in **-ant,** which may function as the equivalent of a subordinate clause; it is traditionally known as the present participle or gerund. In the case of many verbs, the same form may function as an adjective as well.

A. Formation

1. The stem of the **-ant** form is the same as that of the first person
    plural present indicative.

chanter	nous chantons	chantant	*singing*
finir	nous finissons	finissant	*finishing*
partir	nous partons	partant	*leaving*
attendre	nous attendons	attendant	*waiting*

    Note that three verbs have an irregular stem.

avoir	nous avons	ayant	*having*
être	nous sommes	étant	*being*
savoir	nous savons	sachant	*knowing*

2. **Ayant** and **étant** may be combined with past participles to form
    compound, or perfect, participles.

ayant chanté	*having sung*
étant parti(e)(s)	*having left*
s'étant souvenu(e)(s)	*having remembered*

3. When used as an adjective, the **-ant** form shows normal agreement
    in gender and number.

un village charmant	*a charming village*
des villages charmants	*charming villages*
une ville charmante	*a charming city*
des villes charmantes	*charming cities*

Note that **soi-disant,** however, is invariable.

Ces soi-disant docteurs ne sont que des charlatans.
These so-called doctors are only charlatans.

4. Certain verbs have verbal adjectives whose form differs from that of
    the corresponding participles or gerunds.

a. Adjectives with a slightly different stem.

convaincant	*convincing, cogent*	convainquant	*convincing*
fatigant	*tiring, tiresome*	fatiguant	*tiring, fatiguing*
intrigant	*intriguing, scheming*	intriguant	*plotting, scheming*
navigant	*sailing, flying*	naviguant	*navigating, sailing*
provocant	*provocative*	provoquant	*provoking*
suffocant	*stifling*	suffoquant	*choking, smothering*

b. Adjectives ending in **-ent.**

adhérent	*adherent, adhesive*	adhérant	*adhering*
convergent	*convergent, converging*	convergeant	*converging*
différent	*different, differing*	différant	*differing, postponing*
divergent	*divergent, diverging*	divergeant	*diverging*
émergent	*emergent, emerging*	émergeant	*emerging*
équivalent	*equivalent*	équivalant	*being equivalent*
influent	*influential*	influant	*influencing*
négligent	*negligent, neglectful*	négligeant	*neglecting*
précédent	*preceding, previous*	précédant	*preceding*
somnolent	*somnolent*	somnolant	*dozing*

c. Other adjectives.

ennuyeux	*boring, tiresome*	ennuyant	*boring, annoying*
flatteur	*flattering*	flattant	*flattering*
menteur	*mendacious, lying*	mentant	*lying*
pleureur	*weeping, tearful*	pleurant	*weeping*
puissant	*powerful*	pouvant	*being able*
savant	*learned*	sachant	*knowing*

B. Uses of the *-ant* form

1. As adjectives, **-ant** forms behave like any other adjectives; they are almost always placed after the nouns they modify.

a. In most cases, the adjective has an active sense and is the equivalent of a relative clause with the noun as subject.

Il a dû abandonner la chirurgie parce qu'à la suite de sa maladie il avait les mains tremblantes (= qui tremblaient).
He had to give up surgery because as a result of his illness he had trembling hands.

Pour moderniser le vieux château, ils y ont mis l'électricité et
 l'eau courante.
*To modernize the old chateau, they installed electricity and running
 water.*

b. In certain fixed cases, the relation of the adjective to its noun is different
from that of an active verb to its subject.

Mes enfants ont été invités à une soirée dansante chez l'ambassadeur
 pour le 14 juillet.
*My children have been invited to a dance at the ambassador's for Bastille
 Day.*

In this case, **dansante** is the equivalent of **où l'on danse.** Other phrases
of this type follow.

musique dansante (= m. à faire danser)	*dance music*
thé dansant (= t. où l'on danse)	*tea dance*
café chantant	*café with entertainment*
soirée chantante	*musical evening*
couleur voyante	*loud color*
argent comptant	*cash*
chaise pliante	*folding chair*
rue passante	*busy street*
place payante	*seat for which admission is charged*
entrée payante	*admission charged, no free admission*

Note, too, the following related phrases.

rue commerçante	*business street*
quartier commerçant	*business district*
peuple commerçant	*trading nation*
médecin consultant	*consulting physician*
avocat consultant	*consulting attorney*
poste restante	*general delivery*

2. As verbs, **-ant** forms may or may not be introduced by the preposition **en.** In either case, they are equivalent to subordinate clauses of
various types. Like the verbs in such clauses, they may govern objects and be modified by adverbs.

Lui ayant souvent parlé (= Du fait qu'il lui avait parlé) de cette
 affaire, il s'attendait à une réponse plus prompte.
*Having often spoken to her (him) about the matter, he was expecting a
 more prompt reply.*

Il a découvert le testament de son père en feuilletant (= pendant
 qu'il feuilletait) un vieux livre.
He discovered his father's will while leafing through an old book.

a. There are numerous instances, sometimes overlapping, in which
the **-ant** form is used without **en.**

i. When the **-ant** form has its own explicit subject.

   Les fraises étant hors de saison, nous avons dû repenser notre menu. / Nous avons dû repenser notre menu, les fraises étant hors de saison.
   Strawberries being out of season, we had to rethink our menu. / We had to rethink our menu, strawberries being out of season.

   Le cas échéant, je demanderai votre aide.
   If need be, I'll ask for your help.

ii. When the subject of the **-ant** form is a noun or pronoun in the main clause other than the subject. In this case, the **-ant** phrase cannot precede the main clause.

   Nous l'avons remarqué parlant avec la concierge.
   We noticed him speaking with the concierge.

   Je viens de recevoir une lettre annonçant l'arrivée imminente de mon neveu.
   I've just received a letter announcing my nephew's imminent arrival.

   Note that if the **-ant** form is introduced by **en,** its subject is necessarily the same as that of the main clause.*

   Nous l'avons remarqué en parlant avec la concierge.
   We noticed him while [we were] speaking with the concierge.

   En parlant avec la concierge, nous avons remarqué pour la première fois son petit-fils.
   As we were speaking (While speaking) with the concierge, we noticed her grandson for the first time.

iii. When the function of the **-ant** phrase is adjectival, that is, when it is equivalent to a relative clause.

   Une lettre annonçant (= qui annonçait) l'arrivée imminente de mon neveu m'est parvenue ce matin.
   A letter announcing my nephew's imminent arrival reached me this morning.

   Nous l'avons remarqué parlant (= qui parlait) avec la concierge.
   We noticed him speaking with the concierge.

---

*There are some proverbial expressions in which this rule is not observed.

L'appétit vient en mangeant.   *Appetite grows with eating.*
La fortune vient en dormant.   *Good luck comes when you're not looking for it.*

iv. When the function of the **-ant** phrase is to express cause, that is, when it is equivalent to a clause beginning with **parce que, puisque,** or the like.

Sachant (= Comme elle savait) la vérité sur l'affaire, elle ne se sentait pas le droit de se taire.
Knowing the truth about the matter, she did not feel she had the right to remain silent.

Le vieux représentant, souffrant (= parce qu'il souffrait) de la goutte, a dû limiter ses déplacements.
The elderly salesman, suffering from gout, had to limit his traveling.

v. When the function of the **-ant** phrase is to express an action relatively independent of the main verb and capable of being conveyed in a parallel main clause.

Prenant les six œufs restés dans le frigo, il nous en a fait un repas plus que décent.
He took the six eggs left in the refrigerator and made us a more than acceptable meal.

In this construction, the action expressed in the main clause often defines or concretizes the action expressed in the **-ant** phrase.

Cédant à la tentation de faire l'important, il révéla à la presse les intentions du directeur.
Yielding to the temptation of looking important, he revealed the director's intentions to the press.

Un jeune militant, adoptant la technique kamikaze, prit un avion et alla s'écraser sur le toit de l'ambassade.
A young militant, adopting the kamikaze technique, took an airplane and crashed into the roof of the embassy.

vi. When a conjunction introduces the **-ant** form. The only conjunctions that may occur here are those expressing concession.

Quoiqu' (Bien qu') observant les règles de la pratique religieuse, il restait profondément fermé à la spiritualité.
Although observing the rules of religious practice, he remained fundamentally untouched by spirituality.

vii. When a compound, or perfect, **-ant** form is used.

Ayant travaillé pendant six mois, il peut maintenant s'offrir un voyage à la Martinique.
Having worked for six months, he can now treat himself to a trip to Martinique.

b. There are instances, sometimes overlapping, in which the **-ant** form is introduced by **en.**

   i. To avoid ambiguity, when the subject of the **-ant** form is the same as that of the main verb but the **-ant** phrase follows the main clause.

Nous l'avons remarqué en parlant avec la concierge.
We noticed him while [we were] speaking with the concierge.

See Section a.ii. above.

  ii. When the **-ant** phrase is incorporated into the idiomatic stress construction **c'est . . . que . . . .**

C'est seulement en agrandissant la photo que vous trouverez la preuve que vous cherchez.
Only by enlarging the photo will you find the evidence that you're looking for.

 iii. When the **-ant** phrase has various adverbial functions, i.e., when it is equivalent to a subordinate clause expressing manner or means, a hypothesis, or simultaneity or near simultaneity.

Il est amusant de voir ces oiseaux se nettoyer en se roulant dans la poussière.
It's amusing to see those birds clean themselves by rolling around in the dust.

Vous arriverez à la poste en prenant la rue à gauche.
You will get to the post office by taking the street to the left.

En renonçant au tabac, tu tousserais moins.
If you gave up smoking, you would cough less.

Nous avons été ravis, en arrivant, d'apprendre que nos amis étaient déjà là.
We were delighted, upon arriving, to learn that our friends were already there.

Ma tante est formidable! Elle a su broder une nappe et huit serviettes en regardant la télévision.
My aunt is terrific! She managed to embroider a tablecloth and eight napkins while watching television.

To underscore the simultaneity of the two actions, **en -ant** may be introduced by **tout.**

Figurez-vous, elle est capable de broder tout en regardant la télévision.
Just imagine, she's able to embroider even while watching television.

The same construction may express concession or contrast.

Tout en abhorrant certaines idéologies, les défenseurs de la
   Constitution en protègent la libre expression.
*Although abhorring certain ideologies, the defenders of the Constitu-
   tion protect the free expression of them.*

c. Sometimes, particularly at the beginning of a sentence, it is
    possible to use either **-ant** or **en -ant** with little or no difference
    in meaning. Note that this variation has its parallel in English.

[En] feuilletant un vieux livre, il a découvert le testament de
   son père.
[While] leafing through an old book, he discovered his father's will.

[En] descendant la rue, elle a glissé sur une peau de banane.
[While] going down the street, she slipped on a banana peel.

[En] apercevant les cerisiers en fleur, nous avons cru à l'avène-
   ment du printemps.
*[While] noticing the cherry trees in bloom, we believed spring had
   come.*

Note that **aller** and **s'en aller** may be followed by an **-ant** form, with or without **en**,
to denote action in progress.

Cette inflation est interminable; les prix vont toujours [en] montant.
This inflation is endless; prices are constantly rising.

C. Special remarks

1. Certain **-ant** forms function as prepositions when used before a
    noun; see Chapter 15, Section I.B.

2. English present participles denoting physical position are rendered
    in French by past participles or adverbs.

sitting	*assis*
standing	*debout*
kneeling	*à genoux, agenouillé*
lying	*couché, allongé*
bending	*penché*
leaning	*appuyé, accoudé*

Note that physical position is expressed in French only if there is some need for specification.

Standing at the window, he looked pensively at the barges going by.
Pensif devant la fenêtre, il regardait les péniches qui passaient.

Why are you sitting there reading instead of getting dinner ready?
Qu'est-ce que tu fais là à lire plutôt que de préparer le dîner?

The editor-in-chief, standing behind his desk, appeared larger than life-size to the
new reporter.
**Le rédacteur-en-chef, debout derrière son bureau, paraissait au nouveau re-
porter plus grand que nature.**

3. English frequently expresses motion by combining a verb that denotes a type of movement with an adverb or preposition that indicates the direction of the movement. The French equivalent of such
an utterance usually expresses the direction in the verb and the type
of movement—if it needs to be specified—in an **en -ant** phrase or
other adverbial modifier.

While we rowed across the lake, the lifeguard swam across.
**Alors que nous avons traversé le lac en canot, le maître-nageur
l'a fait à la nage.**

He had no sooner walked out of the house than he heard cries for
help; he ran back in and found his wife lying on the floor.
**Il était à peine sorti de la maison qu'il entendit crier au secours;
il rentra en courant et trouva sa femme par terre.**

XII. THE SUBJUNCTIVE

A. Forms

1. **The present.** The present subjunctive is formed by adding the following endings to the verb stem.

Singular	Plural
-e	-ions
-es	-iez
-e	-ent

a. *One-stem verbs.* The stem of most one-stem verbs can be found by
dropping the **-ent** ending of the third-person plural of the present
indicative: **donnent → donn-, finissent → finiss-, partent →
part-, vendent → vend-,** etc.

je donne	nous donnions	je finisse	nous finissions
tu donnes	vous donniez	tu finisses	vous finissiez
il donne	ils donnent	on finisse	elles finissent
je parte	nous partions	je vende	nous vendions
tu partes	vous partiez	tu vendes	vous vendiez
il parte	elles partent	elle vende	ils vendent

The following one-stem verbs have an irregular stem.

faire   je fasse, tu fasses, etc.
pouvoir   je puisse, tu puisses, etc.
savoir   je sache, tu saches, etc.

b. *Two-stem verbs.* Verbs which have two plural stems in the present indicative, such as **boire, venir, prendre,** have two stems in the present subjunctive as well. One stem is used in the singular and the third person plural; the other is used in the first and second persons plural.

je boive	nous buvions	je prenne	nous prenions
tu boives	vous buviez	tu prennes	vous preniez
il boive	elles boivent	elle prenne	ils prennent

The following verbs show some irregularity.

aller   j'aille, tu ailles, il aille, elles aillent, nous allions, vous alliez

avoir   j'aie, tu aies, elle ait, ils aient, nous ayons, vous ayez

être   je sois, tu sois, on soit, ils soient, nous soyons, vous soyez

vouloir je veuille, tu veuilles, elle veuille, ils veuillent, nous voulions, vous vouliez

2. **The imperfect.** The stem of the imperfect subjunctive is the first person singular of the **passé simple** minus the last letter. To that stem are added the following endings.

Singular	*Plural*
-sse	-ssions
-sses	-ssiez
-ˆt	-ssent

Chanter and **vivre,** for example, are conjugated as follows.

je chantasse	je vécusse
tu chantasses	tu vécusses
il chantât	elle vécût
nous chantassions	nous vécussions
vous chantassiez	vous vécussiez
elles chantassent	ils vécussent

The only exception is the verb **haïr,** which in the third-person singular retains the dieresis instead of taking the circumflex: **il haït.**

3. **The past.** The past subjunctive is formed by combining the present subjunctive of the auxiliary **avoir** or **être** with the past participle of the verb in question.

prendre	j'aie pris, tu aies pris, elle ait pris, etc.
venir	je sois venu(e), tu sois venu(e), etc.
se lever	je me sois levé(e), tu te sois levé(e), etc.

4. **The pluperfect.** The pluperfect is formed by combining the imperfect subjunctive of the auxiliary with the past participle of the verb in question.

prendre	j'eusse pris, tu eusses pris, il eût pris, etc.
venir	je fusse venu(e), tu fusses venu(e), etc.
se lever	je me fusse levé(e), tu te fusses levé(e), etc.

B. Tense usage

Only the present and past subjunctive are normally used in ordinary discourse, while all four subjunctive tenses are found in formal usage.

1. **Formal usage.** The following tables and examples show the usual sequences of tenses in complex sentences using the subjunctive.

a. *Main verb*   *Subordinate verb*

present indicative	present subjunctive
imperative	or
future	past subjunctive
future perfect	

Je regrette qu' { il ne soit pas ici { maintenant. / demain

il n'ait pas été ici hier.

I am sorry that { he is not here now. / he will not be here tomorrow. / he was not here yesterday.

Ordonnez qu' { il prenne ces précautions immédiatement. / il ait pris ces précautions avant demain.

Order him to take those precautions { immediately. / before tomorrow.

J'ordonnerai qu' { il parte le plus tôt possible. / il soit parti avant l'aube.

I shall order him { to leave as soon as possible. / to be gone by dawn.

J'aurai ordonné avant ton retour qu'il parte sans tarder.
Before your return I shall have ordered him to leave without delay.

b. *Main verb*   *Subordinate verb*

imperfect indicative
passé composé   imperfect subjunctive
simple past   or
pluperfect indicative   pluperfect subjunc-
passé antérieur   tive

Je { regrettais / ai regretté / regrettai / avais regretté } qu' { il partît / il fût parti la veille. } { sur-le-champ. / le lendemain. }

I { was / had been } sorry that { he was leaving immediately. / he would be leaving the next day. / he had left the day before. }

Quand j'eus ordonné qu' { il partît tout de suite, / il fût parti avant midi, } il céda.

When I had ordered him { to leave right away, / to be gone before noon, } he gave in.

c. *Main verb*   *Subordinate verb*

                                          present subjunctive
present conditional   past subjunctive
                                          imperfect subjunctive
                                          pluperfect subjunctive

past conditional   { imperfect subjunctive / pluperfect subjunctive }

Je voudrais qu' { il vienne / il vînt / il soit venu / il fût venu } { tout de suite. / avant trois heures. }

I should like him { to come immediately. / to have come by three o'clock. }

J'aurais voulu qu' { il vînt avec moi. / il fût venu avant moi. }

I should have liked him { to come with me. / to have come before me. }

2. **Ordinary discourse.** As the preceding examples show, precise time reference in the subjunctive is less significant than subjunctiveness

itself. This is particularly striking in ordinary discourse, where, with regard to real time, the imperfect and pluperfect are replaced by the other tenses of the subjunctive.

J'ai peur que cette herbe sèche ne prenne feu.

I am afraid that this dry grass $\begin{cases} may\ catch \\ may\ be\ catching \\ will\ catch \end{cases}$ *fire.*

J'avais peur que cette herbe sèche ne prenne (= prît) feu.

I was afraid that this dry grass $\begin{cases} might\ catch \\ might\ be\ catching \\ would\ catch \end{cases}$ *fire.*

J'ai peur que cette herbe sèche n'ait pris feu.

I am afraid that this dry grass $\begin{cases} has \\ may\ have \\ will\ have \end{cases}$ *caught fire.*

J'avais peur que cette herbe sèche n'ait (= eût) pris feu.

I was afraid that this dry grass $\begin{cases} had \\ might\ have \\ would\ have \end{cases}$ *caught fire.*

C. Uses of the subjunctive

In some cases, the use of the subjunctive is obligatory; in others, the choice of mood—subjunctive, indicative, or conditional—depends upon the nuance to be expressed.

1. Obligatory uses of the subjunctive

a. In clauses governed by the following verbs and verbal expressions. (Note that the subordinating conjunction is **que** unless otherwise noted.)

aimer	*like*
aimer mieux	*prefer*
approuver	*approve*
attendre	*wait*
s'attendre à ce que	*expect*
avoir hâte	*be eager*
avoir honte	*be ashamed*
avoir peur	*be afraid*

commander	*order*
conseiller	*advise*
consentir à ce que	*consent*
craindre	*fear*
défendre	*forbid*
demander	*ask, request*
déplorer	*deplore*
désirer	*want, desire*
détester	*hate, detest*
s'émerveiller	*marvel*
s'étonner	*be surprised, astonished*
éviter	*avoid*
exiger	*demand, require*
faire attention à ce que	*take care*
insister pour que	*insist*
mériter	*deserve, merit*
s'opposer à ce que	*object, oppose*
ordonner	*order, command*
permettre	*allow, permit*
se plaindre	*complain*
préférer	*prefer*
prendre garde	*take care (lest)*
prier	*ask, beg, pray*
proposer	*propose, suggest*
regretter	*be sorry, regret*
se réjouir	*be delighted, rejoice*
souhaiter	*wish*
tâcher	*try, endeavor*
tenir à ce que	*insist*
travailler à ce que	*work toward*
veiller à ce que	*take care*
vouloir	*want, wish*
être bien aise	*be pleased*
content	*happy, glad*
désolé	*very sorry*
enchanté	*delighted*
ennuyé	*annoyed*
étonné	*surprised, astonished*
fâché	*upset, annoyed*
furieux	*furious, angry*
heureux	*happy*
inquiet	*worried*
navré	*very sorry, crushed*
ravi	*delighted*
satisfait	*satisfied*
surpris	*surprised*
triste	*sad*

Avant de songer à la couleur des rideaux, il faut attendre que les travaux soient achevés.
Before thinking about the color of the curtains, we have to wait for the construction to be finished.

Indisposée, elle demanda qu'on lui servît le déjeuner dans sa chambre.
Feeling ill, she asked that her lunch be served in her room.

Nous n'avions nullement l'intention de l'offenser. Je suis désolé qu'il ait pu le penser.
We had no intention whatever of offending him. I am very sorry that he could have thought we did.

Note that stative verbs such as **devenir, rester, paraître, sembler** may replace **être** in the expressions above.

Elles semblent contentes que vous ayez offert de les aider.
They seem happy that you offered to help them.

Note that the main and subordinate clauses have different subjects; if the same subject is intended, an infinitive is used instead of a subordinate clause.

Je veux que tu sois là à huit heures.
I want you to be there at eight.

Je veux être là à huit heures.
I want to be there at eight.

b. In clauses governed by the following impersonal verbs and verbal expressions.

il convient	*it is fitting, appropriate*
il faut	*it is necessary*
il s'en faut de beaucoup	*(see Section X.A.1.f.)*
de peu	
peu s'en faut	
il importe	*it is important*
peu importe	*it is not important*
il se peut	*it may be*
it semble	*it seems*
il suffit	*it suffices*
il vaut mieux	*it is preferable*
cela m' (t', l', etc.) agace	*it annoys me (you, etc.)*
cela m' (t', l', etc.) ennuie	*it annoys me (you, etc.)*
cela me (te, le, etc.) fâche	*it upsets me (you, etc.)*
cela m' (t', l', etc.) irrite	*it irritates me (you, etc.)*
cela (il) me (te, lui, etc.) plaît	*it pleases me (you, etc.)*
cela me (te, le, etc.) vexe	*it annoys me (you, etc.)*
c'est dommage	*it is too bad, a pity*

il est bizarre	it is peculiar
convenable	fitting, proper
désirable	desirable
essentiel	essential
étonnant	surprising
étrange	strange
exceptionnel	unusual, exceptional
extraordinaire	extraordinary
fâcheux	irritating
faux	false
heureux	fortunate
honteux	shameful
important	important
impossible	impossible
inadmissible	unacceptable
incroyable	unbelievable, incredible
indispensable	necessary, indispensable
inévitable	inevitable
injuste	unfair, unjust
inutile	useless
juste	fair, right, just
malheureux	unfortunate
mauvais	bad
naturel	natural
nécessaire	necessary
possible	possible
préférable	preferable
peu probable	unlikely
rare	unusual, rare
regrettable	regrettable
souhaitable	desirable
temps	time
urgent	urgent
utile	useful

Ils sont en retard; il se peut qu'ils se soient trompés d'adresse.
They're late; it may be they've gone to the wrong address.

Ça l'ennuie qu'on fasse tant d'attention à ses affaires de famille
     dans le village.
*It annoys him that in the village people pay so much attention to his
     family affairs.*

N'est-il pas honteux qu'au vingtième siècle la famine fasse tou-
     jours ses victimes?
*Isn't it disgraceful that in the twentieth century famine still claims its
     victims?*

Note that the verbs **considérer (comme), croire, estimer, juger,** and **trouver** may be followed by the same adjectives (+ subordinate clause) as **il est** in the above list.

Nous trouvons extraordinaire que le coupable n'ait pas été puni.
We find it extraordinary that the guilty party has not been punished.

Les ingénieurs considéraient comme indispensable que les marécages fussent asséchés.
The engineers considered it indispensable that the marshes be drained.

   c.   In clauses introduced by the following conjunctions.

afin que	*so that, in order that*
à moins que	*unless*
au lieu que	*instead*
avant que	*before*
bien que	*although*
de crainte que	*for fear that*
de peur que	*for fear that*
encore que	*although*
jusqu'à ce que	*until*
non que	*not that*
pour que	*so that, in order that*
pourvu que	*provided*
quoique	*although*
sans que	*without*

La spirale des prix et salaires ne prendra jamais fin sans que le gouvernement prenne des mesures exceptionnelles.
The wage-price spiral will never end without the government taking (unless the government takes) extraordinary measures.

Veux-tu bien me garder ce fauteuil jusqu'à ce que le déménageur vienne le chercher?
Would you mind keeping this chair for me until the mover comes for it?

Note that when **que** replaces a conjunction requiring the subjunctive or replaces **si,** the verb in the subordinate clause is in the subjunctive.

Nous irons ce soir à l'observatoire pourvu qu'il fasse beau et qu'il n'y ait pas de nuages.
Nous irons ce soir à l'observatoire s'il fait beau et qu'il n'y ait pas de nuages.
We'll go to the observatory this evening provided (if) the weather is nice and there are no clouds.

Note that any clause introduced by **que** which opens the sentence normally takes the subjunctive.

Qu'il ait bien compris ce livre est évident; il est tout aussi évident qu'il n'en admet pas la thèse.
That he has fully understood this book is obvious; it is just as obvious that he does not accept its thesis.

d.   In clauses introduced by the following indefinite constructions.

$$\left.\begin{array}{l} \textbf{pour} \\ \textbf{quelque} \\ \textbf{si} \end{array}\right\} + \text{adjective or adverb} + \textbf{que}$$

quelque(s) + noun + **que**
quel (-le, -s, -les) que

$$\left.\begin{array}{l} \textbf{qui} \\ \textbf{quoi} \end{array}\right\} \textbf{que ce} \left\{\begin{array}{l} \textbf{soit} \\ \textbf{fût} \end{array}\right\} \left\{\begin{array}{l} \textbf{qui} \\ \textbf{que} \end{array}\right.$$

où que
qui que
quoi que

$$\textbf{que} + \text{clause } \textbf{ou} \left\{\begin{array}{l} \textbf{non} \\ \textbf{que} + \text{clause} \end{array}\right.$$

Quelque gentiment que vous le priiez, vous n'obtiendrez jamais
   rien de lui.
*No matter how (However) nicely you ask him, you'll never get any-
   thing from him.*

Quelque (Si, Pour) pratiques que soient les verres de contact, ils
   ne sont pas à conseiller à tout le monde.★
*However (No matter how) practical contact lenses may be, they are
   not advisable for everyone.*

Quelques injures qu'il ait lancées, ses adversaires les lui ont par-
   données.
Whatever insults he may have hurled, his opponents forgave him.

Quelles que soient nos hésitations, nous ne nous opposerons pas à
   vos projets.
Whatever hesitations we may have, we will not oppose your plans.

Ces normes s'appliquent à qui que ce soit qui veuille importer des
   marchandises.
These norms apply to anyone wishing to import merchandise.

Dans cette galerie, où que vous regardiez, il y a des merveilles à
   voir.
In this gallery, wherever you look, there are wonders to be seen.

★Note that the almost synonymous construction **tout** + adjective or adverb + **que** normally takes the indicative.

Tout violent qu'il est, il a quand même bon cœur.
As violent as he is, he still has a good heart.

Qu'on l'entende ou non, l'arbre qui tombe ne fait-il pas de bruit?
Whether it is heard or not, does the falling tree not make noise?

Que ce soit par téléphone, que ce soit par télégramme, il faut le
toucher dans les vingt-quatre heures.
*Whether [it be] by telephone or by wire, you must contact him within
the next twenty-four hours.*

e. In independent clauses introduced by **que** and expressing a command or a wish.

Et Dieu dit: Que la lumière soit!
And God said: Let there be light!

Que je meure si je mens!
Hope to die if I'm lying!

For further examples, see Section V.C.1. above. Note that, in
certain fixed expressions and constructions, **que** is omitted.

Ainsi soit-il!
So be it!

Dieu soit loué!
God be praised!

A Dieu ne plaise!
God forbid!

Dieu vous garde!
God keep you!

Sauve qui peut!
Every man for himself.

Vive la République (la France, le roi)!
Long live the Republic (France, the King)!

n'en déplaise à + noun or pronoun

N'en déplaise à mes collègues, je ne saurais approuver cette nouvelle politique.
*With all due respect to my colleagues, I cannot give my approval to
this new policy.*

Moi, ne vous en déplaise, je préfère l'hédonisme à l'ascétisme.
I for one, if you don't mind, prefer hedonism to asceticism.

pouvoir + subject + infinitive

Puissiez-vous jouir de longues années de bonheur.
May you enjoy long years of happiness.

Puisse la postérité garder le souvenir de leur noble sacrifice.
May posterity keep the memory of their noble sacrifice.

plût à + noun + **que** + clause

Plût au Seigneur que la paix se rétablisse bientôt.
May it please the Lord that peace return soon.

2.   Uses of the subjunctive in which the choice of mood depends upon the nuance to be expressed.

    a.   When the following verbs simply state a fact, they take the indicative. When, however, they express an order or a wish, approval or a hypothesis, they take the subjunctive.

avertir	*warn*	admettre	*grant*
crier	*shout*	comprendre	*understand*
dire	*say, tell*	concevoir	*conceive*
écrire	*write*	consentir	*consent*
entendre	*hear; expect*	être d'avis	*be of the opinion*
faire	*do, make*	[s']imaginer	*imagine, conceive*

J'ai dit qu'il se faisait couper les cheveux.
I said he was getting his hair cut.

Je lui ai dit qu'il fasse (de se faire) couper les cheveux.
I told him to get his hair cut.

Nous entendons que vous partez tout de suite.
We understand (hear) that you're leaving immediately.

Nous entendons que vous partiez tout de suite.
We expect (want) you to leave immediately.

Leur traitement a fait qu'elle a guéri en peu de temps.
The result of their treatment was that she recovered rapidly.

Docteur, je vous supplie, faites qu'elle guérisse!
Doctor, I beg you, make her well!

Nous admettons tous que les filles mères ont besoin d'aide, mais de quelle source?
We all grant that unwed mothers need assistance, but from what source?

Admettons pour l'instant que le gouvernement soit cette source.
Let us suppose for the moment that the government is that source.

Je comprends que tu vas te marier. Je n'en savais rien, je suis ravi de l'apprendre!
I understand you're going to get married. I didn't know; I'm delighted to hear it!

Je comprends que tu veuilles te marier. On n'est plus si jeunes.
I understand your wanting to get married. We're not so young any-
more.

J'ai supposé, à le voir si agité, qu'il avait reçu une mauvaise nouvelle.
I assumed, seeing him so upset, that he had received bad news.

Suppose que tu aies reçu une mauvaise nouvelle. Ne serais-tu pas
agité, toi aussi?
Suppose you received bad news. Wouldn't you be upset, too?

b. The following verbs and verbal expressions tend to take the subjunctive. When used negatively, however, they may take the indicative.

contester	*deny, dispute*
dissimuler	*hide, conceal*
douter	*doubt*
nier	*deny*
avoir des doutes	*have doubts*
il est douteux	*it is doubtful*

Je doute que nos enfants puissent goûter le plaisir de traverser
l'océan en paquebot.
I doubt our children will be able to enjoy the pleasure of crossing the
ocean by ship.

Nous ne doutons pas, étant donné qu'il s'agit d'une première
mondiale, qu'il n'y ait dans l'assistance bon nombre de cri-
tiques distingués.
We don't doubt, given that it's a world première, that there will be a
goodly number of distinguished critics in the audience.

Vu sa gourmandise, je n'ai aucun doute qu'il viendra à notre réception.
Given his love for food, I have no doubt he'll come to our reception.

c. When the following subordinating conjunctions introduce a result, they take the indicative. When, however, they introduce a
purpose, they take the subjunctive.

de façon que
de manière que
de [telle] sorte que
tel (-le, -s, -les) que

Le chef du labo a tout arrangé de façon qu'on a pu observer
toutes les souris en même temps.
The head of the lab arranged everything in such a way that all the
mice could be observed at the same time.

Le chef du labo aurait voulu tout arranger de façon qu'on puisse (pût) observer toutes les souris en même temps.
The head of the lab would have liked to arrange everything in such a way that all the mice could be observed at the same time.

Il voulait lancer une campagne publicitaire telle que le succès du livre soit (fût) assuré.
He wanted to launch the kind of advertising campaign that would ensure the success of the book.

On a mené une campagne publicitaire telle que le succès du livre a été assuré.
They ran the kind of advertising campaign that ensured the success of the book.

d. In a relative clause, the verb is in the indicative when the noun modified by the clause represents an entity whose existence is real. The verb is in the subjunctive when that existence is somehow in question.

i. The subjunctive is used when the relative clause modifies **personne, rien,** or any noun made negative. Negation within the relative clause is expressed by **ne** without **pas.**

Nous n'avons trouvé malheureusement personne qui sache traduire ce document finlandais.
We have unfortunately not found anyone able to translate this Finnish document.

Il n'y a pas un monument dans cette ville qui ne soit d'une laideur extraordinaire.
There is no monument in this city which is not extraordinarily ugly.

Je n'ai jamais dressé un chien qui mette tant de temps à apprendre les ordres les plus simples.
I've never trained a dog that took so much time to learn the simplest commands.

Note that the same situation applies with **peu de, rare,** and similarly restrictive expressions.

Il y a de moins en moins d'épiciers qui veuillent bien livrer à domicile.
There are fewer and fewer grocers who are willing to make home deliveries.

ii. When the noun modified by the relative is also modified by a superlative or by **seul, unique, premier, dernier** or is restricted by **ne . . . que,** the subjunctive is normally used.

Cette basse est le chanteur le moins doué que j'aie jamais entendu.
This bass is the most untalented singer I have ever heard.

C'est drôle, ces costauds, l'unique chose dont ils aient peur
c'est de se faire vacciner.
*These big guys are funny; the only thing they're afraid of is getting
vaccinated.*

Merci d'être venu. Il n'y a que toi qui puisses me remonter le
moral à un moment pareil.
*Thank you for coming. Only you can cheer me up at a time like
this.*

Note that the indicative is often used if the superlative expresses not a judgment but
an objective fact.

Ce gratte-ciel est le plus haut qu'on a (*or* ait) construit depuis dix ans.
This skyscraper is the tallest that has been built in the past ten years.

    iii. When the noun modified represents an entity whose existence
or attainability is in doubt, the verb in the relative clause is in
the subjunctive.

Y a-t-il dans ce quartier un restaurant où l'on puisse manger
pour pas cher?
*Is there any restaurant in this neighborhood where you can eat for
not much money?*

Il y a dans ce quartier plusieurs restaurants où l'on peut bien
manger pour pas cher.
*There are several restaurants in the neighborhood where you can eat
well for not much money.*

Je voudrais mettre dans ce coin un divan qui fasse double emploi comme lit.
*In that corner I'd like to put a couch that will do double duty as a
bed.*

Ma grand-mère avait un divan qui faisait double emploi comme
lit.
My grandmother had a couch that did double duty as a bed.

   3. Uses of the subjunctive in which the choice of mood is determined
by the form of the main clause: positive or negative, declarative or
interrogative.

    a. The following verbs and impersonal constructions take the indica-
tive when they convey an affirmative sense and the subjunctive
when they convey a negative sense. Note that affirmativeness includes negative questions and that negativeness includes affirmative questions; the determining factor is the kind of reply the
speaker expects.

affirmer	*assert, state, affirm*
croire	*think, believe*
dire	*say*
espérer	*hope, expect*
être sûr	*be sure*
être certain	*be certain*
juger	*judge*
penser	*think*
prétendre	*claim*
savoir	*know*
sentir	*feel*

trouver	*think, believe*
voir	*find, consider, see*
il est certain	*it is sure, certain*
clair	*evident, clear*
évident	*obvious*
exact	*true, correct*
hors de doute	*beyond doubt*
incontestable	*undeniable, indisputable*
indiscutable	*indisputable, undeniable*
probable	*probable*
sûr	*certain, sure*
vrai	*true*
il paraît	*it appears*
il me (te, lui, etc.) semble*	*it seems to me (to you, to him, etc.)*
il s'ensuit	*it follows*

Je ne prétends pas que l'enseignement par la télévision soit une panacée, mais il peut être très utile dans certaines conditions.

I do not claim that television teaching is a panacea, but it can be very useful under certain conditions.

Malgré ses deux heures de piscine par jour, je ne crois pas qu'elle fasse des progrès.

Despite her two hours in the pool every day, I don't think she is making progress.

Est-il exact que le pétrole de l'Alaska puisse subvenir à nos besoins énergétiques?

Is it true that Alaskan oil can supply our energy needs?

Il est indiscutable que la campagne mondiale contre la variole a réussi.

It is undeniable that the worldwide campaign against smallpox has been successful.

---

*For **il semble** without an indirect object, see Section C.1.b.

Il a juré qu'il ignorait les machinations de ses agents. Ne croyez-vous pas qu'il mentait?

He swore he did not know about his agents' machinations. Don't you think he was lying?

Note that the indicative may be substituted for the subjunctive in order to emphasize the speaker's conviction.

Figure-toi, il y a toujours quelques cinglés qui ne croient pas que la terre est ronde.

Just imagine, there are still some crackpots who do not believe that the earth is round.

b. The following constructions take the subjunctive when the main clause is negative or interrogative. Otherwise, they are followed by the indicative.

si . . . que	*so . . . that*
tant . . . que	*so much . . . that*
tellement . . . que	*so . . . that*
au point que	*to the extent (point) that*
à ce point que	*to the extent (point) that*
à [un] tel point que	*to such an extent (point) that*

Ce volcan ne risque pas d'être si actif qu'on doive évacuer les environs.

This volcano is not likely to be so active that the area will need to be evacuated.

Ont-ils tant d'obligations qu'ils ne puissent nous recevoir lundi prochain?

Have they so many commitments that they cannot see us next Monday?

Dans les grandes entreprises, on craint les espions «industriels» à tel point qu'on prend des mesures de sécurité exceptionnelles.

Big businesses fear "industrial" spies to such an extent that they take extraordinary security measures.

4. Use of the subjunctive in which the choice of mood is a matter of literary style. The pluperfect subjunctive may be substituted for the pluperfect indicative or the past conditional or both in hypothetical utterances.

$$\text{S'il en} \begin{cases} \text{avait} \\ \text{eût} \\ \text{avait} \\ \text{eût} \end{cases} \text{prévu les conséquences, il ne se}$$

$$\begin{cases} \text{serait} \\ \text{serait} \\ \text{fût} \\ \text{fût} \end{cases} \text{pas fait couronner.}$$

If he had foreseen the consequences, he would not have had himself crowned.

Note that such substitutions may occur in other uses of the past conditional as well.

Elle, si délicate, a abandonné son foyer pour aller faire des fouilles. Qui l'eût cru!
She, so fastidious, left her family to go on a dig. Who would have thought it?

La veille de son départ, elle a presque changé d'avis. C'eût été une erreur.
On the eve of her departure, she almost changed her mind. It would have been a mistake.

D. Pleonastic (redundant) *ne*

After the following verbs and conjunctions, all of which take the subjunctive, the verb in the subordinate clause may be preceded by **ne** with no negative value. This **ne** is more frequent in literary than in colloquial usage.

craindre	*fear*	ne pas contester	*not deny, not dispute*
empêcher	*prevent*	ne pas douter	*not doubt*
éviter	*avoid*	ne pas nier	*not deny*
avoir peur	*be afraid, fear*	à moins que	*unless*
prendre garde	*take care (lest)*	avant que	*before*
il s'en faut	(see Section	de crainte que	*lest, for fear that*
peu s'en faut	X.A.1.f.)	de peur que★	*lest, for fear that*

Il faut à tout prix éviter que les journalistes [ne] soient avisés de ces négotiations.
We must at all costs avoid having journalists informed of these negotiations.

Achetons une nouvelle chaîne stéréo avant que ça [ne] devienne inabordable.
Let's buy a new stereo system before they're priced out of reach.

★There is a strong tendency to use **ne** in a **sans que** clause if the main clause contains a negative.

Negation

Total negation, independent of any clause, is expressed in French by **non**. Most other forms of negation entail the use of **ne** and a specifying particle in a clause or, independently, the specifying particle alone. The particle may be an adverb, adjective, pronoun, or conjunction.

As-tu vu le facteur? —Non.	*Have you seen the mailman? —No.*
Je n'ai pas vu le facteur.	*I have not seen the mailman.*
Je n'ai vu personne.	*I have not seen anyone.*
Qui as-tu vu? —Personne.	*Whom have you seen? —No one.*

I. NEGATIVE ADVERBS

A. **Non** is used in the following ways.

1. Independently, as the equivalent of a clause.

   Tu veux regarder le débat télévisé ce soir? —Non, merci. J'ai trop à faire.
   You want to watch the panel discussion on TV this evening? —No, thanks, I have too much to do.

2. To replace a clause after verbs of communication and thinking, such as **dire, répondre,** and **croire.**

   A-t-il encore décidé de démissionner? —Il prétend que non.
   Has he decided to resign yet? —He claims not to have (that he has not).

3. To express contrast between two syntactically similar elements in an utterance.

   Mais vous vous trompez. —C'est un meuble de style, [et] non d'époque.
   I'm afraid you're mistaken. —The piece is a reproduction, [and] not an original.

   C'est un danseur non éblouissant, mais techniquement parfait.
   He is not a dazzling dancer, but he is technically perfect.

Note that in this use **non** may be replaced by **pas** or **non pas**.

4. To negate nouns and adjectives, including participles.

les non-croyants	*nonbelievers*
un non-sens	[*a piece of*] *nonsense*
un pacte de non-agression	*a nonaggression pact*
les métaux non-ferreux	*nonferrous metals*
des objets non réclamés	*unclaimed objects*
une quantité non négligeable	*an appreciable amount*
Il plaide non coupable.	*He pleads not guilty.*

5. To negate **seulement, loin, moins,** and **sans.**

Non loin d'ici vous trouverez non seulement une auberge mais un garage aussi.
Not far from here you will find not only an inn but a garage as well.

B. Negation of a clause is expressed by the combination of **ne** with one (or more) of the following adverbs

ne . . . pas	*not*
point	*not, not at all*
aucunement	*not at all, by no means*
nullement	*not at all, by no means*
guère	*scarcely, hardly*
jamais	*never, not ever*
plus	*no longer, not any more*
nulle part	*nowhere, not anywhere*

1. **Ne** precedes the conjugated verb and any conjunctive pronouns. The adverb follows the conjugated verb, except that in a compound tense **nulle part** follows the past participle.

Malgré toutes ses explications, nous ne comprenons nullement les mobiles de son acte.
Despite all his explanations, we don't by any means understand the motives for his act.

Il ne s'est jamais servi du service de thé qu'il a hérité de sa grand-mère.
He has never used the tea service that he inherited from his grandmother.

J'ai cherché partout mon acte de naissance, mais je ne l'ai trouvé nulle part.
I looked everywhere for my birth certificate, but I didn't find it anywhere.

Note that for the sake of emphasis **jamais** may begin a statement.

Encore en panne! Jamais machine n'a fonctionné si mal!
Broke again! Never has a machine worked so badly!

Jamais je n'ai vu [une] machine fonctionner si mal.
Never have I seen a machine work so badly.

2. When an infinitive is negated, both **ne** and the adverb precede the verb and any conjunctive pronouns, except that **aucunement, nullement,** and **nulle part** follow.

Pour éviter toute explication désagréable, je te conseille de ne jamais la revoir.
To avoid any unpleasant scene, I advise you never to see her again.

C'est un étourdi. Il vaut mieux ne compter nullement sur lui.
He's scatterbrained. It's better not to count on him at all.

Note that two constructions are possible with a past or a passive infinitive.

Mon permis de conduire, je crains de ne $\left\{\begin{array}{l}\text{l'avoir pas}\\\text{pas l'avoir}\end{array}\right\}$ réussi.
I'm afraid I didn't get my driver's license.

Ils sont persuadés de $\left\{\begin{array}{l}\text{n'être pas}\\\text{ne pas être}\end{array}\right\}$ suffisamment appréciés par le public.
They are convinced they are not sufficiently appreciated by the public.

3. **Ne . . . pas** may be combined with other adverbs.

ne . . . pas encore	*not yet*
pas du tout	*not at all*
pas non plus	*not . . . either*

Mon confrère n'a pas encore lu ton rapport et malheureusement je ne l'ai pas étudié non plus.
My colleague has not yet read your report and unfortunately I have not studied it either.

4. **Ne** may be used without **pas** in certain constructions and still have full negative force.

a. With **oser, cesser, pouvoir** followed by an infinitive.

Malgré toutes ses déceptions, il ne cesse de croire à la démocratie.
Despite all his disappointments, he does not stop believing in democracy.

J'avoue ne pouvoir le suivre dans son raisonnement.
I admit I cannot follow him in his reasoning.

b. With **savoir, pas** may be omitted if the meaning is *know* but not if it is *know how.*

La décision reste à prendre; ils ne savent s'ils veulent rester ou partir.
The decision has yet to be made; they don't know whether they want to stay or leave.

Même les choses les plus simples sont difficiles pour ceux qui ne savent pas lire.
Even the simplest things are difficult for those who do not know how to read.

For conditional **savoir** with **ne** alone, see Chapter 1, Section VII.D.2.

  c. In a relative clause modifying a noun or pronoun in a negative, dubitative, or interrogative clause.

On n'a pas encore créé une tulipe noire qui ne soit en réalité d'un violet très foncé.
No one has yet developed a black tulip which is not really very deep purple.

Je doute qu'il y ait quelqu'un parmi nous qui ne sache nager.
I doubt there is anyone among us who does not know how to swim.

Y a-t-il quelqu'un qui ne craigne la cécité?
Is there anyone who does not fear blindness?

  d. After **que** meaning *why* and sometimes after **si** (*if*).

Que n'avions-nous prévu les graves conséquences de la construction de ce barrage?
Why had we not foreseen the serious consequences of building this dam?

Si je ne me trompe, il en est à son deuxième roman.
If I'm not mistaken, he is on his second novel.

  e. In a few set expressions.

un je ne sais quoi
a certain something

N'importe.
It doesn't matter. (Never mind.)

ne vous (lui, leur, etc.) en déplaise
with all due respect

n'avoir garde de + infinitive
to be far from + . . . ing
to take care not to + infinitive

n'avoir que faire de + noun or pronoun
to have no use for + noun or pronoun

n'avoir que faire de + infinitive
to have no business + . . . ing

Il lui manque ce je ne sais quoi qui distingue le génie de l'intelligence.
He lacks that certain something which distinguishes genius from intelligence.

II. NEGATIVE ADJECTIVES

Ne . . . **aucun(e)**   no, not any
        nul(le)   no, not any

  A. The negative adjectives may modify any noun in the clause; they precede the noun.

Dans ces circonstances, le comptable n'a eu aucun conseil utile à nous donner.
In these circumstances, the accountant had no useful advice to give us.

Jusqu'ici, nulle victime de cet accident du travail n'a été indemnisée.
So far no victim of that job-related accident has been compensated.

Note that after **sans, aucun** may follow the noun it modifies.

Le commissaire-priseur estime que ce tapis est sans valeur aucune.
The appraiser judges this carpet to be of no value at all.

B. The plural forms of **aucun** and **nul** are used exclusively with nouns that occur only in the plural or have a special meaning in the plural.

La vendeuse dit: —Je regrette, il ne me reste plus aucuns ciseaux.
The saleswoman said: "I'm sorry; I haven't a single pair of scissors left."

Pour tous les soins que ce médecin fournit aux pauvres, il ne reçoit aucuns honoraires.
For all the care that this doctor gives to the poor, he receives no fees.

C. **Nul** and **aucun** may be used as negative pronouns; see Section III.C.

III. NEGATIVE PRONOUNS

ne . . . personne		*no one, nobody, not anyone*
	rien	*nothing, not anything*
ne . . . qui que ce soit		*nobody, not one at all*
	quoi que ce soit	*nothing, not anything at all*
ne . . . aucun(e)		*none, not one*
	nul(le)	*no one, none, not one*

A. **Personne** and **rien** may serve any noun or pronoun function in the clause: subject, object of verb, object of preposition. With compound tenses, direct object **personne** follows the past participle, whereas direct object **rien,** like negative adverbs, precedes.

La grenade a explosé mais heureusement n'a blessé personne.
The grenade exploded but luckily did not wound anyone.

Il a le sommeil si profond qu'il n'a rien entendu pendant le cambriolage.
He sleeps so soundly that he heard nothing during the burglary.

Nous ne céderons à leur pression pour rien au monde.
We will not yield to their pressure for anything in the world.

Personne ne saura me convaincre qu'il faille dépenser de telles sommes pour un nouveau stade.
No one will be able to convince me that it is necessary to spend such sums for a new stadium.

For modification of **personne** and **rien** by an adjective, see Chapter 5, Section II.B.8.

B. **Qui que ce soit** and **quoi que ce soit** may replace **personne** and **rien** for emphasis, but not as subjects. With compound tenses, they follow the past participle.

Etant enfant unique, il n'aura à partager la propriété avec qui que ce soit.
As an only child, he will not have to share the property with anyone at all.

Les touristes ont fait du lèche-vitrines tout l'après-midi, mais ils n'ont acheté quoi que ce soit.
The tourists window-shopped all afternoon, but they didn't buy a thing.

C. **Nul** and **aucun**

1. **As subjects**

   a. Masculine singular **nul** may be used absolutely, like the synonymous **personne**; it refers only to human beings.

   Nul n'est censé ignorer la loi.
   No one is supposed to be ignorant of the law.
   Ignorance of the law is no excuse.

   b. **Nulle, aucun,** and **aucune** always refer to one out of a given group; **nul** may also be so used. Reference is not necessarily to human beings.

   Parmi les opéras français, nul (aucun) n'enthousiasme plus le grand public que *Carmen.*
   Of all French operas, none is more enthusiastically received by the general public than Carmen.

   Les forces de l'ordre ont voulu disperser les mères manifestant devant le ministère. Nulle (Aucune) n'a bougé.
   The police tried to disperse the mothers demonstrating in front of the ministry. Not one budged.

2. In functions other than subject, **nul(le)** is virtually never used. Direct object **aucun(e)** is necessarily complemented by a **de** (or **d'entre**) phrase or by an equivalent pronoun (**en, dont,** etc.).

   La vendeuse lui a montré dix paires de gants, dont il n'a acheté aucune.
   The saleswoman showed him ten pairs of gloves, but he didn't buy any [of them].

   Cherchez si vous voulez dans tous les dictionnaires, vous ne trouverez ce mot dans aucun.
   Look if you wish in all the dictionaries; you won't find that word in any.

IV. NEGATIVE CONJUNCTIONS

ne . . . que	*only, but*
ne . . . ni . . . ni	*neither . . . nor, not either . . . or*
ne . . . ni ne	*neither . . . nor, not . . . or*

A. **Ne . . . que** is negative in form but restrictive in meaning; unlike real negatives, it does not bring about a change in the partitive or indefinite determiner of a direct object. It may limit any part of the sentence except the subject and except the verb if it is in a simple tense.

Il suit un régime végétarien très stricte, ce qui veut dire qu'il ne mange que des céréales et des légumes.
He adheres to a very strict vegetarian diet, which means he eats only grains and vegetables.

Notre fille adore tant nager qu'elle ne sort de l'eau que pour manger et dormir.
Our daughter adores swimming so much that she doesn't get out of the water except to eat and sleep.

Tu crois avoir evité le danger; tu n'as que retardé ses effets.
You think you've avoided the danger; you have only (but) delayed its effects.

La vie normale ne reprendra que lorsque les peintres auront quitté l'appartement.
Normal life won't return until the painters have left the apartment.
Normal life will return only when the painters have left the apartment.

1. To limit a verb in a simple tense, **ne faire que** + infinitive or the verb + **seulement** must be used.

   Ne t'en fais pas pour les clés. Je ne perds jamais mes affaires;

   je $\begin{cases} \text{ne fais que les égarer.} \\ \text{les égare seulement.} \end{cases}$

   Don't worry about the keys. I never lose my things; I only misplace them.

2. To limit a subject, **il n'y a que** + noun or pronoun, or noun or pronoun modified by **seul** must be used.

   Parmi les créatures aquatiques, il n'y a que les cétacés qui soient vivipares.
   Parmi les créatures aquatiques, seuls les cétacés sont vivipares.
   Among the aquatic creatures, only the cetaceans are viviparous.

   Lui seul, de toute notre bande, sait distinguer entre les champignons comestibles et les vénineux.
   Only he (He alone), in our whole group, can distinguish between edible and poisonous mushrooms.

B. **Ne . . . ni . . . ni** is used to coordinate any two (or more) parts of a sentence except verbs in a simple tense and except conjunctive pronouns.

Quel dommage! Ni les amandiers ni les cerisiers ne seront en fleur lors de notre visite.
What a shame! Neither the almond trees nor the cherry trees will be in bloom at the time of our visit.

Le porte-parole de la centrale nucléaire n'a ni confirmé ni nié les bruits d'un accident survenu cette nuit.
The spokesman for the nuclear power plant has neither confirmed nor denied the rumors of an accident last night.

Ils sont allés au théâtre pleins d'enthousiasme, mais le spectacle ne leur a plu ni à lui ni à elle.
They went to the theater full of enthusiasm, but neither of them liked the show.

Elle ne cacha le nom de son amant ni par pudeur ni par discrétion, mais par crainte des conséquences.
She concealed the name of her lover out of neither delicacy nor discretion, but out of fear of the consequences.

C. **Ne . . . ni ne . . .** is used to coordinate verbs in a simple tense.

L'administration n'autorisera ni n'approuvera l'innovation que vous proposez.
The administration will neither authorize nor approve the innovation you are proposing.

V. NEGATIVE PARTICLES WITHOUT *NE*

A. Negative particles except **pas** (unmodified), **qui que ce soit,** and **quoi que ce soit** may be used independently of a clause, where, although **ne** is absent, they retain their negative meaning.

Qui est venu? —Personne.
Who came? —No one.

Qu'a-t-il fait? —Rien.
What did he do? —Nothing.

As-tu rencontré des amis? —Aucun.
Did you meet any friends? —Not one.

Tu ne l'as pas fait? [Ni] moi non plus.
You didn't do it? I didn't either.

Y tenez-vous? —Certainement pas!
Do you really care about it? —Certainly not!

B. **Aucun, jamais, personne,** and **rien** have a positive meaning when
    used without **ne** in interrogative sentences, after verbs of doubting,
    after a negative main clause, in a hypothetical clause, after such prep-
    ositions as **sans** and **avant de** and such conjunctions as **sans que** and
    avant que, and following a comparison of inequality.

Dans tout ce flot de paroles, y-a-t-il aucun argument qui soit probant?
In this whole spate of words, is there any argument which is conclusive?

Etant donné la condition du marché, je doute qu'on puisse rien ac-
complir sans tout risquer.
*Given the condition of the market, I doubt that we can accomplish any-
thing without risking everything.*

Il est incapable de partager les responsabilités; il ne veut pas que rien
se fasse sans lui.
*He is incapable of sharing responsibilities; he does not want anything to be
done without him.*

Si jamais tu en parlais à qui que ce soit, je ne te pardonnerais pas.
If ever you spoke about it to anyone, I wouldn't forgive you.

Ils se sont mariés pendant leurs vacances sans souffler mot à personne.
*They got married during their vacation without breathing a word to any-
one.*

Je ne comprends pas le succès qu'a eu cet acteur; il a moins de talent
que personne au monde.
*I don't understand the success this actor has had; he has less talent than
anyone in the world.*

VI. NEGATIVE PARTICLES IN COMBINATION

With the exception of **pas,** it is possible to use two or more negative
particles in a single clause without expressing double negation. Only one
of them is to be understood as having negative value.

Elle ne dit rien.
She says nothing.

Elle ne dit plus rien.
She says nothing anymore.
She no longer says anything.

Elle ne dit jamais plus rien.
She never says anything anymore.

Elle ne dit jamais plus rien à personne.
She doesn't ever say anything anymore to anyone.

Nulle part vous ne trouverez personne qui veuille admettre aucune de
ces hypothèses.
Nowhere will you find anyone willing to accept any of these hypotheses.

A.   In a negative context, the conjunction **ni** is used where English would
have *or.*

Pensez donc, cet homme a débarqué ici il y a cinquante ans sans argent ni amis.
*Just think; that man landed here fifty years ago without money or friends
(with neither money nor friends).*

Par ces soirs nuageux, on ne voit guère [ni] les planètes ni les étoiles.
On these cloudy evenings, you can hardly see the planets or the stars.

B.   To express double negation (equivalent, as in English, to a positive
utterance), French combines **pas** with another of the negative particles.

Mais tu te trompes! Il ne dit pas rien, mais bien quelque chose d'important.
But you're wrong! He's not saying nothing, but something important.

Note, however, the construction **ne . . . pas non plus,** which does not express double
negation.

Beaucoup d'étudiants détestent les examens; bien des professeurs ne
les aiment pas non plus.
Many students hate exams; many teachers don't like them either.

C.   **Ne . . . pas que** expresses the opposite of **ne . . . que.**

A la différence d'autres régions, celle-ci n'a pas que des champs de blé
mais des collines et des bois aussi.
*Unlike other regions, this one has not only wheat fields but hills and woods
also.*

Note that, combined with negative particles other than **pas, ne . . . que** retains its
restrictive sense.

Il est si malade qu'il ne prend plus rien que de la soupe.
He is so ill that he no longer eats anything but soup.

Il n'y a jamais eu que deux sopranos qui puissent rivaliser avec elle.
There have been only two sopranos who could ever rival her.

3

Articles

I. FORMS

The forms of the articles vary according to the number and gender of the nouns that they determine.

	SINGULAR		PLURAL
	MASCULINE	FEMININE	MASC./FEM.
DEFINITE	le, l'	la, l'	les
INDEFINITE	un	une	des, de, d'
PARTITIVE	du, de l' de, d'	de la, de l' de, d'	—

A. The elided forms are used before nouns beginning with a vowel or a mute h.

l'arbre *the tree*   l'hôpital *the hospital*
l'étoile *the star*   l'héroïne *the heroine*

BUT

le héros *the hero*   la hiérarchie *the hierarchy*

B. The forms **le** and **les** are combined with the prepositions **à** and **de** to form the monosyllables **au, aux** and **du, des.** This occurs even when the article is part of a proper noun or a title, but not a family name.

le marché aux fleurs   *the flower market*
le bureau du directeur   *the director's office*
aller au Havre   *go to Le Havre*

venir du Caire	*come from Cairo*
la renommée des *Fleurs du mal*	*the fame of the* Flowers of Evil
les édifices de Le Corbusier	*the buildings of Le Corbusier*

Note that, when there are two parallel articles within a title, contraction is normal only for the first.

la renommée du *Rouge et le Noir*
the fame of The Red and the Black

II. USE OF THE ARTICLES

A. The use of the articles is broader in French than in English. Compare **Les chevaux sont des animaux** with *Horses are animals;* compare **Je prendrai du café avec du lait et du sucre** with *I'll have coffee with milk and sugar.* Again, while *The father, mother and children have all left on vacation* has only one article, there is an article in front of each noun in **Le père, la mère et les enfants sont tous partis en vacances.**

B. Principal omissions of articles

1. Idiomatic expressions: verb + direct object

avoir besoin (de)	*need*
bonne/mauvaise mine	*look well/ill*
chaud/froid	*be hot/cold*
confiance (en)	*have confidence*
conscience (de)	*be conscious*
coutume (de)	*be in the habit*
droit (à)	*be entitled*
envie (de)	*feel like*
faim/soif	*be hungry/thirsty*
hâte (de)	*be eager, in a hurry*
honte (de)	*be ashamed*
lieu	*take place*
mal (à)	*hurt, have a pain*
peur (de)	*be afraid*
raison/tort (de)	*be right/wrong*
soin (de)	*take care*
sommeil	*be sleepy*
chercher fortune	*seek one's fortune*
querelle (à)	*pick a fight*
demander congé (à)	*ask leave*
conseil (à)	*ask advice*

	grâce (à)	beg for mercy
	pardon (à)	ask for pardon
donner	congé (à)	discharge
	envie (à)	make one feel like
	libre cours (à)	give free rein
faire	appel (à)	appeal
	attention (à)	pay attention
	envie (à)	arouse envy
	face (à)	face, cope
	fortune	succeed
	jour/nuit	be day/night
	part (de)	announce
	partie (de)	be part
	peur (à)	frighten
	plaisir (à)	please
	preuve (de)	demonstrate
perdre	connaissance	lose consciousness
	patience	lose patience
prendre	congé (de)	take leave
	fin	come to an end
	froid	catch cold
	garde (à)	watch out
	goût (à)	acquire a taste
	part (à)	share
rendre	compte (de)	give an account
	hommage (à)	pay homage
	service (à)	be helpful
trouver	asile/refuge	find a haven
	moyen (de)	find a way
y avoir	+ *abstract noun*	
	il y a erreur	there is an error
	il y avait unanimité	there was unanimity

2. Idiomatic expressions: preposition + object.

aller/venir, etc.	*go/come, etc.*
à bicyclette	by bicycle
à cheval	on horseback
à pied	on foot
en auto	by car
en autobus	by [city] bus
en car, autocar	by bus
en moto, motocyclette	by motorcycle
en vélo	by bicycle

en voiture	by car
en/par avion	by air, by plane
en/par bateau	by ship, by boat
par mer	by sea
par terre	by land
à travers champs	through fields

aller/être, etc.	go/be, etc.
en ville	to/in town
en province	to/in the provinces
avoir à cœur de	be intent upon
envoyer sous pli séparé	send under separate cover
mettre sous clef	lock up
perdre de vue	lose sight of
prêter sur gages	lend against security
d'après nature	true to life
contre nature	unnatural
pour mémoire	for the record
sauf erreur	if I am not mistaken
sous serment	under oath
sous peine de	on/under penalty of

3. **Noun + preposition + noun.** The second noun in this construction is adjectival. Such phrases are extremely numerous, as they are not confined to fixed expressions.*

la tasse à café	coffee cup
le quatuor à cordes	string quartet
les sports d'hiver	winter sports
la chemise de coton	cotton shirt
la montre en or	gold watch
l'étudiant en médecine	medical student
le coiffeur pour hommes	barber
le costume sur mesures	custom-made suit

4. The article is omitted before almost any noun governed by the preposition **en;** the exceptions are very rare.

en briques	made of brick
en Italie	in/to Italy
en l'absence de	in the absence of
en l'air	in the air

---

*See Chapter 15, Section III.A.

en l'espèce	*in this case*
en l'honneur de	*in honor of*
en l'occurrence	*specifically, in these circumstances*

5. There is no article before abstract nouns which, governed by **de, par, avec,** or **sans,** have an adverbial function.

Il a pleuré de rage.	*He wept with frustration.*
Nous sommes venus par curiosité.	*We came out of curiosity.*
Elle se bat avec courage.	*She fights bravely.*
Je suis entré sans hésitation.	*I walked in unhesitatingly.*

Note that it is often possible to add a descriptive adjective to a noun preceded by **par** or **avec.** In that case, the indefinite article is used, unless **avec** is followed by **bon, mauvais,** or especially, **grand** before the noun. Note, too, that with a superlative the definite article is used.

par hasard	*by chance*
par un hasard malheureux	*by an unfortunate chance*
avec tristesse	*sadly, with sadness*
avec une profonde tristesse	*with [a] deep sadness*
avec grande tristesse	*very sadly, with [a] great sadness*
avec le plus grand empressement	*with the greatest urgency*

6. Before a noun in apposition, the article is omitted if the apposition provides a characterization offered as new information; the definite article is used to recall information.

Ce château, bijou architectural du 17e siècle, a été endommagé par une bombe.
This castle, an architectural gem of the 17th century, was damaged by a bomb.

Après des années de travail ardu, elle gagna le prix Nobel, honneur qu'elle méritait bien.
After years of arduous work, she won the Nobel Prize, an honor she richly deserved.

Il y a à New York une célèbre statue de Balzac, le grand écrivain romantique.
There is in New York a famous statue of Balzac, the great Romantic writer.

7. In a series of nouns, the article is frequently omitted either for conciseness or for stylistic effect. This may also occur with nouns grouped in antithetical or parallel pairs.

Ecoliers, lycéens, apprentis, jeunes ouvriers, tous adorent les nouvelles bandes dessinées.
Schoolchildren, high-school students, apprentices, young workers, all adore the new comic strips.

Ils ont déniché au grenier divers objets du siècle dernier: articles de toilette, vêtements, jouets, albums de photos.
In the attic they discovered various objects from the last century: toilet articles, clothes, toys, and photograph albums.

Journalists et policiers suivaient avec un même intérêt la vendetta des gangsters.
Reporters and police followed the gangsters' vendetta with equal interest.

8.   There is no article before the name of a month, except when modified.

Juillet a été pluvieux et nous avons eu un août torride.
July was rainy and we had a torrid August.

III. THE DEFINITE ARTICLE

The definite article serves to particularize persons, things, and ideas in French as in English.

Les voleurs ont emporté le téléviseur pendant que les locataires de l'appartement dormaient.
The thieves carried off the television set while the tenants of the apartment were sleeping.

Demain matin, le soleil se lèvera à cinq heures précises.
Tomorrow morning, the sun will rise at exactly five o'clock.

La liberté que vous cherchez n'est pas facile à atteindre.
The freedom you seek is not easy to attain.

In addition, however, the French definite article has a number of uses which the English article does not have.

A.   Before abstract and generic nouns

L'union fait la force.
Unity is strength.

J'aime bien la musique de chambre.
I like chamber music.

Les roses blanches sont plus rares que les roses rouges.
White roses are rarer than red roses.

Il a consacré sa vie aux livres.
He has dedicated his life to books.

Le fer ne résiste pas à l'oxydation.
Iron is not resistant to oxidation.

B. Before names of languages, except when used adjectivally with **de** or introduced by **en**

L'anglais est une langue germanique.
English is a Germanic language.

Il n'a pas suivi beaucoup de cours de japonais.
He hasn't taken many Japanese courses.

Le document a été rédigé en anglais et en français.
The document was drawn up in English and French.

Note that, after the verb **parler,** the article may be omitted if there is no intervening word.

Ici on parle [l']italien et [le] russe.
Italian and Russian are spoken here.

Elles parlent couramment l'italien et le russe.
They speak Italian and Russian fluently.

C. Before proper nouns modified by a title, a preposed adjective, or a prepositional phrase

le président Washington	*President Washington*
le général Leclerc	*General Leclerc*
la reine Elisabeth	*Queen Elizabeth*
le docteur Paré	*Doctor Paré*
le professeur Pasteur	*Professor Pasteur*
le petit Philippe	*little Philip*
la vieille Madame Defarge	*old Mrs. Defarge*
le vieux New York	*old New York*
le Paris d'avant guerre	*pre-war Paris*

1. The article is omitted before the titles **monsieur, madame, mademoiselle, monseigneur, maître,** and **saint(e).**

monsieur Dufour	*Mr. Dufour*
madame Defarge	*Mrs. Defarge*
saint Pierre	*Saint Peter*

2. When used as vocatives, titles are often combined with **monsieur le** or **madame/mademoiselle la.**

Bonjour, monsieur le curé.	*Hello, Father.*
Bonsoir, madame la directrice.	*Good evening, [Madam].*

3. When used as vocatives, the words **oncle, tante, cousin(e), grand-père,** and **grand-mère** do not take the article if they are followed by a first name or a family name. When these nouns are not used as vocatives, the use of the article is optional.

Bonjour, oncle Paul.   *Hello, Uncle Paul.*
Bonsoir, tante   *Good evening, Aunt Laura.*
  Laure.

Nous venons de voir [la] grand-mère Dupont.
We have just seen Grandmother Dupont.

Papa et [l']oncle Xavier reviendront demain.
Father and Uncle Xavier will come back tomorrow.

D. Days of the week

1. The definite article is used to express repetition but not a single, undated occurrence.

   La boulangerie est fermée le(s) lundi(s).
   The bakery is closed on Mondays.

   Il viendra dîner avec nous lundi.
   He will come to dine with us on Monday.

2. The definite article may precede the day of the week if the date is specified.

   Je viendrai vous voir $\begin{cases} \text{mardi} \\ \text{le mardi} \\ \text{mardi le} \end{cases}$ 5 octobre.

   I shall come to see you Tuesday, October 5.

3. The names of saints' days are always introduced by the article **la,** with the noun **fête** understood.

   la Sainte-Catherine   *Saint Catherine's Day*
   la Saint-Sylvestre   *Saint Sylvester's Day (Dec. 31)*

   Aux pays anglophones, la veille de la Toussaint est une fête populaire.
   In the English-speaking countries, the eve of All Saints' Day (Hallowe'en) is a popular holiday.

E. Before nouns of measurement, weight, or quantity when a price is quoted. With a unit of time, however, the preposition **par** is used without article.

40 francs le mètre   *40 francs a meter*
3 000 lires le kilo   *3000 lire a kilo*
100 dollars la paire   *100 dollars a pair*
5 marks la bouteille   *5 marks a bottle*
6 000 yen la livre   *6000 yen a pound*

2 livres [la] pièce	*2 pounds apiece*
trois fois par jour	*three times a day*
1 000 francs par mois	*1000 francs a month*
deux voyages par an	*two trips a year*
cinq répétitions par semaine	*five rehearsals a week*

Note that the phrase **[de] l'heure** is used in statements about hourly remuneration and **à l'heure** in statements about speed per hour.

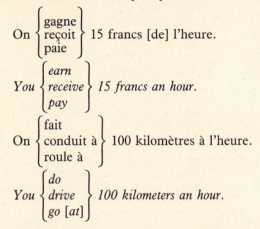

On {gagne / reçoit / paie} 15 francs [de] l'heure.

You {earn / receive / pay} 15 francs an hour.

On {fait / conduit à / roule à} 100 kilomètres à l'heure.

You {do / drive / go [at]} 100 kilometers an hour.

F. Almost all geographic names except those of cities have a definite article: continents (**l'Asie**), countries (**le Mexique**), mountains (**les Alpes**), bodies of water (**la Méditerrannée**), departments of France (**le Calvados**), provinces (**l'Ontario**), and states (**le Kentucky**).

1. The article does not occur with **Israël,** with masculine singular names of islands (**Cuba, Madagascar, Bornéo,** etc.), and certain feminine singular names of islands (**Malte, Chypre,** etc.).

2. The article does not occur with names of cities unless they are modified (see Section C. above) or unless the article is an integral part of the name and may never be omitted.

Le Havre	*Le Havre*
La Rochelle	*La Rochelle*
Le Bourget	*Le Bourget*
Le Mans	*Le Mans*
La Haye	*The Hague*
Le Caire	*Cairo*
La Mecque	*Mecca*
La Havane	*Havana*
La Nouvelle-Orléans	*New Orleans*

3. Names of continents, countries, islands, provinces, departments, and states following the prepositions **en, à, dans,** and **de.**

a. **En** (*to* and *in*). **En** is used without the article before all feminine names and before those masculine names of countries that begin with a vowel.★

en Europe	*in/to Europe*
en Tchécoslovaquie	*in/to Czechoslovakia*
en Sicile	*in/to Sicily*
en Sardaigne	*in/to Sardinia*
en Inde	*in/to India*
en Provence	*in/to Provence*
en Lombardie	*in/to Lombardy*
en Pennsylvanie	*in/to Pennsylvania*
en Afghanistan	*in/to Afghanistan*
en Israël	*in/to Israel*
en Iran	*in/to Iran*
en Equateur	*in/to Ecuador*

Note the occasional use of **en Danemark** and **en Portugal**. Masculine names of former French provinces may also be found with en (**en Limousin, en Poitou**). For American states whose names are masculine and begin with a vowel, see Section c.i. below.

b. **A** (*to* and *in*). **A** is used with the article before all masculine names beginning with a consonant (except American states) and before plural names. With names of islands, à is used with or without the article, depending upon the particular name (see Section 1. above).

au Danemark	*in/to Denmark*
au Japon	*in/to Japan*
aux Baléares	*in/to the Balearic Islands*

★Aside from names of cities, whose gender cannot be determined by any clear rule, geographic names are feminine if they end in mute **-e** and masculine if they end otherwise.

la Colombie	*Colombia*
la Hollande	*Holland*
la Floride	*Florida*
l'Egypte	*Egypt*
le Pérou	*Peru*
le Niger	*Niger*
le Québec	*Quebec*
l'Irak	*Iraq*

Exceptions:

le Mexique	*Mexico*
le Cambodge	*Cambodia*
le Zaïre	*Zaire*
le/la Nigeria	*Nigeria*
la Haute-Volta	*Upper Volta*

aux Etats-Unis   *in/to the United States*
aux Indes   *in/to India (before 1947)*
aux Pays-Bas   *in/to the Netherlands*
à la Martinique   *on/in/to Martinique*
à Malte   *on/in/to Malta*

Note that numerous feminine names of large islands (some of which are nations as well) take **en.**

en Islande   *in/to Iceland*
en Irlande   *in/to Ireland*
en Corse   *in/on/to Corsica*
en Sardaigne   *in/to Sardinia*
en Sicile   *in/to Sicily*
en Crète   *in/on/to Crete*
en Nouvelle-Guinée   *in/to New Guinea*

   c. **Dans** (*to* and *in*)

      i. Used with the article before all names of French departments and before masculine names of American states.

dans le Gard   *in/to [the] Gard*
dans la Gironde   *in/to [the] Gironde*
dans le Texas   *in/to Texas*
dans l'Indiana   *in/to Indiana*
dans l'Etat de New York   *in/to New York [State]*

     ii. Used with the article before all internally modified geographic names. There is, however, a growing tendency to use **en** and no article before feminine names.

dans le Dakota du Nord   *in/to North Dakota*
dans la Caroline du Sud   *in/to South Carolina*

dans l' } Union Soviétique   *in/to the Soviet Union*
en

dans l' } Afrique du Nord   *in/to North Africa*
en
en Allemagne Orientale   *in/to East Germany*

    iii. Used with the article before all geographic names modified by a descriptive adjective or its equivalent.

dans l'Ethiopie septentrionale   *in/to northern Ethiopia*
dans la France du Nord   *in/to northern France*
dans la Turquie byzantine   *in/to Byzantine Turkey*
dans la vieille Russie   *in/to old Russia*

dans le Cambodge d'avant la révolution
in/to pre-revolutionary Cambodia

dans le Japon qui vit naître les samouraïs
in/to the Japan which saw the rise of the samurai

d. De (*of* and *from*)

    i. Used with the article before masculine singular names beginning with a consonant and before all plural names.

revenir du Venezuela	*to return from Venezuela*
les produits du Mali	*the products of Mali*
la géographie des Etats-Unis	*the geography of the United States*

    ii. Used without the article before feminine singular names and before masculine singular names beginning with a vowel.

revenir de Bulgarie	*to return from Bulgaria*
importé de Thaïlande	*imported from Thailand*
les produits d'Irak	*the products of Iraq*
du fromage de Hollande	*cheese from Holland, Dutch cheese*
le gouvernement de Norvège	*the government of Norway, the Norwegian government*

Note that the article is used when the country must be thought of as a geo-political entity, in contrast to the case where the **de** phrase is simply the equivalent of an adjective of nationality.

l'invasion de la Somalie	*the invasion of Somalia*
l'avenir de l'Australie	*the future of Australia*

G. The definite article is very often used in French before the names of parts of the body and sometimes before nouns denoting clothes, where English uses the possessive adjective. See Chapter 8.

IV. THE INDEFINITE AND PARTITIVE ARTICLES

The indefinite article and the partitive article serve mainly to present a noun which has not been previously uttered or is not particularized and which represents an entity considered apart from its generic class.

    The singular indefinite article in French has the same meaning as English *a* or *an*.

Tout à coup, j'ai entendu un bruit étrange.
Suddenly, I heard a strange noise.

    The plural indefinite article and the partitive article in French express the same notions as English *some* or *any* or the absence of any determiner.

Tout à coup, j'ai entendu des bruits étranges.
Suddenly, I heard [some] strange noises.

On nous a servi du riz.
We were served [some] rice.

On ne prend pas de vin ce soir.
We are not having [any] wine this evening.

Note that stressed *some* in the subject of a clause cannot be expressed by **des,** but requires **certain(e)s.**

Certains cochons sont capables de déterrer les truffes.
Some (Certain) pigs are able to unearth truffles.

A.   The indefinite article occurs with nouns designating entities which can be counted, while the partitive article is used with nouns denoting entities which cannot be counted. Sometimes the distinction between "count" nouns and "mass" nouns stems, not from the nouns themselves, but from the context in which they are uttered or from the particular idea being expressed.

COUNT NOUNS	MASS NOUNS
Il a une pomme. *He has an apple.* Il a des pommes. *He has apples.*	
	Il a de la patience. *He has patience.*
La France produit des vins. *France produces wines (different kinds of wine).*	La France produit du vin. *France produces wine.*
On a vu naître un veau. *We saw a calf born.*	Nous mangeons du veau. *We are eating veal.*
Sortons prendre un café. *Let's go out for a [cup of] coffee.*	Il a pris du café une fois dans sa vie. *He has had coffee once in his life.*

B.   The indefinite and partitive articles are often reduced to the form **de** alone or are omitted altogether. In addition to the instances in Section II.B. above, there are the following.

1. When a plural noun is preceded by an adjective, the indefinite article is **de.** This is true even when the noun is represented by **en.**

des tragédies	*tragedies*
d'excellentes tragédies	*excellent tragedies*
des conseils	*advice*
de bons conseils	*good advice*

    Parmi ces coureurs, il y en a de faibles ainsi que d'infatigables.
    Among these runners, there are weak ones as well as indefatigable ones.

    a. If the plural adjective and noun constitute a compound, the article remains **des.**

des gens	*people*
des jeunes gens	*young men*
des mots	*words*
des bons mots	*witticisms*
des magasins	*stores*
des grands magasins	*department stores*

    b. The preposed plural adjectives **certain(e)s, différent(e)s,** and **divers(es)** express approximately the same idea as the plural indefinite article; the article is therefore not used with them.

        Certains arbres ne perdent jamais leurs feuilles.
        Certain (Some) trees never lose their leaves.

        Elles s'intéressent à $\begin{Bmatrix} \text{diverses} \\ \text{différentes} \end{Bmatrix}$ œuvres de bienfaisance.
        They are interested in various charities.

2. The indefinite article, singular, or plural, is normally omitted when the noun shows *all* of the following characteristics:

    —it has an adjectival function;
    —it follows a form of **devenir, se faire, rester,** or **être** with a subject other than **ce;**
    —it is not modified by a descriptive adjective;
    —it denotes a recognized social category, such as profession, nationality, religion, family status.

    Elle est étudiante. C'est une étudiante.
    She is a student.

    Il est ancien combattant. C'est un ancien combattant.
    He is a war veteran.

    Son père voudrait qu'il se fasse médecin.
    His father would like him to become a doctor.

Leurs ancêtres luttèrent pour rester protestants.
Their ancestors fought to remain Protestants.

Elle a hâte de devenir grand-mère.
She is eager to become a grandmother.

C'est un violoniste, oui, mais il est aussi chef d'orchestre.
He is a violinist, it's true, but he is also a conductor.

a. This construction may be used with certain other nouns when the intention is to characterize rather than identify.

Nous sommes [très] amis, Laurent et moi.
Lawrence and I are [good] friends.

Ce garçon nous fait rire tout le temps; il est très clown.
That fellow keeps us laughing; he's quite a clown.

Elle⎫
Il ⎭ est très femme.
She is very much a woman.
He is very womanish.

b. When the noun is modified by a descriptive adjective or the equivalent, the indefinite article is used. If the verb is **être,** the neuter pronoun **ce** tends to replace **il(s), elle(s).**

Vous êtes un écrivain éminent.
You are an eminent writer.

Elle est devenue un peintre de tout premier ordre.
She became a first-rate painter.

Tu es un élève qui réussiras.
You're a pupil with a future.

C'est un chef d'orchestre avec une réputation mondiale.
He is a conductor with a world reputation.

C'étaient des protestants très conservateurs.
They were very conservative Protestants.

3. The indefinite and partitive articles normally occur as **de** alone when the noun is the direct object in a negative clause.

Elle n'a pas de manteau.
She has no coat.

Il ne fait jamais de fautes.
He never makes mistakes.

Vous ne prenez plus de café?
You don't drink coffee any more?

Note that this rule does not apply after **être**, since **être** does not take a direct object.

Ce n'est pas de la soie, c'est du nylon.
It's not silk; it's nylon.

    a. Negation does not necessarily rule out the form **un(e)**, particularly when it may mean *a single*.

Dans le monde entier, il n'y a pas un homme qui sache ce secret.
In the whole world, there is no man (not a single man) who knows that secret.

    b. The reduction to **de** alone does not occur when the negation refers not to the direct-object noun but to some other element of the statement or when, despite the presence of a negative, the statement expresses an essentially affirmative idea.

Maintenant qu'il est directeur, il ne rend plus des comptes, il en demande.
Now that he is director, he no longer gives accounts; he asks for them.

Ton grand-père ne t'a pas légué de l'argent pour que tu le gaspilles.
Your grandfather did not leave you money for you to waste [it].

Nous ne collectionnons pas des tableaux anciens, mais des modernes.
We do not collect old paintings, but modern ones.

Non, tu ne peux pas aller au cinéma. N'as-tu pas des devoirs à faire?
No, you can't go to the movies. Don't you have homework to do?

    c. The reduction to **de** alone does not occur when the object follows **ne . . . que.**

Du balcon on ne voyait au loin que des montagnes.
From the balcony you could see only mountains in the distance.

A cause de son allergie, il ne porte que du coton.
Because of his allergy, he wears only cotton.

4. After prepositional **de,** there is no plural indefinite (**des**) or partitive (**du, de la, de l'**) article.

    a. Nouns and adverbs of quantity + **de**

Elle voit souvent des films. Beaucoup de films la déçoivent.
She sees films often. Many films disappoint her.

Tu as peut-être du temps à perdre. Il me reste, à moi, peu de temps.
You perhaps have time to waste. I have little time left.

Il nous fallait des œufs. On a acheté une douzaine d'œufs.
We needed eggs. We bought a dozen eggs.

Vouz avez du thon? Je voudrais une boîte de thon.
Have you any tuna? I'd like a can of tuna.

i. The definite article may be used to particularize the noun.

Beaucoup des films qu'elle voit lui plaisent.
She likes many of the films she sees.

Il me reste peu du temps que j'avais prévu pour cette tâche.
Little of the time I had allotted for this task is left.

On a acheté une douzaine des œufs les plus frais.
We bought a dozen of the freshest eggs.

Je voudrais une boîte du meilleur thon.
I'd like a can of the best tuna.

ii. The nouns of quantity **la plupart, la majorité, la moitié, le quart,** and the like are followed by **de** + definite article even when no particularization is intended.

La plupart des lecteurs comprendront sans difficulté les allusions mythologiques.
Most readers will understand the mythological allusions with no difficulty.

Il avait si faim qu'il a dévoré la moitié du rôti.
He was so hungry that he devoured half of the roast.

Note that **la plupart de** is used before plural nouns, **la plupart du temps** being a rare exception. Normally, with singular nouns, **la plus grande partie de** is used.

La plus grande partie de la population n'exerce souvent pas son droit de vote.
The majority of the population often fails to exercise its right to vote.

iii. The adverbs of quantity **encore** and **bien** do not entail the use of prepositional **de,** and any noun following them is introduced by the normal plural indefinite or partitive article.

Veux-tu me passer du pain? Veux-tu me passer encore du pain?
Will you pass me some bread? Will you pass me some more bread?

Il a eu de la peine à faire cela. Il a eu bien de la peine à faire cela.
He had difficulty doing that. He had great (much) difficulty doing that.

Il a visité des pays exotiques. Il a visité bien des pays exotiques.
He visited exotic lands. He visited many exotic lands.

Note, however, that the rule which calls for **de** alone before a plural adjective (see Section 1. above) remains operative after **encore** and **bien**.

encore de tristes nouvelles   bien d'autres personnes
more sad news   *many other people*

In the latter case, the context often permits the noun to be deleted, but the phrase **bien d'autres** remains unchanged.

Certains bateaux capoteront, mais bien d'autres finiront la course.
Certain boats will capsize, but many others will finish the race.

b. Other constructions containing preposition **de**.

Elle veut vous donner des conseils. Sauriez-vous vous passer de conseils?
She wants to give you advice. Can you do without advice?

Il a de la patience. Vous aussi, vous avez besoin de patience.
He has patience. You too need patience.

Il y a de la neige partout. La route est couverte de neige.
There is snow everywhere. The road is covered with snow.

Il y avait de l'eau dans l'évier. Il était plein d'eau.
There was water in the sink. The sink was full of water.

Note that prepositional **de** may be combined with the definite article to particularize the noun.

Sauriez-vous vous passer des conseils d'un médecin?
Can you do without the advice of a doctor?

Vous avez besoin de la patience d'un ange.
You need the patience of a saint.

La route est couverte de la neige tombée hier soir.
The road is covered with the snow that fell last evening.

L'évier est plein de l'eau la plus sale imaginable.
The sink is full of the dirtiest water imaginable.

5. The indefinite and partitive articles are omitted in the constructions **ni . . . ni . . .** and **sans . . . ni . . .** and after the preposition **sans**.

Depuis l'inondation, ni fleurs ni herbe n'ont poussé dans ce jardin.
Since the flood, neither flowers nor grass have grown in this garden.

Il a été dévalisé pendant son voyage et est rentré sans bagages ni argent.
He was robbed during his trip and came home without luggage or money.

Il est très difficile de préparer un gâteau sans sucre.
It is very hard to bake a cake without sugar.

6. The indefinite and partitive articles are omitted after the phrases **en sa (ma, ta, etc.) qualité de** and **en tant que,** as well as the prepositions **comme** and, in certain phrases, **pour.**

L'auteur parle de cette vedette en tant que vraie femme plutôt que symbole de la femme.
The author speaks of this star as a real woman rather than a symbol of womanhood.

En ma qualité de (Comme) commissaire de police, je suis dans l'obligation de vous avertir que vous avez le droit de garder le silence.
In my capacity as (As) police officer, I am required to warn you that you have the right to remain silent.

Qu'est-ce que vous prenez comme dessert?
What will you have for dessert?

avoir pour effet	*result in*
avoir pour conséquence	*result in*
avoir pour maître	*have as (for) one's mentor*
avoir pour élève	*have as (for) a pupil*
prendre pour femme	*wed, marry*

Il a eu pour maître un très grand philosophe.
He had a great philosopher for (as) his teacher.

Nouns in French are unlike those in English in that they all, irrespective of what they designate, have gender—feminine or masculine—as well as number—singular or plural. The gender of nouns, whatever their etymologies, remains a largely arbitrary matter, apart from the obvious nouns denoting persons or animals: **un homme, une femme, une vache, un taureau.**

I. GENDER

A. Motivated gender

There are two sorts of nouns with motivated gender in French: 1) pairs of words with different roots and 2) words of a single root where only the ending indicates whether the noun is feminine or masculine.

la femme	l'homme	*woman/man*
la fille	le garçon	*girl/boy*
la poule	le coq	*hen/rooster*
la jument	le cheval	*mare/horse*
la chèvre	le bouc	*nanny-goat/billy-goat*
la vache	le taureau	*cow/bull*
le chat	la chatte	*cat*
le loup	la louve	*wolf/she-wolf*
le veuf	la veuve	*widower/widow*
le coiffeur	la coiffeuse	*barber/hairdresser*
l'avocat	l'avocate	*lawyer*
le pharmacien	la pharmacienne	*pharmacist*

1. While the male and female of many animals are designated by distinctive forms, there are numerous cases where one gender or the other prevails. In such cases **mâle** or **femelle** must be added.

une fourmi	*ant*
une souris	*mouse*
un rat*	*rat*
un éléphant	*elephant*

---

*The form **la rate,** obsolete, is now used only jocularly.

L'éléphant femelle porte son petit 21 mois.
The female elephant carries her young 21 months.

Au terme de l'expérience, les souris mâles ont succombé d'un cancer à l'estomac.
At the end of the experiment, the male mice died of stomach cancer.

2. There are certain nouns of person which change gender only by a change of article. The following are among the most common.

-iste: un/une artiste, chimiste, dentiste, pianiste
        artist, chemist, dentist, pianist
-aire: un/une adversaire, bibliothécaire, libraire, secrétaire
        adversary, librarian, bookseller, secretary

un/une camarade	*friend, comrade*
un/une collègue	*colleague, co-worker*
un/une complice	*accomplice*
un/une concierge	*concierge*
un/une élève	*pupil*
un/une enfant	*child*

Note that **bébé** (*baby*) is always masculine.

3. Certain nouns of profession occur only in masculine form. For the feminine, there is compounding with **femme.**

la femme médecin★	*(woman) doctor*
la femme professeur	*(woman) professor, teacher*
la femme écrivain	*(woman) writer*
la femme député, etc.	*(woman) representative*

a. Forms of address

Madame/Mademoiselle le professeur
Madame/Mademoiselle le docteur
Madame/Mademoiselle le maire
Madame le Ministre de la Santé
Madame le conservateur des musées de Paris

b. Some feminine forms have traditionally designated not an officer but his wife. Today these forms are used more and more to designate the officer herself.

la générale
l'amirale
la colonelle

★Forms such as **la doctoresse, la sénatrice, la mairesse** are used only for special stylistic effect.

la préfète
la présidente

4. The gender of certain nouns may not always reflect the sex of the person denoted.

le (*or* la) soprano, le contralto, la basse
soprano, contralto, bass

la sentinelle, la recrue
sentry, recruit

la victime, la dupe
victim, dupe

J'ai entendu hier une des plus grandes basses de notre époque.
Yesterday I heard one of the greatest basses of our time.

La victime du hold-up est un septuagénaire.
The victim of the holdup is a seventy-year-old man.

B. Unmotivated gender

Most nouns in French have a grammatical gender which has nothing to do with what the noun expresses (**la table, le crayon**) or with its form (**un drame, une âme, un musée, une idée**). However, gender may be predicted within certain groups.

1. Classes of nouns which are always masculine

a. All days of the week, months, seasons

Il est né un lundi.
He was born on a Monday.

Elle passe tous ses septembres au bord de la mer.
She spends all her Septembers at the seashore.

Il faut planter les choux au printemps.
Cabbage should be planted in the spring.

b. All languages

le roumain	*Rumanian*
le sarde	*Sardinian*
le farsi	*Farsi*

c. All elements, metals, Latin scientific names of plants and animals.

le carbone	*carbon*
le chlorure	*chlorine*
le cuivre	*copper*
le fer	*iron*
le fluor	*fluorine*
l'iode	*iodine*
le soufre	*sulphur*
l'argent massif	*sterling silver*
l'or fin	*pure gold*
l'oxygène comprimé	*compressed oxygen*
le bronze	*bronze*
le laiton	*brass*
l'acier trempé	*tempered steel*
le cannabis	*cannabis*
le viola odorata	*viola odorata (sweet violet)*
le rhésus	*rhesus monkey*

d. All nouns created from other parts of speech, except when they designate a female person

le boire et le manger	*food and drink*
les parlers régionaux	*regional dialects*
le nécessaire	*the necessary, what is necessary*
le fini	*the finite, what is finite*
le qu'en-dira-t-on	*gossip*
le bouche-à-l'oreille	*word of mouth*
le tranquillisant	*tranquilizer*
le moi	*ego, self*

Il est si violent qu'il tuerait pour un oui ou un non.
He is so violent that he would kill for no reason at all.

Définir le beau, le bien, et le vrai est une préoccupation de la philosophie.
Defining the beautiful, the good, and the true is a concern of philosophy.

La brune assise près de la fenêtre est ma belle-sœur.
The dark-haired woman sitting near the window is my sister-in-law.

e. All cardinal numbers

le onze	*number eleven*
le cent	*number one hundred*
le milliard	*billion*

J'avais misé sur le huit, mais c'est le un qui a gagné.
I had bet on [the] eight, but [the] one won.

f. All trees

le chêne	*oak*
le saule pleureur	*weeping willow*
le peuplier	*poplar*
le poirier	*pear tree*

Note that there is one exception: **l'yeuse** (*holly-oak*).

2. Noun endings which denote masculine gender

a. **-age**

le nettoyage	*cleaning*
le dépistage	*tracking down*
le voyage	*trip, voyage*

Note that there are only six exceptions.

la cage	*cage*
l'image	*image, picture*
la nage	*swimming*
la page	*page*
la plage	*beach*
la rage	*rabies; rage*

b. **-ment**

le changement	*change*
le parlement	*parliament*
le battement du cœur	*heartbeat*

Note that there is only one exception: **la jument** (*mare*).

c. **-isme**

le catholicisme	*Catholicism*
le romantisme	*Romanticism*
le je-m'en-fichisme (pop.)	*indifference*
le strabisme	*cross-eyedness, strabismus*

d. **-as**

le tas	*heap*
le fracas	*loud noise*
le repas	*meal*

e. **-at.** Most nouns in suffixal **-at** designate an office, function, or body of people.

le chat	*cat*
le secrétariat	*secretaryship, secretariat*
le professorat	*teaching profession, teachers*
l'odorat	*sense of smell*

Le patronat refuse de porter tous les frais des nouvelles mesures
de sécurité.
*The employers refuse to assume all the costs of the new safety
measures.*

f. -oir. Most nouns in suffixal **-oir** designate an instrument of some
kind.

le soir	*evening*
le miroir	*mirror*
le battoir (à tapis)	*(carpet) beater*

g. -eur. Most nonabstract nouns in suffixal **-eur** designate an instrument or a person.

le cœur	*heart*
l'aspirateur	*vacuum cleaner*
le batteur	*(electric) beater; drummer*
l'aiguilleur du ciel	*air traffic controller*

Note that abstract nouns in suffixal **-eur** are feminine, with only
a few exceptions.

| la fadeur | *insipidity* |
| la fraîcheur | *freshness, coolness* |

le bonheur	*happiness*
le malheur	*unhappiness, misfortune*
le labeur	*labor*
l'honneur	*honor*
le déshonneur	*dishonor*
le facteur	*factor*

Note that there are two nonsuffixal feminines in **-eur.**

| la fleur | *flower* |
| la peur | *fear* |

h. -ier. Many of these nouns designate a container, instrument, or
person.

le sucrier	*sugar bowl*
le clavier	*keyboard*
le luthier	*lutemaker*
l'atelier	*workshop, studio*
le rosier	*rosebush*

i. -et. Most of these nouns are or were once diminutives.

le garçonnet	*little boy*
le livret	*booklet; opera libretto*
le chevalet de peintre	*easel*

j. -ot. The suffix **-ot** serves to form diminutives of masculine names.

le pot	*small jar; drink*
le chiot	*puppy*
le tricot	*knitting; knitted garment*
Pierrot	*Pete*
Jeannot	*Johnny*

Note that there is one exception: **la dot** [dɔt] (*dowry*).

k. -ain

le nain	*dwarf*
l'écrivain	*writer*
le sacristain	*sacristan*

Note that there are two exceptions.

la main	*hand*
la putain	*whore*

l. -ail

l'ail	*garlic*
le travail	*work*
l'éventail	*fan; range*

m. -eau

le château	*castle*
le souriceau	*baby mouse*
le panneau	*panel; sign*

Note that there are two exceptions.

la peau	*skin*
l'eau	*water*

n. -if

le canif	*pocket knife*
le tarif	*rate, charge*
l'if	*yew*

o. **-in**

le lin	*flax; linen*
le bassin	*basin, pool*
le marin	*sailor*

Note that there is one exception: **la fin** (*end*).

3. There is one class of nouns which are always feminine: names of sciences and analogous fields of study.

la psychologie	*psychology*
la biologie	*biology*
l'astronomie	*astronomy*
l'économie	*economics*
la physique	*physics*
l'informatique	*computer science*
la médecine	*medicine*
la jurisprudence	*jurisprudence*

4. **Noun endings which denote feminine gender**

a. **-tion** and **-sion**

la nation	*nation*
la climatisation	*air conditioning*
l'extension	*extension*

Note that there is one exception: **le bastion** (*bastion*).

b. **-ance** and **-ence**

la chance	*luck, chance*
l'assistance	*audience; assistance*
la compétence	*competence*
l'exigence	*exigency, demand*

c. **-ie**

la biographie	*biography*
la philologie	*philology*
la bigamie	*bigamy*
la polyphonie	*polyphony*
l'hérésie	*heresy*
la sympathie	*sympathy*
la démocratie [si]	*democracy*
la boulangerie	*bakery*

Note that there are two exceptions.

le génie	*genius; engineering*
l'incendie	*fire*

d. -esse

la tresse	*braid*
l'adresse	*address; skill*
la princesse	*princess*

e. -elle. Most of these nouns are or once were diminutives.

la selle	*saddle*
la coccinelle	*ladybug*
la tourelle	*turret*

Note that there is one exception: **le libelle** (*broadside*).

f. -ette. Most of these nouns are or once were diminutives. The suffix **-ette** serves to form diminutives of feminine names or feminine counterparts of masculine names.

l'assiette	*dish, plate*
la fillette	*young girl*
l'amourette	*passing fancy*
Jeannette	*Jeanie, Jeannette*
Antoinette	*Antoinette*

Note that there is one exception: **le squelette** (*skeleton*).

g. -ade

la parade	*ostentation*
l'escalade	*scaling, climbing; escalation*
la noyade	*drowning*

h. -té and -tié in abstract nouns

la vérité	*truth*
la culpabilité	*guilt*
la bonté	*goodness, kindness*
la pitié	*pity*
l'amitié	*friendship*

Note the exception **le doigté** (*fingering, touch; tact*).

    i. **-ée.** As a suffix, **-ée** usually indicates quantity.

la bouchée	*mouthful*
la brassée	*armful, armload; swimming stroke*
la poignée	*fistful, handful; handle*
la journée	*day*
l'idée	*idea*
la diarrhée	*diarrhea*

Note that there are a few exceptions.

le lycée	*secondary school*
le mausolée	*mausoleum*
le musée	*museum*
le trophée	*trophy*

    j. **-ière.** Many of these nouns designate a container, instrument, or person.

la bière	*beer; bier*
la théière	*teapot*
la souricière	*mousetrap*
la cuisinière	*stove; cook*
la pâtissière	*pastry maker*

    k. **-trice.** Most of these nouns designate a machine, tool, or person.

la génératrice	*generator*
la calculatrice	*adding machine, calculator*
la cantatrice	*(opera) singer*

    l. **-euse.** These nouns tend to designate a person or a machine or other instrument.

la chanteuse	*(popular) singer*
la coiffeuse	*hairdresser; dressing table*
la tondeuse	*lawnmower*

    m. **-eur** in abstract nouns

la grandeur	*grandeur; size*
la hauteur	*haughtiness; height*
la splendeur	*splendor*

Note that there are a few exceptions; see Section 2.g. above.

    n. **-aie.** Nouns with suffixal **-aie** designate a place where something grows.

la plaie	*wound*
la cerisaie	*cherry orchard*
la roseraie	*rose garden*
la ronceraie	*bramble patch*

o.   **-aille.** As a collective suffix, **-aille** is usually pejorative.

la caille	*quail*
la bataille	*battle*
la canaille	*rabble*
la marmaille	*brood, bunch of kids*
la ferraille	*scrap-iron*

p.   **-aine** and **-eine**

la laine	*wool*
la quinzaine	*two-week period, fortnight*
la baleine	*whale*
la seine	*net*

q.   **-ite** in nouns designating an illness

la bronchite	*bronchitis, chest cold*
la poliomyélite	*poliomyelitis*
l'appendicite	*appendicitis*

r.   **-ose** in nouns designating an illness

| la tuberculose | *tuberculosis* |
| la brucellose | *brucellosis, anthrax* |

5.   **Nouns with double gender.** In the case of a few nouns, a slight change of meaning is signaled by a change of gender. In a few other cases, singular and plural are of different genders.

a.   **Gens** (*people*) is always plural and masculine. However, any adjective with a distinctive feminine form placed immediately before **gens** takes that feminine form; any other preceding adjectives in the same phrase take the feminine form as well. All other words referring to **gens** are masculine.

Quelles honnêtes et bonnes gens!/Quels bons et honnêtes gens!
What honest, good people!/What good, honest people!

Marqués par une vie de privations, les vieilles gens de ces photos laissent voir une dignité toute particulière.
Marked by a lifetime of privation, the old people in these photos reveal a very special dignity.

Que vont-ils faire maintenant, ces bonnes gens?
What are these good people going to do now?

b. Other nouns.

	MASC. SINGULAR	FEM. SINGULAR	MASC. PLURAL	FEM. PLURAL
aigle(s)	male eagle; superior; medal with an eagle	female eagle; heraldic symbol	(like masculine singular)	(like feminine singular)
amour(s)★	love; cupid	—	cupids	loves
délice(s)★	treat, delight	—	—	joy(s), delights
foudre(s)	lightning, as attribute of Jupiter	lightning	—	lightning, condemnation
hymne(s) [imn]	national anthem; song of praise	religious hymn	(like masculine singular)	(like feminine singular)
orgue(s) (musical)	organ	—	organs	organ
Pâque(s)	Easter Day; Easter (season)	Passover (Jewish); Easter (Orthodox)	—	Easter (religious holiday); Easter communion

Ce n'est pas un aigle, mon cousin, mais il est bien sympathique.
My cousin's no genius, but he's very nice.

L'enseigne des armées de Napoléon arborait l'aigle impériale.
The standard of Napoleon's armies bore the imperial eagle.

Tu es un amour d'avoir apporté des fleurs.
You're a dear to have brought flowers.

Les petits amours peints au plafond semblaient nous regarder.
The little cupids painted on the ceiling seemed to be watching us.

Dans ses mémoires, elle parle des folles amours de sa jeunesse.
In her memoirs, she speaks of the mad love affairs of her youth.

★With **un de, un des, le plus** + adjective + **des,** the masculine is used.

Le plus beau des amours ne résiste pas à l'avarice.
The most beautiful of loves is no match for greed.

Ce melon est un délice!
This melon is a treat!

Ce romancier a imaginé un lieu de délices inouïes.
This novelist invented a place of unheard-of delights.

On lui a commandé une toccata pour inaugurer les grandes orgues de la cathédrale.
He was commissioned to compose a toccata to inaugurate the organ of the cathedral.

Nous aimerions acheter un orgue portatif pour notre fille.
We'd like to buy a portable organ for our daughter.

6. **Gender of nouns recently borrowed from other languages.** Their gender tends to be masculine, especially if they come from English and end in a consonant.

le marketing	*marketing*
le standing	*status*
le basket	*basketball*

Note that assimilation by meaning to an existing feminine class may result in feminine gender.

la jeep	*jeep*	(la voiture)

7. **Homonyms.** There are pairs of identical nouns distinguished only by gender.

un aide	*male assistant*
une aide	*female assistant; assistance*
le critique	*critic*
la critique	*criticism*
le garde	*watchman, guard*
la garde	*action of watching; person or group*
le guide	*masculine guide; guidebook*
la guide	*female guide*
le livre	*book*
la livre	*500 grams; pound*
le manche	*handle*
la manche	*sleeve; water channel*
La Manche	*English Channel*
le martyre	*martyrdom*
la martyre	*female martyr*
le martyr	*male martyr*

| le mémoire | *paper, report* |
| la mémoire | *memory* |

| le mode | *mode; musical mode; verb mode* |
| la mode | *fashion* |

le mort	*dead man*
la mort	*death*
la morte	*dead woman*

| le moule | *mold* |
| la moule | *mussel* |

| le mousse | *cabin boy* |
| la mousse | *foam; moss; pudding* |

| le page | *page (boy)* |
| la page | *page* |

| le physique | *physical appearance* |
| la physique | *physics* |

| le poêle | *heating stove* |
| la poêle | *skillet* |

| le politique | *politician* |
| la politique | *politics; policy* |

| le poste | *job; position; set (radio, TV)* |
| la poste | *mail* |

| le radio | *radiogram; male radio operator* |
| la radio | *radio; x-ray* |

le solde	*bank balance; sale*
la solde	*pay (in army)*
les soldes	*merchandise on sale*

| le somme | *sleep, nap* |
| la somme | *sum, total* |

| le souris | *smile* |
| la souris | *mouse* |

| le tour | *tour; turn; trick* |
| la tour | *tower* |

| le vase | *vase* |
| la vase | *mud (in body of water)* |

| le voile | *veil* |
| la voile | *sail* |

8.   Compound nouns

a.   *Noun + noun:* the gender is determined by the first noun.

la comédie-ballet	*comedy with ballet*
le bateau-mouche	*sightseeing boat (Paris)*

b.   *Noun + adjective or adjective + noun:* Gender is determined by the noun.

le raton-laveur	*raccoon*
le bas-bleu	*blue stocking*
la chauve-souris	*bat*
le petit-fils	*grandson*

Note the exception **le rouge-gorge** (*robin redbreast*).

c.   Other compounds (noun + preposition + noun, preposition + noun, preposition + infinitive, verb + noun, verb + verb, adjective + adjective) are usually masculine.

un arc-en-ciel	*rainbow*
le tête-à-tête	*private conversation*
un en-tête	*letterhead*
le pourboire	*tip*
le portefeuille	*wallet*
le passeport	*passport*
le gâte-sauce	*kitchen-boy; apprentice, helper*
le trouble-fête	*wet blanket*
le va-et-vient	*coming and going*
le laissez-passer	*pass, permit*
le laisser-aller	*unconstraint; carelessness, neglectfulness*
le chrétien-démocrate	*Christian-Democrat*
le clair-obscur	*chiaroscuro*

Note that with **contre** and **sous** the compound takes the gender of the noun, whether or not there is a hyphen.

la contrebasse	*double bass*
le contrebasson	*contrabassoon*
le contrespionnage	*counterespionage*
la contre-attaque	*counterattack*
la souslocation	*subletting*
la sous-classe	*subclass*
la sous-consommation	*underconsumption*

II. NUMBER

Most nouns in French, masculine and feminine, form the plural by adding **-s**.

| le nom, les noms | *name, names* |
| la rose, les roses | *rose, roses* |

There are, however, several exceptional formations.

A. Plural and singular have the same form when the singular noun ends in **-s**, **-x**, or **-z**.

le mois, les mois	*month*★
le pays, les pays	*country*
la croix, les croix	*cross*
le nez, les nez	*nose*
un os [ɔs], les os [o]	*bone*

B. Plural ending in **-x**

    1. Nouns with singular ending in **-au, -eau, -eu, -œu.**

le tuyau, les tuyaux	*pipe; conduit;* pop. *tip*
le chapeau, les chapeaux	*hat*
le jeu, les jeux	*game; set*
le vœu, les vœux	*wish*

Note the exceptions **le pneu, les pneus** (*tire*); **le bleu, les bleus** (*blue*) or (*bruise*); **le landau, les landaus** (*baby stroller*).

    2. There are seven nouns in **-ou** with plural in **-x.**

le bijou, les bijoux	*jewel*
le caillou, les cailloux	*pebble*
le chou, les choux	*cabbage*
le genou, les genoux	*knee*
le hibou, les hiboux	*owl*
le joujou, les joujoux	*toy* (*dim. of* jouet)
le pou, les poux	*louse*

Note that other **-ou** nouns take a plural in **-s**: **le clou, les clous** (*nail*); **le fou, les fous** (*madman*).

C. Plural ending in **-aux**

    1. Nouns with singular ending in **-al.**

le mal, les maux	*ache; harm; evil*
le cheval, les chevaux	*horse*
le piédestal, les piédestaux	*pedestal*

Note that there are numerous plurals in **-s**, including: **le bal, les bals** (*dance*); **le ré-**

★English translations will henceforth usually appear only in the singular.

cital, les récitals (*recital*); **le festival, les festivals** (*festival*). Note that **l'idéal** (*ideal*) gives either **les idéals** or **les idéaux.**

2. Nouns with singular ending in **-ail.** There are seven common nouns with plural in **-aux.**

le bail, les baux	*lease*
le corail, les coraux	*coral*
l'émail, les émaux	*enamel*
le soupirail, les soupiraux	*air hole, vent*
le travail, les travaux	*work*
le vantail, les vantaux	*leaf (of door, shutter, sluice gate); folding panel of triptych*
le vitrail, les vitraux	*stained glass window*

Note that other **-ail** nouns take a plural in **-s: le détail, les détails** (*detail*); **le chandail, les chandails** (*sweater*).

D. Nouns with two plural forms

A few nouns have two plural forms expressing different meanings.

un œil	*eye*
les yeux	*eyes*
les œils-de-bœuf	*bull's-eye windows*
les œils-de-chat	*cat's-eyes (semi-precious stone)*
le ciel	*sky*
les cieux	*skies; heavens*
les ciels	*skies (in painting); climate*
un aïeul	*grandfather*
les aïeux	*ancestors*
les aïeuls	*grandfathers; grandparents*

C'est un Américain de vieille souche, dont les aïeux furent parmi les premiers colonistes.
He is an American of old stock, whose ancestors were among the early colonists.

Mes aïeuls ont débarqué à New York peu avant la naissance de mon père.
My grandparents landed in New York shortly before the birth of my father.

E. Nouns with different meanings in plural and singular

The plural of these nouns has the double function of expressing the plural of the singular as well as a distinct idea.

le ciseau	*chisel*
les ciseaux	*scissors; chisels*

| un échec | *failure* |
| les échecs | *chess; failures* |

| le gage | *pledge* |
| les gages | *wages; pledges* |

| la lunette | *spyglass* |
| les lunettes | *eyeglasses; spyglasses* |

| la vacance | *vacancy* |
| les vacances | *vacation; vacancies* |

F.   Nouns regularly used only in the plural

les affres (*f*)	*agony*
les alentours (*m*)	*environs*
les arrhes (*m*)	*deposit*
les confins (*m*)	*borders*
les dépens (*m*)	*expenses*
les entrailles (*f*)	*bowels, entrails; womb*
les environs (*m*)	*environs*
les fiançailles (*f*)	*engagement*
les frais (*m*)	*expenses*
les funérailles (*f*)	*funeral*
les honoraires (*m*)	*fee*
les mœurs (*f*)	*mores*
les obsèques (*m*)	*funeral*
les pourparlers (*m*)	*negotiations*
les représailles (*f*)	*reprisal*
les ténèbres (*f*)	*darkness*
les vivres (*m*)	*food supplies, victuals*

G.   Plural of proper nouns

These usually show the same formations as common nouns, except that they are invariable when designating families.

| l'Amérique, les Amériques | *America, the Americas* |
| les Smith | *the Smiths* |

Note that princely family names and family names used generically take the mark of the plural.

| les Bourbons | *the Bourbons* |

Les Cicérons sont rares à notre époque.
Ciceros are rare in our time.

H.   Plural of compound nouns

1.   Compounds written as one word form the plural regularly.

le passeport, les passeports	*passport*
le portefeuille, les portefeuilles	*wallet*
le pourboire, les pourboires	*tip*

Note that titles of address and a few other one-word compounds isolate their components in forming the plural.

monsieur, messieurs
madame, mesdames
mademoiselle, mesdemoiselles
monseigneur, messeigneurs

le bonhomme, les bonshommes	*fellow*
le gentilhomme, les gentilshommes	*gentleman*

2. **Noun + noun**

   a. When the two nouns are in apposition, both become plural.

le chou-fleur, les choux-fleurs	*cauliflower*
le porc-épic, les porcs-épics	*porcupine*

   b. When the second noun is adjectival, only the first noun becomes plural.

le bain-marie, les bains-marie	*double-boiler*
le timbre-poste, les timbres-poste	*postage stamp*

3. **Noun + preposition + noun.** With or without hyphen, only the first noun becomes plural.

un arc-en-ciel, les arcs-en-ciel	*rainbow*
la pomme de terre, les pommes de terre	*potato*
le pot-de-vin, les pots-de-vin	*bribe*
le ver à soie, les vers à soie	*silkworm*

Note that there are some compounds of this type that are invariable.

le/les pied-à-terre	*pied-à-terre*
le/les pot-au-feu	*stew*
le/les tête-à-tête	*private conversation*

4. **Noun + adjective or adjective + noun.** Both components change in the plural.

le raton-laveur, les ratons-laveurs	*raccoon*
la basse-cour, les basses-cours	*farmyard*
le grand-père, les grands-pères	*grandfather*

Note that saints' names used as common nouns are invariable.

le/les saint-bernard   *Saint Bernard (dog)*
le/les saint-honoré   *(type of pastry)*

Note that **demi-** is always invariable and that **grand-** is invariable in gender before feminine nouns.

le demi-frère, les demi-frères   *half-brother*
la demi-mesure, les demi-mesures   *half-measure*

la grand-mère, les grands-mères   *grandmother*
l'arrière-grand-tante, les arrière-grands-tantes *great-aunt*

5. **Adjective + adjective.** Both components change in the plural.

la douce-amère, les douces-amères   *bittersweet (plant)*
le chrétien-démocrate, les chrétiens-démo-   *Christian-Democrat*
  crates
le sourd-muet, les sourds-muets   *deaf mute*

6. **Verb + direct object noun**

a. When the noun which is the direct object does not or cannot denote several entities, the compound is invariable.

l'/les abat-jour   *lampshade*
le/les coupe-papier   *paper knife*
le/les crève-cœur   *heartbreak*
le/les gratte-ciel   *skyscraper*
le/les pare-brise   *windshield*
le/les porte-bonheur   *good luck charm*
le/les trouble-fête   *wet blanket*

b. When the noun which is the direct object can denote several entities, it takes the sign of the plural.

le couvre-lit, les couvre-lits   *bedspread*
le prête-nom, les prête-noms   *figurehead, straw man*
le protège-tibia, les protège-tibias *shin guard*
le tire-bouchon, les tire-bouchons   *corkscrew*

c. In certain compounds, the noun which is the direct object is plural even when the compound is singular.

le/les casse-noisettes   *nutcracker*
le/les compte-gouttes   *medicine dropper*
le/les porte-cigarettes   *cigarette case*

7. **Preposition + noun.** Usage varies.

l'après-midi, les après-midi(s)   *afternoon*
l'en-tête, les en-tête(s)   *letterhead*

8. Compound nouns with **garde-**.

    a. When **garde** designates a person, it takes **-s** to mark the plural; the second noun may be singular or plural.

        le/la garde-malade, les gardes-malades   *nurse-companion*
        le/la garde-barrière, les gardes-barrière(s)   *railroad crossing guard*

    b. When garde refers to an object, it is invariable.

        le garde-côte, les garde-côte(s)   *coast guard vessel*
        le garde-fou, les garde-fou(s)   *railing*

Descriptive Adjectives

French adjectives, except for certain classes, show agreement in number and gender with the nouns they modify.

le feu vert   *green light*
les feux verts   *green lights*

The descriptive adjectives of French comprise not only true adjectives but also certain other parts of speech used adjectivally: present* and past participles, nouns, and adverbs.

une nouvelle surprenante   *surprising bit of news*
des tissus importés   *imported fabrics*
des réunions monstres   *huge meetings*
un monsieur très bien   *distinguished man*
des gens comme il faut   *proper people*

I. FORMS

While some adjectives are invariable, most vary according to one or another of three patterns. Two-form adjectives distinguish only between singular and plural; three-form adjectives have only one form for masculine singular and plural, and distinct forms for feminine singular and plural; four-form adjectives mark both genders and both numbers.

A. Invariable adjectives

1. Nouns used as adjectives

Florence et Venise sont de véritables villes musée.
The cities of Florence and Venice are true museums.

Note that there are many words which are both nouns and real adjectives; they are not invariable. (See, too, the plural of compound nouns, Chapter 4, Section II.G.)

C'est une musicienne renommée, mais ses enfants ne sont pas du tout musiciens.
She is a famous musician, but her children are not at all musical.

---

*See Chapter 1, Section XI.A.4.

2.   Certain adjectives of foreign or slang origin

une chèvre angora	*angora goat*
des chandails angora	*angora sweaters*
une femme chic	*elegant woman*
des manteaux chic	*fashionable coats*
une petite fille gnangnan	*whiny little girl*
des garçons gnangnan	*whiny boys*
Elle est radin.★	*She is stingy.*
Ils sont radin.	*They are stingy.*
une cheminée rococo	*Rococo mantelpiece*
des vêtements rococo	*outmoded clothes*
une livre sterling	*one pound sterling*
cinq livres sterling	*five pounds sterling*
une fille sympa	*likeable girl*
Ils sont sympa.	*They're nice.*

3.   Color adjectives. Most are true adjectives and show the expected agreement. Some, however, originally nouns, are invariable.

une soie bordeaux	*deep red silk*
des écharpes cerise	*cherry-colored scarves*
des uniformes kaki	*khaki uniforms*
des velours lie-de-vin	*maroon velvets*
une étoffe marron	*brown fabric*
des rideaux orange	*orange curtains*
des cheveux poivre et sel	*salt-and-pepper hair*

Note that certain common nouns of color have come to function as true adjectives and are thus variable.

des cheveux châtains	*chestnut-colored hair*
un tapis à fond écarlate	*scarlet-grounded carpet*
des tissus mauves	*mauve fabrics*
des manteaux pourpres	*bright red coats*
des joues roses	*pink cheeks*

a.   *Compounds: adjective + adjective or adjective + noun.* These are invariable.

Il a les yeux bleu clair et les cheveux châtain foncé.
He has light blue eyes and dark brown hair.

★The feminine form **radine** exists but is rare.

Ce printemps on a vu énormément de robes vert pomme, jaune
paille, bleu marine et rose bonbon.
*This spring, apple green, straw yellow, navy blue, and candy pink
dresses were popular.*

b. *Series.* When an ordinarily variable color adjective is used in a
series with an invariable color term, the variable one tends to become invariable.

une statue blanche	*white statue*
une statue or et blanc	*gold and white statue*
des reliures rouges	*red bindings*
des reliures rouge(s) et or	*red and gold bindings*

de vieilles écharpes figurées, brique, vert et jaune
old brick-red, green, and yellow printed scarves

Note that the series **blanc et noir** functions as a fixed, invariable compound.

des chats blanc et noir	*black-and-white cats*
une chatte blanc et noir	*black-and-white cat*

4. Adverbs used as adjectives. These are invariable.

J'ai fait la connaissance d'une jeune fille très bien.
I met a very nice girl.

Il a fait cette année des tableaux pas mal.
He has done some quite good paintings this year.

Note that, in combinations of two adjectives where one is used adverbially, that adjective does not agree.

des enfants mort-nés	*stillborn children*

Les nouveau-nées ont un bracelet rose.
The newborn girls have pink bracelets.

Elle était très court vêtue. *She wore very short skirts.*

B. Two-form adjectives

These do not mark gender; they end in **-e** in the singular and **-es** in
the plural.

un air artiste	*artistic look*
une image horrible	*horrible picture*
des personnes aimables	*likeable people*
un récit historique	*historical account*
une lueur jaunâtre	*yellowish gleam*
des véhicules prioritaires	*vehicles with right of way*
un homme mollasse	*lethargic man*
une imagination pauvre	*weak imagination*

Note the exceptional feminine forms of **traître** and **maître**.

Ces routes de montagne sont traîtresses.
These mountain roads are treacherous.

Il nous a exposé les idées maîtresses de l'impressionnisme.
He presented the key ideas of Impressionism to us.

C.   Three-form adjectives

Adjectives ending in **-s** and **-x** have the same form for the masculine singular and plural, and different forms for the feminine singular and feminine plural.

1.   Masculine in **-s**: feminine in **-se(s)** or, in the case of seven adjectives, **-sse(s)**.

divers, diverse(s)	*diverse, different*
gris, grise(s)	*grey*
sournois, sournoise(s)	*sly*
bas, basse(s)	*low*
épais, épaisse(s)	*thick*
exprès, expresse(s)	*explicit*
gras, grasse(s)	*fat; oily*
gros, grosse(s)	*thick; fat; coarse*
las, lasse(s)	*weary*
métis, métisse(s)	*half-breed, mongrel*

Note certain exceptions: **frais, fraîche(s)** (*cool* or *fresh*); **tiers, tierce** (*third*).

2.   Masculine in **-x**: feminine in **-se(s)**.

galeux, galeuse(s)	*mangy, scabby*
jaloux, jalouse(s)	*jealous*
peureux, peureuse(s)	*fearful, timid*

Note that there are three exceptions: **faux, fausse(s)** (*false*); **roux, rousse(s)** (*red-haired*); **doux, douce(s)** (*sweet, gentle, soft*). For **vieux** (*old*), see Section E below.

D.   Four-form adjectives

1.   Adjectives with plural in **-s** in both masculine and feminine.

   a.   *Adjectives ending in* **-ai, -i, -é, -u, eu★** *add* **-e** *to form the feminine.*

★Note that **hébreu** (*Hebrew*) has a masculine plural in **-x** and that the feminine counterpart is **hébraïque(s)**.

un vrai singe	*real monkey*
des histoires vraies	*true stories*
des gens peu polis	*impolite people*
des surfaces polies	*polished surfaces*
un nez violacé	*purplish nose*
une peau violacée	*purplish skin*
un homme ventru	*paunchy man*
une commode ventrue	*bombé chest*
un pantalon bleu	*blue pants*
des écharpes bleues	*blue scarves*

Note that adjectives in **-gu** add **-ë** for the feminine: **aigu, aiguë; ambigu, ambiguë**.

des réactions ambiguës	*ambiguous reactions*
des cris aigus	*shrill cries*

Note that there are two exceptions in **-te**: **coi, coite** (*quiet*); **favori, favorite** (*favorite*).

b. With the exception of certain classes, adjectives ending in **-d, -t, -r, -l, -ain, -ein, -in, -un** add **-e** to form the feminine.

des visages laids	*ugly faces*
une laide grimace	*ugly grimace*
un esprit dément	*mad wit*
une idée démente	*crazy idea*
un air idiot	*idiotic look*
des histoires idiotes	*idiotic stories*
un nombre pair	*even number*
les maisons impaires	*odd-numbered houses*
un vil mensonge	*foul lie*
une action vile	*vile action*
un corps sain	*healthy body*
une nourriture saine	*healthful food*
des verres pleins	*full glasses*
une vie pleine	*full life*
un lainage fin*	*fine woolen*
des observations fines	*keen observations*

---

*Note the feminine of **malin(s)** (*perverse, malignant*) and **bénin(s)** (*benign*): **maligne(s), bénigne(s)**.

| des yeux bruns | *brown eyes* |
| une bière brune | *dark beer* |

i. **-et:** feminine in **-ette** or, in the case of nine adjectives, **-ète**

blet, blette	*overripe*
net, nette	*clean*
muet, muette	*mute*

complet, complète	*complete*
concret, concrète	*concrete*
désuet, désuète	*outmoded*
discret, discrète	*discreet*
incomplet, incomplète	*incomplete*
indiscret, indiscrète	*indiscreet*
inquiet, inquiète	*worried*
replet, replète	*full*
secret, secrète	*secret, secretive*

ii. **-ot:** feminine in **-otte**

pâlot, pâlotte	*rather pale*
sot, sotte	*foolish*
vieillot, vieillotte	*old-fashioned*

iii. **-er** and **-ier:** feminine always in **-ère** and **-ière**

| amer, amère | *bitter* |
| léger, légère | *light* |

| fier, fière | *proud* |
| premier, première | *first* |

For **-eur,** see Section e.

iv. **-el** and **-eil:** feminine always in **-elle** and **-eille**

| cruel, cruelle | *cruel* |
| mortel, mortelle | *fatal; mortal* |

| pareil, pareille | *similar* |
| vermeil, vermeille | *red* |

Note that **gentil** and **nul** become **gentille** and **nulle** in the feminine.

c. Adjectives ending in **-an, -en, -ien, -on**

i. **-en** and **-ien:** feminine always in **-enne** and **-ienne**

| méditerranéen, méditerranéenne | *Mediterranean* |
| moyen, moyenne | *average* |

chrétien, chrétienne	*Christian*
ancien, ancienne	*antique; former*

ii. **-an:** feminine sometimes in **-anne,** sometimes in **-ane**

paysan, paysanne	*peasant*
toscan, toscane	*Tuscan*

iii. **-on:** feminine in **-onne,** with a few exceptions in **-one**

bon, bonne	*good*
maigrichon, maigrichonne	*skinny*
saxon, saxonne	*Saxon*
lapon, lapone	*Lappish*
letton, lettone	*Latvian, Lettish*
mormon, mormone	*Mormon*
nippon, nippone	*Nipponese*

d. Adjectives ending in **-c, -f, -g** show a change in final consonant as well as **-e** in the feminine.

i. **-c:** feminine in **-che** or **-que** or, in one case, **-cque.**

des cheveux blancs	*white hair*
une jument blanche	*white mare*
un aveu franc	*frank avowal*
une franche hostilité	*overt hostility*
un vin sec	*dry wine*
des feuilles sèches	*dry leaves*
les jardins publics	*public parks*
l'opinion publique	*public opinion*
des bains turcs	*Turkish baths*
la cuisine turque	*Turkish cooking*
un philosophe grec	*Greek philosopher*
des tragédies grecques	*Greek tragedies*

ii. **-ef:** feminine in **-ve**

naïf, naïve	*ingenuous*
vif, vive	*lively; live*
bref, brève	*brief*

iii. **-g:** feminine in **-gue**

long, longue	*long*
oblong, oblongue	*oblong*

e. Adjectives ending in **-eur:** feminine in **-eure, -euse, -esse,** or **-trice.**

i. **-eure** occurs only in ten comparative adjectives.

antérieur, antérieure	*anterior, preceding*
postérieur, postérieure	*posterior, following*
ultérieur, ultérieure	*later, beyond*
intérieur, intérieure	*interior*
extérieur, extérieure	*exterior*
supérieur, supérieure	*superior, upper*
inférieur, inférieure	*inferior, lower*
majeur, majeure	*major*
mineur, mineure	*minor*
meilleur, meilleure	*better*

ii. **-euse** occurs in adjectives derived directly from the stem of a present participle.

(mentant) menteur, menteuse	*lying, mendacious*
(rouspétant) rouspéteur, rouspéteuse	*grumbling*

Méfiez-vous des apparences; elles sont souvent trompeuses.
Beware of appearances; they are often deceiving.

Note that there are a few exceptions in **-esse.**

(chassant) chasseur, chasseresse	*hunting*
(enchantant) enchanteur, enchanteresse	*enchanting*
(vengeant) vengeur, vengeresse	*avenging*

iii. **-trice** is the feminine for **-teur** in adjectives not derived from the stem of a present participle.

(créant) créateur, créatrice	*creative*
(consolant) consolateur, consolatrice	*consoling*
(—) moteur, motrice	*motor, driving*

2. Adjectives with masculine plural in **-x** and feminine plural in **-s**

a. Masculine singular in **-al:** masculine plural in **-aux** and feminine in **-ale(s)**

un ami loyal	*loyal friend*
une tenue estivale	*summer attire*
des ennuis familiaux	*family problems*

i. A few adjectives have a masculine plural in **-als.**

banal, banals	*banal*
bancal, bancals	*limping, lame*
choral, chorals	*choral*
fatal, fatals	*fated; fatal*
final, finals	*final*
natal, natals	*native*
naval, navals	*naval*

ii. A few adjectives have a masculine plural in either **-als** or **-aux.**

glacials or glaciaux	*glacial*
idéals or idéaux	*ideal*
jovials or joviaux	*jovial*

b. Masculine singular in **-eau:** masculine plural in **-eaux** and feminine in **-elle(s).**

jumeau(x), jumelle(s)	*twin*
morvandeau(x), morvandelle(s)	*from Morvan*
tourangeau(x), tourangelle(s)	*from Touraine*

E.   Five-form adjectives

There are five adjectives that have a special, fifth form for use with an immediately following masculine singular noun beginning with a vowel or mute **h.**

beau(x), bel, belle(s)	*beautiful*
nouveau(x), nouvel, nouvelle(s)	*new*
fou(s), fol, folle(s)	*mad, foolish*
mou(s), mol, molle(s)	*soft*

un bel enfant	*beautiful child*
un nouvel an	*new year*
un vieil ami	*old friend*
un fol espoir	*foolish hope*
un mol oreiller	*soft pillow*

Note that in the singular **vieux** (*old*) shows the same pattern as the other adjectives in this group; it has two masculine forms **vieux** and **vieil.**

II. USE OF ADJECTIVES

A. Certain adjectives are used in only one gender, some of them, more-over, only in one fixed expression

bouche bée	*mouth agape*
la dent œillère	*eyetooth*
la rose trémière	*hollyhock*
une œuvre pie	*charitable deed*
un vent coulis	*draft*
le hareng saur	*smoked herring*
benêt	*foolish*
fat	*fatuous*
preux	*valiant, heroic*
vainqueur	*victorious, conquering*

B. Agreement

1. One adjective modifying more than one noun is always plural.

    a. When the nouns are of one gender, the adjective shows the same gender.

    Il portait un chapeau et un manteau neufs.
    He was wearing a new hat and coat.

    La synagogue et l'église ont été détruites par la même bombe.
    The synagogue and the church were destroyed by the same bomb.

    b. When the nouns are of different genders, the adjective is masculine. If the masculine and feminine plural forms of the adjective are pronounced differently, it is usual to place the masculine noun closer to the adjective. If there is no difference in sound, the nouns may be placed in any order.

    Il s'est acheté une table et un fauteuil anciens.
    He bought himself an antique table and armchair.

    Elle portait des chaussures et un sac violets.
    She was wearing purple shoes and bag.

    Il faisait tout avec un doigté et une sensibilité exceptionnels.
    He did everything with exceptional tact and sensitivity.

2. A single noun in the plural may be modified by several adjectives in the singular.

    Aux dix-huitième et dix-neuvième siècles, l'Europe a connu plusieurs révolutions.
    In the eighteenth and nineteenth centuries, there were several revolutions in Europe.

Les littératures française, italienne et anglaise ont toutes subi l'influence de l'antiquité.
French, Italian, and English literature have all been influenced by antiquity.

3. When an adjective follows a noun + **de** + noun construction, agreement depends on the meaning.

des lambeaux d'étoffe noire	*shreds of black cloth*
un groupe de soldats blessés	*group of wounded soldiers*
un poisson d'eau douce	*fresh-water fish*
un poisson de mer frais	*fresh salt-water fish*
un tas de livres très haut	*very high stack of books*
des journées de travail joyeuses	*joyous days of work*

4. In the expression **avoir l'air** + adjective, the adjective may be masculine singular, agreeing with **air,** or else may vary with the subject of **avoir.**

Cette vedette a l'air sot.
Cette vedette a l'air sotte. ⎫ *That star looks stupid.*

5. **Compound adjectives**

   a. When an adjective used adverbially is joined to a following adjective, only the second shows agreement.

   Il a des relations haut-placées.
   He knows people in high places.

   b. The adjectives **frais** and **grand** may be used adverbially with a following past participle, in which case they show agreement.

des cerises fraîches cueillies	*freshly picked cherries*
une fleur fraîche éclose	*newly opened flower*
une fenêtre grande ouverte	*wide-open window*
des yeux grands ouverts	*wide-open eyes*

   c. **Demi, semi, mi** placed before an adjective and linked to it by a hyphen are invariable.

des poutres demi-pourries	*half-rotted beams*
une membrane semi-perméable	*semi-permeable membrane*
des pierres semi-précieuses	*semi-precious stones*
des yeux mi-clos	*half-closed eyes*

6. The literary or ironic adjective **feu** (*late*) is rarely used in the plural and is usually invariable. It shows agreement, however, if the article or a possessive adjective precedes.

Feu la mère de Madame est une pièce de Feydeau.
Madam's Late Mother is a play by Feydeau.

feu le roi	*the late king*
feu son père	*his late father*
la feue reine	*the late queen*
l'enfant de ma feue sœur	*my late sister's child*

7. **Drôle de** + noun (*funny, odd . . .*): **drôle** takes the number and gender of the noun following **de**.

un drôle de type	*funny guy, queer duck*
une drôle de vie	*peculiar life*
des drôles de têtes	*odd faces*

8. Adjectives and participles modifying interrogative, negative, and indefinite pronouns are normally introduced by **de** and retain masculine singular form.

Qui d'instruit aurait écrit une telle phrase?
Who with any education would have written such a sentence?

Quoi de plus révélateur?
What could be more revealing?

Qu'est-ce qu'il y a de parfait au monde?
What is there that is perfect in the world?

personne d'intéressant
no one interesting

rien de nocif
nothing harmful

quelque chose de précieux
something precious

N'importe qui de renseigné saurait ce qu'il y a de faux dans ces discours.
Anyone informed could tell what is false in these speeches.

n'importe quoi de nourrissant
anything nourishing

Note that an adjective or participle modifying a form of **quelqu'un** is also introduced by **de** but agrees with the form of the pronoun.

Entre les bêtises qu'il a débitées, il y avait quelques-unes de vraiment étonnantes.
Among the stupidities he uttered, there were some really astonishing ones.

Note, too, that, if the modifier has a complement, **de** tends to be omitted.

J'ai vu des mosaïques romains qui ressemblaient à quelques-uns faits par des artistes modernes.
I have seen Roman mosaics which resembled some done by modern artists.

C. Position of adjectives

1. As a general rule, descriptive adjectives are placed after the noun they modify.

la nature humaine	*human nature*
un déjeuner champêtre	*picnic*
une pierre précieuse	*precious stone*
la table ronde	*round table*

2. Two adjectives modifying the same noun and having equal, or parallel, importance in that function are either placed in their normal position and linked by **et** or placed on either side of the noun.

   des années paisibles et tranquilles
   peaceful and calm years

   une jeune et jolie femme
   a young, pretty woman

   d'immenses perspectives alléchantes
   vast inviting prospects

3. When a noun and adjective form a unit modified by another adjective, no conjunction is used.

   une éclipse solaire, une éclipse solaire célèbre
   a solar eclipse, a famous solar eclipse

   une jeune fille, une belle jeune fille
   a young girl, a beautiful young girl

4. Adjectives normally placed before the noun

   a. Certain common adjectives

bon, mauvais	*good, bad*
vieux, jeune	*old, young*
gros, grand, petit	*big, great, small*
long	*long*
beau, joli	*beautiful, pretty*
gentil	*nice*

   b. Adjectives denoting qualities perceived as inherent

le sage Nestor	*wise Nestor*
la frivole Marie-Antoinette	*frivolous Marie-Antoinette*

5. Adjectives whose meaning changes with position. Before the noun, they tend to be subjective, figurative, or attenuated; after the noun, they have their full literal and objective value.

ancien

C'est un ancien boxeur qui s'est fait marchand de vins.
He is a former boxer who has become a wine dealer.

La ville de Rome foisonne de monuments anciens.
The city of Rome abounds in ancient monuments.

Nous aimons regarder les meubles anciens au marché aux puces.
We like to look at the antique furniture at the flea market.

brave

Ce sont de braves gens qui méritent tout succès.
They are fine people who deserve every success.

C'est un combattant brave qui n'a jamais fléchi devant le danger.
He is a brave fighter who has never shrunk from danger.

certain

D'un certain point de vue, il a raison.
From one (a certain) point of view, he is right.

Ne pourriez-vous pas me fournir des preuves certaines de vos allé-
    gations?
Couldn't you provide me with sure proof of your allegations?

cher

Elle est non seulement une collègue mais une chère amie.
She is not only a colleague but a dear friend.

C'est l'épicier le plus cher du quartier.
He is the most expensive grocer in the neighborhood.

curieux

Il a la curieuse habitude de se coucher avec le soleil.
He has the peculiar habit of going to bed with the sun.

C'est une femme curieuse qui ne cesse de se mêler des affaires des
    autres.
*She is an inquisitive woman who is always mixing into other people's
    business.*

dernier

Le 31 décembre est le dernier jour de l'année.
December 31 is the last day of the year.

Le dernier roman de cet auteur est de loin son meilleur.
This author's latest (last) novel is by far his best.

As-tu reçu le numéro de la semaine dernière?
Did you receive last week's issue?

différent

J'ai différentes choses à vous donner.
I have various things to give you.

Dans des conditions différentes, il aurait mieux réussi.
In different circumstances, he would have had greater success.

jeune

Ce jeune garçon est très précoce.
This young boy is very precocious.

Bien qu'elle soit dans la soixantaine, elle a le visage jeune.
Although she is in her sixties, she has a youthful face.

méchant

Elle a été étonnée de voir le méchant deux-pièces où il habitait.
She was surprised to see the wretched two-room apartment that he lived in.

Il a publié sur cette pièce une critique particulièrement méchante.
He published a particularly vicious review of the play.

même

Nous avons, vous et moi, les mêmes goûts.
You and I have the same tastes.

C'est effrayant, et la pensée même me fait frissonner.
It's frightening, and the very thought makes me shudder.

Vous pouvez vous fier à lui, il est la discrétion même.
You can trust him; he is discretion itself.

nombreux

Le chimiste a trouvé la formule après de nombreuses expériences.
The chemist found the formula after numerous experiments.

Les familles nombreuses sont en train de disparaître.
Large families are in the process of disappearing.

nouveau

Je viens de dénicher une nouvelle pièce pour ma collection de vieilles porcelaines.
I've just dug up a new (another) piece for my collection of old porcelain.

Le médecin lui a conseillé un traitement nouveau qui a eu du succès
à l'étranger.
*The doctor advised a newly developed treatment which has been success-
ful abroad.*

pauvre

C'est la troisième fois que cette pauvre bête a failli se faire écraser.
That's the third time that poor animal has almost been run over.

Les ressortissants des pays pauvres constituent une fraction importante de la main-d'œuvre européenne.
*Nationals of poor countries constitute a large segment of the European
labor force.*

prochain

Le prochain avion pour votre destination part dans 30 minutes.
The next plane for your destination leaves in 30 minutes.

L'année prochaine* nous passerons nos vacances au bord de la mer.
Next year we shall spend our vacation at the seashore.

propre

Maintenant qu'elle a atteint sa majorité, elle prendra son propre appartement.
Now that she is of age, she will get her own apartment.

Prenez un torchon propre pour essuyer la vaisselle.
Take a clean towel to dry the dishes.

sacré

Ce sacré menteur nous a trompés une fois de plus.
That darned liar has fooled us once again.

Le livre sacré des musulmans c'est le Coran.
The sacred book of the Moslems is the Koran.

sale

Ce sale individu n'a pas de principes.
This nasty creature has no principles.

L'enfant est rentré, les mains et la figure sales.
The child came home with dirty hands and face.

---

*When *next* is not used in relation to the moment of speaking, it is expressed in French by
suivant.

Il a dit qu'il le ferait la semaine suivante.
He said he would do it the next (following) week.

seul

Ne perdez pas ce livre; c'est le seul exemplaire qui me reste.
Don't lose that book; it's the only copy I have left.

Il n'a qu'un seul défaut: c'est la prétention de ne pas en avoir.
He has only one (a single) flaw: claiming not to have any.

La bonne volonté seule (La seule bonne volonté) ne saurait prévaloir contre la malveillance.
Good will alone cannot prevail against malevolence.

Les enfants seuls ne sont pas admis au cinéma.
Unaccompanied children are not admitted to this movie theater.

simple

Ne vous offensez pas; c'est une simple formalité.
Don't be offended; it is a mere formality.

Elle prépare pour les autres une cuisine compliquée mais elle-même ne mange que des mets simples.
She does complicated cooking for others but eats only simple dishes herself.

triste

Malgré ton air de bravade, tu joues un triste personnage.
Despite your bravado, you cut a wretched (sorry) figure.

Les scènes tristes de ce drame ont fait pleurer l'assistance entière.
The sad scenes of this drama made the whole audience cry.

unique

Il prétend que son unique souci est de nous éviter des ennuis.
He claims his sole (only) concern is to spare us difficulties.

Les enfants uniques ne sont pas forcément égoïstes.
Only children are not necessarily selfish.

Il a un talent unique pour nouer des liens d'amitié.
He has a unique talent for creating bonds of friendship.

6

Adverbs

French adverbs, like those in English, modify verbs, adjectives, and other adverbs, and are invariable.

I. FORMS

There are three classes of forms: those derived from adjectives, simple nonderived forms, and phrases.

A. Adverbs derived from adjectives

For many adjectives, the addition of the suffix **-ment** forms the corresponding adverb. With the exceptions given below, **-ment** is added to the feminine singular form, unless the masculine ends in **-ai, -é, -i,** or **-u.**

pur, pure	purement	*pure, purely*
strict, stricte	strictement	*strict, strictly*
faux, fausse	faussement	*false, falsely*
nouveau, nouvelle	nouvellement	*new, newly*
fou, folle	follement	*mad, madly*
rapide, rapide	rapidement	*rapid, rapidly*
vrai, (vraie)	vraiment	*true, truly*
aisé, (aisée)	aisément	*easy, easily*
poli, (polie)	poliment	*polite, politely*
absolu, (absolue)	absolument	*absolute, absolutely*
dû, (due)	dûment	*due, duly*

1. Certain adjectives change **-e** to **-é** before **-ment.**

aveugle, aveugle	aveuglément	*blind, blindly*
commode, commode	commodément	*comfortable, comfortably*
conforme, conforme	conformément	*similar, in conformity*
énorme, énorme	énormément	*enormous, enormously*
uniforme, uniforme	uniformément	*uniform, uniformly*

commun, commune	communément	*common, commonly*
confus, confuse	confusément	*confused, confusedly*
exprès, expresse	expressément	*direct, expressly*
importun, importune	importunément	*importunate, importunately*
obscur, obscure	obscurément	*obscure, obscurely*
précis, précise	précisément	*precise, precisely*
profond, profonde	profondément	*deep, deeply*
profus, profuse	profusément	*profuse, profusely*

2. Adjectives in **-ant** or **-ent** become adverbs in **-amment** or **-emment**.

constant	constamment	*constant, constantly*
élégant	élégamment	*elegant, elegantly*
intelligent	intelligemment	*intelligent, intelligently*
prudent	prudemment	*prudent, prudently*

Note that there are three exceptions: **lent, lentement** (*slow, slowly*); **présent, présentement** (*present, at present*); **véhément, véhémentement** (vehement, vehemently).

3. A few adverbs are formed by adding a circumflex to the final vowel of the masculine singular and then adding **-ment**.

assidu	assidûment	*assiduous, assiduously*
continu	continûment	*continuous, continuously*
cru	crûment	*crude, crudely*
incongru	incongrûment	*incongruous, incongruously*
gai	gaîment (also gaiement)	*gay, gaily*

4. **Irregular formations**

(bref, brève)	brièvement	*brief, briefly*
(gentil, gentille)	gentiment	*nice, nicely*
(impuni, impunie)	impunément	*unpunished, with impunity*

5. A few **-ment** adverbs are unrelated to any existing adjective.

notamment	*notably*
nuitamment	*by night*
sciemment	*knowingly*

B. **Simple, nonderived adverbs**

maintenant	*now*
déjà	*already*
ici	*here*
partout	*everywhere*

peu	*little*
même	*even*
environ	*approximately*
bien	*well*
très	*very*
vite	*fast*

Note that, unlike other adverbs, **tout** (*all, very*) agrees in number and gender with a following feminine adjective or past participle which begins with a consonant or aspirate **h**. In the case of a feminine adjective which begins with a vowel or mute **h** and is singular, agreement is optional.

Elle est toute seule.	*She is all alone.*
Elles sont toutes seules.	*They are all alone.*
Elle est tout(e) étonnée.	*She is very surprised.*
Elles sont tout étonnées.	*They are very surprised.*
Ils sont tout seuls.	*They are all alone.*
Ils sont tout étonnés.	*They are very surprised.*

For similar agreement of **frais** and **grand** used adverbially, see Chapter 5, Section II.B.5.b.

C. Phrases

1. Fixed phrasal adverbs

tout de suite	*immediately*
là-dessus	*thereupon*
en haut	*above*
quelque part	*somewhere*
tout à fait	*quite, entirely*
à peu près	*approximately*
d'ailleurs	*besides*

2. Idiomatic adverbial phrases

à l'improviste	*unexpectedly*
à contre-cœur	*reluctantly*
à tâtons	*gropingly*
de pied ferme	*resolutely*
d'instinct	*instinctively*
en cachette	*secretly*

3. Phrases with *sans* and *avec*

Il a répondu sans hésitation (sans hésiter).
He answered unhesitatingly.

Toute la matinée, la radio a répété sans cesse la même nouvelle.
All morning, the radio endlessly repeated the same news.

Nous avons écouté le conférencier avec scepticisme.
We listened to the speaker skeptically.

Ils débitaient des idioties avec le plus grand sérieux du monde.
They were uttering stupidities with the utmost seriousness.

4. The constructions **d'un air** + masculine adjective and

$$
\left.\begin{array}{l} \textbf{de} \\ \textbf{d'une} \end{array}\right\} + \left\{\begin{array}{l} \textbf{façon} \\ \textbf{manière} \end{array}\right\} + \text{feminine adjective}
$$

Se levant de son siège, il se dirigea d'un air menaçant vers la cabine
de pilotage.
Rising from his seat, he walked threateningly toward the cockpit.

Il conduit de façon trop dangereuse pour que je voyage avec lui.
He drives too dangerously for me to travel with him.

Ces vauriens mentent d'une manière éhontée.
Those good-for-nothings lie shamelessly.

D. Fixed locutions composed of verb and adjective used adverbially. (The
adjective is invariable.)

aller [tout] droit	*go straight ahead*
(s') arrêter court, net	*stop short*
chanter faux/juste	*sing out of tune/in tune*
coûter cher	*be expensive*
frapper ferme/juste	*strike hard/hit the mark*
parler bas/ferme/haut	*speak in a low voice/firmly/loudly*
refuser net	*refuse flatly*
sentir bon/mauvais	*smell good/bad*
sonner faux	*ring false*
tenir bon	*hold firm*
travailler dur, ferme	*work hard*
vendre cher	*sell at a high price*
viser droit, juste/haut	*aim straight/high*
voir clair	*see clearly*

Avec vos renseignements, nous verrons plus clair dans cette histoire
de fraude.
With your information, we'll understand this case of fraud better.

Elle a une voix admirable mais malheureusement elle chante toujours
faux.
She has an admirable voice but unfortunately always sings out of tune.

II. POSITION OF ADVERBS

A.   Adverbs modifying an adjective or another adverb generally precede the word they modify. When modifying a past participle, the adverb may precede or follow.

Il a une écriture parfaitement illisible.
He has a perfectly illegible handwriting.

N'hésitez point; c'est une mission que vous accomplirez fort honorablement.
Do not hesitate; it is a mission that you will accomplish very honorably.

La vieillesse, conçue autrefois (autrefois conçue) comme un état honorable, jouit aujourd'hui de peu de considération.
Old age, once thought of as an honorable state, is held in low regard today.

B.   Adverbs modifying a verb or an entire clause

1.   When modifying an entire clause, the adverb may occupy the initial position or occur after the verb.

Malheureusement, j'ai perdu leur adresse.
Unfortunately, I lost their address.

J'ai perdu malheureusement leur adresse.
I unfortunately lost their address.

a.   In initial position, certain adverbs are always followed by inversion of subject and verb.

à peine	*scarcely*
aussi	*and so*
d'autant moins	*all the less*
d'autant plus	*all the more*
encore	*yet*
peut-être	*perhaps*
sans doute	*no doubt*

Il voulait faire plaisir à ses parents, aussi est-il devenu avocat.
He wanted to please his parents, and so he became a lawyer.

A peine eut-il sauté que l'avion explosa.
Hardly had he jumped when the plane blew up.

Peut-être l'Histoire se souviendra-t-elle de cette triste époque.
Perhaps history will remember this unhappy time.

b. In initial position, certain other adverbs may be followed by inversion.

ainsi	*thus*
à plus forte raison	*all the more reason*
du moins	*at least*
en vain	*in vain*
vainement	*in vain*
(tout) au moins	*at least, at the (very) least*
(tout) au plus	*at most, at the (very) most*

Elle est morte dans un accident de la route; du moins le prétend-on (on le prétend).
She died in an automobile accident; at least they claim so.

Ce projet a demandé trop de temps; ainsi nous faudra-t-il (il nous faudra) nous méfier de tels projets à l'avenir.
This project has taken too much time; we'll thus have to be wary of such projects in the future.

c. There are a few adverbs regularly used in initial position with **que** and without inversion.

peut-être que	*perhaps*
probablement que	*probably*
sans doute que	*no doubt*

Peut-être que vous avez raison, mais j'ai des réserves là-dessus.
Perhaps you are right, but I have some reservations.

Note that **apparemment** and **heureusement** may also be used with **que** and with no inversion.

2. In modification of a verb, noninitial placement depends to a great extent upon the particular adverb and whether the verb is simple or compound in tense.

a. Simple tenses and participial and infinitive equivalents: the adverb follows the verb.

Demain, si tu veux, on parlera longuement de cette affaire.
Tomorrow, if you like, we'll speak at length about this matter.

Ce chien a toujours peur quand il y a de l'orage.
That dog is always afraid when it storms.

Croyant fermement à l'authenticité du tableau, il refusa de la revendre.
Firmly believing the painting was authentic, he refused to resell it.

Il s'est juré de garder éternellement le souvenir de leur trahison.
He swore to himself to remember their betrayal forever.

Note that the short, common adverbs **bien, mieux, mal, peu, trop** are generally placed before an infinitive.

Il ne faut pas trop manger.
One must not eat too much.

L'étude des langues étrangères permet de mieux comprendre sa propre langue.
The study of foreign languages allows one to understand one's own language better.

b. Compound tenses and participial and infinitive equivalents. Certain adverbs of time and place always follow the past participle, as do adjectives used adverbially. The position of other adverbs is not fixed.

aujourd'hui	*today*
demain	*tomorrow*
hier	*yesterday*
tard	*late*
tôt	*early*
ici	*here*
là	*there*
partout	*everywhere*
là-haut	*up there*
là-bas	*down there, over there*
dessus	*on top*
dessous	*underneath*

S'il n'avait pas stationné hier devant la maison, il n'aurait pas d'amende à payer.
If he had not parked in front of the house yesterday, he would not have a fine to pay.

Les nageurs se rappellent bien avoir vu des méduses partout cet été-là.
Swimmers well remember seeing jellyfish everywhere that summer.

En reprochant à son camarade son amour du luxe, il avait visé juste.
When he reproached his friend for a love of luxury, his aim had been perfect.

Beaucoup de jeunes gens ont travaillé bénévolement dans les pays sous-développés.
Many young people have worked without pay in underdeveloped countries.

Elle a soigneusement enveloppé les gobelets dans du papier de soie avant le déménagement.
She carefully wrapped the goblets in tissue paper before moving.

Comparison of Adjectives, Adverbs, and Nouns

Comparison involving adjectives, adverbs, and nouns falls into several types:

(1) comparison of equality
(2) comparison of inequality
    (a) comparison of superiority
    (b) comparison of inferiority

Comparison of inequality occurs on two levels, or degrees, of intensity: the comparative, involving two terms, and the superlative, involving three or more.

I. COMPARISON OF EQUALITY

A. Adjectives and adverbs

1. In affirmative utterances, the usual construction is **aussi** + modifier + **que** + second term. **Aussi** may be intensified by **tout**. The construction adjective + **comme** + second term is also used.

   Ayant fait fortune, il a acheté une maison aussi magnifique qu'un palais.
   Having made his fortune, he bought a house as grand as a palace.

   Les vacances sont tout aussi nécessaires au bien-être que les vitamines.
   Vacations are just as necessary to our well-being as vitamins.

   Tout étrangère qu'elle est, elle parle notre langue aussi couramment que nous.
   Although a foreigner, she speaks our language as fluently as we do.

   Le salon de leur appartement est grand comme un mouchoir de poche.
   The living room of their apartment is [as] big as a handkerchief.

2. In negative utterances, **si** is usually substituted for **aussi**.

   La régate de cette année n'a pas été si passionnante que celle de l'année passée.
   This year's regatta was not so exciting as last year's.

Heureusement, le nouveau président ne parle pas si abondamment que l'ancien.
Fortunately, the new president does not speak so lengthily as the old one.

3. With more than one modifier, **aussi** and **si** are normally repeated.

Elle est aussi aimable et aussi charmante que son amie.
She is as pleasant and [as] charming as her friend.

N'étant pas encore tout à fait rétabli, il ne peut courir ni si vite ni si loin qu'il voudrait.
Not yet being completely healed, he cannot run so fast or so far as he would like.

4. The second term of the comparison may be an entire clause, and there may be a verb complement (**le, y,** or **en,** depending on the verb).

Les fils seront bientôt tout aussi ambitieux que leur père [l']a toujours été.
The sons may soon be just as ambitious as their father has always been.

Le paysage s'est révélé aussi beau que je m'y attendais.
The landscape turned out to be as beautiful as I had expected.

5. Adjectives and adverbs may be compared with other adjectives and adverbs; there is no need to repeat the verb.

Les héroïnes des mélodrames étaient aussi bonnes que belles.
The heroines of melodramas were as good as they were beautiful.

Le chevalier aimait aussi discrètement que tendrement.
The knight loved as discreetly as he did tenderly.

B. Nouns

1. In affirmative utterances, comparison is expressed by **autant de** + noun + **que** + second term. **Autant** may be reinforced by **tout.**

Ce tremblement de terre a causé autant de morts que celui de San Francisco.
That earthquake caused as many deaths as the one in San Francisco.

Malgré ses soixante ans, ce professeur de danse a tout autant de vitalité que ses élèves.
Despite her (his) sixty years, this dance teacher has just as much vitality as her (his) pupils.

2. In negative utterances, **tant** is usually substituted for **autant.**

Ma fille n'a pas tant de caries dentaires que ses camarades.
My daughter does not have as many dental cavities as her friends.

Les nouveaux revêtements de sol n'exigent pas tant d'entretien que ceux d'il y a dix ans.
The new floorcoverings do not require so much care as those of ten years ago.

3. With more than one noun, **autant** and **tant** need not be repeated, but **de** must occur before each noun.

Pour moi, la tour moderne peut avoir autant de beauté et de vigueur qu'une cathédrale gothique.
For me, the modern skyscraper can have as much beauty and vigor as a Gothic cathedral.

4. The second term of the comparison may be an entire clause, and there may be a verb complement (**le, y,** or **en,** depending upon the verb).

Avec un peu d'effort, tu auras autant de commandes que ton prédécesseur en avait.
With a bit of effort, you will have as many orders as your predecessor used to have.

Prenez autant de temps qu'il vous faudra pour réussir ce portrait.
Take as much time as you need with this portrait.

5. The second term of comparison may be another object of **autant** (**tant**) **de;** the second noun is introduced by **de.**

L'histoire nous présente autant de scélérats que de héros.
History offers us as many rogues as heroes.

Vu le marché, on n'a pas planté tant de choux que de maïs.
Given the market, we didn't plant as much cabbage as corn.

C. Verbs and clauses

Comparison may involve not only adjectives, adverbs, and nouns, but verbs and larger units as well.

1. Clause + *autant que* **+ clause**

Il joue autant qu'il travaille.
He plays as much as he works.

Elle aime les sports autant que sa sœur les déteste.
She likes sports as much as her sister hates them.

2. *Autant* **+ clause +** *autant* **+ clause**

Autant il se passionne pour la musique, autant il se désintéresse de l'art.
His love of music equals his lack of interest in art.

Comp of inequality in affirmative may use pleon. ne

INEQUALITY

comparative degree of superiority is marked by **plus,** that of inferiority by **moins.** The second term of the comparison is introduced by **que. Plus** and **moins** may be reinforced by **bien, beaucoup, encore,** or **tellement.**

Le lièvre va-t-il courir plus vite que la tortue?
Is the hare going to run faster than the tortoise?

Avec les nouveaux tarifs, on devra se téléphoner beaucoup moins fréquemment.
With the new rates, we'll have to phone each other much less often.

a. The second term of the comparison may be an entire clause, and there may be a verb complement (**le, y,** or **en,** depending upon the verb). In addition, if the clause containing **plus** or **moins** is affirmative, it is normal to add pleonastic **ne** to the following clause.

Il guérit plus lentement que je ne [l']aurais souhaité.
He is getting better more slowly than I would have wished.

b. An adverb may be compared with another adverb.

Ayant appris l'anglais dans l'armée américaine, il le parle plus couramment que correctement.
Having learned English in the U.S. Army, he speaks it more fluently than correctly.

2. The superlative degree is marked by **le plus** for superiority and **le moins** for inferiority.

Toute la région déteste l'idée d'une nouvelle autoroute, mais les habitants de ce village y résisteront le plus férocement.
The whole region hates the idea of a new highway, but the inhabitants of this village will put up the fiercest resistance.

De tous les membres du conseil d'administration, c'est toujours lui qui agit le moins prudemment.
Of all the members of the board of directors, he is always the one who acts the least prudently.

3. There are three adverbs which have synthetic forms for the comparative and superlative.

bien	*well*	mieux	*better*	le mieux	*best*
beaucoup	*much*	plus	*more*	le plus	*most*
peu	*little*	moins	*less*	le moins	*least*

Elle joue bien ce soir, mais elle a mieux joué la semaine dernière.
She is playing well this evening, but she played better last week.

C'est incroyable—un concours pour voir qui pourra manger le plus.
It's incredible—a contest to see who can eat the most.

Note that **mal** (*badly*) has the synthetic forms **pis** (*worse*) and **le pis** (*worst*), but their use is limited to a few fixed expressions.

Tant pis!	*So much the worse!*
aller de mal en pis	*go from bad to worse*
aller de pis en pis	*get worse and worse*
[ce] qui pis est	*what's worse*

Tu dis que tu peins mal, mais je t'assure que je peins plus mal que toi.
You say you paint badly, but I assure you I paint worse than you do.

4. When **plus, moins, le plus, le moins** apply to more than one adverb, they are repeated.

Il sait lancer le disque plus habilement et plus loin que les autres.
He can throw the discus more skillfully and farther than the others.

B. Adjectives

1. The comparative degree of superiority is marked by **plus,** that of inferiority by **moins.** The second term of the comparison is introduced by **que. Plus** and **moins** may be reinforced by **bien, beaucoup, encore,** or **tellement,** as well as various other intensifying adverbs in **-ment.**

    Les Martiens se révéleront-ils plus intelligents que nous?
    Will the Martians prove to be more intelligent than we?

    Il voudrait trouver un système encore plus efficace que celui utilisé actuellement.
    He would like to find a system even more efficient than the one used at present.

    As-tu jamais vu un plus bel instrument que cette guitare?
    Have you ever seen a more beautiful instrument than this guitar?

    Ces jumeaux sont tous les deux musiciens, mais l'un est drôlement moins doué que l'autre.
    These twins are both musicians, but one is a lot less gifted than the other.

    a. A few adjectives are inherent comparatives of superiority, used without **plus.** The second term of the comparison is introduced by à.

supérieur   *superior*
inférieur   *inferior*
antérieur   *prior, earlier*
postérieur   *subsequent, later*

Il fut déshérité par un testament postérieur à celui qu'il connaissait.
He was disinherited by a will postdating the one he knew about.

b. The second term of the comparison may be an entire clause, and there may be a verb complement (**le, y,** or **en,** depending upon the verb). In addition, if the clause containing **plus** or **moins** is affirmative, it is normal to add pleonastic **ne** to the following clause.

Elle s'est révélée plus mesquine que je ne m'en serais douté.
She proved to be more petty than I would have suspected.

Leurs sondages me semblent moins approfondis que ne le sont ceux de la concurrence.
Their polls seem to me less thorough than are those of the competition.

c. There are three constructions for a comparative that involves multiplication.

La France est $\begin{cases} \text{deux fois plus grande que le Royaume Uni.} \\ \text{deux fois aussi grande que le Royaume Uni.} \\ \text{grande comme deux fois le Royaume Uni.} \end{cases}$

France is twice as large as the United Kingdom.

d. An adjective may be compared with another adjective.

Malgré les apparences, elle est moins habile qu'ambitieuse.
Despite appearances, she is less clever than ambitious.

J'avais commandé un papier peint blanc cassé, mais celui-ci est plus jaune que blanc.
I had ordered an off-white wallpaper, but this one is more yellow than white.

2. The superlative degree is marked by **plus** or **moins** preceded by the definite article, which agrees in number and gender with the adjective.

Les plus belles protestations de sincérité n'ont pu la convaincre.
The finest protestations of sincerity could not convince her.

La sauterelle est un des insectes les plus nocifs.
The locust is one of the most harmful insects.

Parmi tous nos amis, c'est lui le moins apte à réussir.
Of all our friends, he is the least likely to succeed.

a.   An adjective normally placed before the noun may, if its meaning is not affected thereby, be placed after the noun when in the superlative.

Il est si peu visuel que même les tableaux les plus beaux le laissent froid.
He is so unvisual that even the most beautiful paintings leave him cold.

b.   With preposed adjectives, the article may be replaced by a possessive adjective. With postposed adjectives, a possessive may precede the noun, but the article is always retained in the superlative construction itself.

Quand je vais à la pêche, je porte mes plus vieux vêtements.
When I go fishing, I wear my oldest clothes.

Le mycologue nous a montré ses spécimens les plus rares.
The mycologist showed us his rarest specimens.

c.   A noun denoting the context within which a given superlative applies is generally introduced by **de.**

Cette tapisserie est la plus précieuse de toute la collection.
This tapestry is the most valuable in the whole collection.

d.   The verb in a relative clause denoting the context within which a given superlative applies is normally in the subjunctive.

Nous venons de faire l'expérience des montagnes russes les plus sensationnelles qui soient.
We have just been on the most thrilling rollercoaster there is.

See, too, Chapter 1, Section XII.C.2.d.ii.

e.   There are two constructions for a superlative that characterizes a noun preceded by an indefinite article or by a number.

$$\left.\begin{array}{l}\text{ind. art.}\\ \text{number}\end{array}\right\} + \textbf{des} + \text{modified noun}$$

$$\left.\begin{array}{l}\text{ind. art.}\\ \text{number}\end{array}\right\} + \text{noun} + \textbf{des plus} + \text{adjective}$$

un des plus beaux châteaux
one of the most beautiful castles

deux des châteaux les plus magnifiques
two of the most magnificent castles

un château des plus beaux
one of the most beautiful castles

deux châteaux des plus magnifiques
two of the most magnificent castles

f. When an adjective in the superlative degree characterizes an entity in comparison not with other entities but with itself under different circumstances, the article preceding **plus** or **moins** is invariable **le.**

Elles sont toujours hargneuses, mais c'est dans les réunions de comité qu'elles sont le plus hargneuses.
They are always cantankerous, but they are most cantankerous in committee meetings.

3. There are three adjectives which have synthetic forms for the comparative and superlative.

bon	*good*	meilleur	*better*	le meilleur	*best*
mauvais	*bad*	pire	*worse*	le pire	*worst*
petit	*small*	moindre	*lesser*	le moindre	*least, slightest*

a. **Meilleur** is almost always used instead of **plus bon** except when **bon** is being compared with another adjective.

Ce poulet au cari est bien meilleur que le coq au vin.
This curried chicken is much better than the coq au vin.

Ils ont la réputation d'être plus bons qu'intelligents.
They have the reputation of being more good than intelligent.

b. **(Le) plus mauvais** is more usual than **(le) pire,** which carries a strong moral tone.

Elle a plus mauvaise mine aujourd'hui qu'hier.
She looks worse today than yesterday.

Le remède est pire que le mal.
The cure is worse than the evil.

c. **(Le) moindre** is used in reference to significance rather than size, which is expressed by **plus petit.**

Il aurait pu dire bonjour; c'est la moindre des choses.
He might have said hello; it doesn't take much.

La cuillère à café est plus petite que la cuillère à soupe.
A coffee spoon is smaller than a soup spoon.

4. When **plus, moins, le plus, le moins** apply to more than one adjective, they are repeated.

Ce sont les propos les plus imbéciles et les plus injurieux qu'on puisse imaginer.
Those are the most imbecilic and insulting remarks one could imagine.

5.   A word expressing the quantitative difference between two entities with respect to an adjective is introduced by **de.**

Il est de loin l'auteur le plus célèbre de nos jours.
He is by far the most famous author of our time.

Ce mur est de trois mètres plus haut que l'autre.
This wall is three meters higher than the other (higher than the other by three meters).

Il est plus âgé qu'elle de cinq ans.
He is five years older than she is.

C.   Nouns

1.   The comparative degree is marked by **plus de** or **moins de.** The second term of the comparison is introduced by **que** or, if it is a second object of **plus (moins) de,** by **que de. Plus** and **moins** may be reinforced by **bien, beaucoup, encore, tellement,** as well as other intensifying adverbs in **-ment.**

Toute la question est de savoir si un pays a plus d'armements que l'autre.
The whole question is whether one country has more arms than the other.

C'était le four de la saison, avec moins de spectateurs dans la salle que d'artistes sur scène.
It was the flop of the season, with fewer people in the hall than artists on stage.

a.   Before a number, **que** (*than*) is replaced by **de.**

Ce pianiste a donné plus de quinze récitals depuis un mois.
This pianist has given more than fifteen recitals in the last month.

Il nous faut deux cents petits fours pour la réception; le traiteur en a livré moins d'une cinquantaine.
We need two hundred petits fours for the reception; the caterer has delivered fewer than fifty.

b.   The second term of the comparison may be an entire clause. Nouns behave here as adjectives do; see Section B.1.b.

La France produit plus de blé qu'elle n'en a besoin.
France produces more wheat than it needs.

Ce puzzle est décevant; il compte moins de pièces que je ne [l']avais pensé.
This jigsaw puzzle is disappointing; it has fewer pieces than I had thought.

2. The superlative degree is marked by **le plus de** or **le moins de;** the article is invariable. **De** must be repeated before every noun it governs. The superlative may be reinforced by such words as **possible, imaginable, concevable;** these follow the adjective + noun or noun + adjective phrase and are invariable.

De tous les quartiers de la ville, celui-ci a le plus d'immeubles en grès rouge.
Of all the neighborhoods in the city, this one has the most buildings in red sandstone.

Il déteste le cinéma et va voir le moins de films possible.
He hates movies and goes to see the fewest films possible (as few films as possible).

Note that the verb in a relative clause denoting the context within which the superlative applies is normally in the subjunctive.

J'adore voir au cirque cette toute petite voiture d'où sortent le plus de clowns qu'on puisse imaginer.
I adore seeing at the circus that tiny car out of which come the greatest number of clowns you can imagine.

D. Verbs and clauses allow comparison no less than the other parts of the sentence

Nous rêvons de voyager plus que nous ne voyageons.
We dream of traveling more than we travel.

E. Other expressions of comparison

1. **Davantage** is a synonym of **plus** used in a limited number of ways.

a. To modify a verb

Nous l'avons toujours admirée, mais depuis sa démission nous l'admirons encore davantage.
We have always admired her, but since her resignation we admire her even more.

b. With a direct object represented by **en**

L'an dernier, ils ont exporté beaucoup de caoutchouc, mais ils comptent en exporter davantage cette année.
Last year, they exported a great deal of rubber, but they count on exporting more this year.

   c.   With an adjective represented by the neuter pronoun **le**

Je suis sans doute têtu, mais vous deux l'êtes davantage [que moi].
I am no doubt stubborn, but you two are more [than I am].

2.   **Autrement** is a synonym of **beaucoup plus, bien plus,** or **encore plus,** used only before an adjective.

Quelle famille! Le fils est autrement antipathique que le père.
What a family! The son is even more antipathetic than the father.

3.   The absolute superlative denotes the highest possible degree of applicability of a modifier, without reference to specific terms of comparison. There are a few adjectives which are inherently absolute superlatives and thus cannot logically be qualified by **(le) plus** or **(le) moins: excellent** (*excellent*), **parfait** (*perfect*), **suprême** (*supreme*), **infime** (*infinitesimal*), **unique** (*unique*). Such adjectives aside, the absolute superlative may be expressed in several ways.

   a.   By means of **des plus (moins)** placed before a plural adjective

Je déteste ce portrait; il est des moins flatteurs.
I hate that portrait; it is extremely unflattering.

   b.   By means of **on ne peut plus (moins)** placed before an adjective or adverb

Le dîner était on ne peut plus simple, mais tout le monde y a pris plaisir.
The dinner was extremely simple, but everyone enjoyed it.

   c.   By means of the adjective prefixes **archi-, extra-, super-, sur-, ultra-**

On a dû rester debout parce que la salle était archicomble.
We had to stand because the hall was filled to bursting.

Il faut une aiguille extra-fine quand on travaille sur de la soie.
You need an extremely fine needle when you work with silk.

   d.   By means of the suffix **-issime,** which is used only with a few adjectives

J'ai trouvé chez un antiquaire un livre rarissime datant du seizième siècle.
I found at an antique dealer's a very rare book dating from the sixteenth century.

C'est un homme richissime, mais qui a un train de vie modeste.
He is an extremely rich man, but one who lives modestly.

4. There are several constructions involving **plus** or **moins** that express change or proportionality as well as comparison.

   a. **de plus (moins) en plus (moins)**

On produit de moins en moins de voitures non automatiques.
Fewer and fewer standard-shift cars are being produced.

Fatigué, il courait de plus en plus lentement.
Tired now, he was running more and more slowly.

Ces malheureux événements nous attristent de plus en plus.
These unfortunate events make us more and more sad.

   b. **d'autant plus (moins) . . . que**

J'ai été d'autant plus étonné de son échec que je considérais sa victoire comme certaine.
I was all the more surprised by his failure as I had considered his victory a certainty.

J'ai été étonné de son échec, d'autant plus que je considérais sa victoire comme certaine.
I was surprised by his failure, all the more as (particularly since) I had considered his victory a certainty.

   c. **Plus (Moins) . . . [et] plus (moins)**

Plus elle danse, [et] plus elle a envie de danser.
The more she dances, the more she feels like dancing.

Plus il travaillera dur, [et] plus il réussira vite.
The harder he'll work, the faster he'll succeed.

Plus la situation dans ce pays-là sera stable, [et] plus nous serons tentés d'y voyager.
The more stable the situation in that country will be, the more tempted we'll be to travel there.

Moins il y a de pollen dans l'atmosphère, [et] moins j'ai d'ennuis.
The less pollen there is in the atmosphere, the fewer problems I have.

Personal Pronouns

I. FORMS

A. The unstressed pronouns are those necessarily bound to a verb. The fact that they are so joined and cannot be used alone is reflected in the term "conjunctive" usually applied to them.

	SINGULAR			PLURAL		
	SUB-JECT	DIRECT OBJECT	INDIRECT OBJECT	SUB-JECT	DIRECT OBJECT	INDIRECT OBJECT
FIRST PERSON *reflexive*	je, j' ⤫	me, m'		nous		
SECOND PERSON *reflexive*	tu ⤫	te, t'		vous		
THIRD PERSON *masculine*	il	le, l'	lui	ils	les	leur	en
feminine	elle	la, l'		elles			y
indefinite	on					
reflexive		se, s'			se, s'	

1. The elided forms (**j'**, **m'**, etc.) are used before words beginning with a vowel or mute **h.**

2. The third-person indefinite pronoun **on*** occurs only as a subject and as a singular. To express an indefinite object, French has re-

---

*For further treatment of **on,** see Chapter 13, Section J.

course to **nous, vous, les gens,** and similar expressions or may omit an object altogether.

Une telle défaite $\left\{\begin{array}{l}\text{nous}\\\text{vous}\end{array}\right\}$ attriste.

Une telle défaite attriste.
Such a defeat saddens one.

3. There are two adverbial forms which function as conjunctive pronouns: **y** (*in that place, to that place; to it, to them*) and **en** (*from that place; of it, of them*).

B. The stressed, or disjunctive, pronouns are those which may function independently of a verb. They include both simple and compound forms.

	SINGULAR	PLURAL
FIRST PERSON	moi moi-même	nous nous-mêmes
SECOND PERSON	toi toi-même	vous vous-même(s)
THIRD PERSON *masculine*	lui lui-même	eux eux-mêmes
feminine	elle elle-même	elles elles-mêmes
indefinite (**on**)	soi soi-même	

II. POSITION

A. Subject pronouns

1. They precede the verb in declarative sentences and subordinate clauses.

Il regardait pensivement l'océan.
He was looking pensively at the ocean.

Pensez-vous qu'il puisse soulever ce poids tout seul?
Do you think he can lift this weight by himself?

2. Subject and verb are inverted in several cases.

    a. To form questions without **est-ce que.**

        Pourquoi divague-t-il toujours?
        Why does he always wander from the subject?

        Sommes-nous condamnés à répéter les erreurs de nos prédéces-
        seurs?
        Are we condemned to repeat the errors of our predecessors?

    b. In clauses beginning with certain adverbs, including **à peine**
        (*hardly*), **aussi** (*and so*), **peut-être** (*perhaps*). See Chapter 6, Sec-
        tion II.B.1.a.-b.

    c. In attributions immediately following direct quotations.

        «Mets un disque, s'il te plaît,» a-t-il dit.
        "Put on a record, please," he said (said he).

        «Je regrette,» balbutia-t-elle, «mais je n'avais pas compris.»
        "I'm sorry," she stammered, "but I hadn't understood."

    d. In wishes expressed with **pouvoir.**

        Puissiez-vous échapper à ce danger!
        May you escape that danger!

3. Subject pronouns are omitted in imperative statements.

    N'oublie pas de renouveler notre abonnement avant la fin du mois.
    Don't forget to renew our subscription before the end of the month.

4. Conjunctive subject pronouns may not be separated from the verb
    by any word other than **ne** and/or object pronouns. If there is any
    other intervening word or phrase, they must be replaced or supple-
    mented with a disjunctive form.

    Moi qui vous parle [je] suis persuadé que cela ne peut arriver.
    I tell you, I am convinced that can't happen.

    Toi seul [tu] es capable de leur faire changer d'avis.
    You alone are capable of making them change their minds.

    Eux, épuisés, [ils] se sont endormis tout de suite, mais moi j'ai
    veillé toute la nuit.
    They, exhausted, fell asleep right away, but I was up all night.

Note that the one exception to this rule is the administrative formula **Je soussigné(e)**
+ verb.

    Je soussigné certifie que ERART Jean a été vacciné contre la variole.
    I the undersigned hereby certify that Jean Erart has been vaccinated against smallpox.

5. Double subjects are treated in various ways, depending upon person, context, and tone. In any case, the verb must agree with the grammatical person representing the combined subject, for example, **vous** + **moi** = **nous** (or **on**).

Mon frère et lui sont allés au cinéma.
Ils sont allés au cinéma, mon frère et lui.
Mon frère et lui, ils sont allés au cinéma.
My brother and he went to the movies.

Elle et eux n'osent plus se voir.
Ils n'osent plus se voir, elle et eux.
Elle et eux, ils n'osent plus se voir.
She and they no longer dare to see one another.

Vous et moi, nous nous connaissons depuis longtemps.
Nous nous connaissons depuis longtemps, vous et moi.
On se connaît depuis longtemps, vous et moi.
You and I have known each other for a long time.

Le pharmacien et moi venons de la même région.
Le pharmacien et moi, nous venons de la même région.
Nous venons de la même région, le pharmacien et moi.
The pharmacist and I come from the same region.

B. Object pronouns

They precede the verb that governs them, except in the case of the affirmative imperative.

1. Single object pronouns

Aimant beaucoup cette sculpture, il passait de longs moments à la contempler.
He liked that sculpture very much and spent long moments gazing at it.

Cette année, pour l'anniversaire de grand-maman, nous lui avons offert des orchidées.
This year, for Grandmother's birthday, we gave her orchids.

Ne se rappelle-t-il pas notre conversation sur les conditions de cette interview?
Doesn't he remember our conversation on the terms of this interview?

Vous ne m'avez jamais raconté l'histoire de votre évasion.
You have never told me the story of your escape.

Pourriez-vous la voir avant lundi pour lui annoncer la nouvelle?
Could you see her before Monday to give her the news?

N'y touchez pas! La peinture est toujours fraîche.
Don't touch! The paint is still wet.

Ecoutez-les bien, ces consignes, il y va de votre vie.
Listen well to these orders; your life is at stake.

Note that in affirmative imperatives, **me** and **te** are replaced by the stressed forms **moi** and **toi.**

Apportez-moi le courrier, s'il vous plaît.
Bring me the mail, please.

Lave-toi les mains, tu les as affreusement sales!
Wash your hands; they're horribly dirty.

2. **Double object pronouns**

a. The forms **me, te, nous, vous, se,** when used as indirect objects, may be combined before the governing verb with the direct object pronouns **le, la, les.** Except in affirmative imperatives, the indirect precedes the direct object.

Il m'a offert la montre. Il me l'a offerte.
He gave me the watch. He gave it to me.

Ne vous présentera-t-elle pas son ami? Ne vous le présentera-t-elle pas?
Won't she introduce her friend to you? Won't she introduce him to you?

Elles s'étaient rappelé les événements. Elles se les étaient rappelés.
They had remembered the events. They had remembered them.

Il n'osait pas me demander ses cent francs. Il n'osait pas me les demander.
He did not dare ask me for his hundred francs. He did not dare ask me for them.

i. In affirmative imperatives, the indirect object follows the direct object.

Racontez-nous ce qui s'est passé. Racontez-le-nous.
Tell us what happened. Tell it to us.

Achète-moi cette belle cravate. Achète-la-moi.
Buy me that beautiful tie. Buy it for me.

ii. If the indirect object in the affirmative imperative statement is reflexive, it precedes the direct object.

Lave-toi les mains. Lave-toi-les.
Wash your hands. Wash them.

Achetons-nous cette voiture. Achetons-nous-la.
Let's buy ourselves that car. Let's buy it for ourselves.

b.   The indirect object pronouns **lui** and **leur** may be used with the direct forms **le, la, les.** Without exception, the indirect object follows the direct.

Il a montré la photo à son frère. Il la lui a montrée.
He showed the photo to his brother. He showed it to him.

Elles distribuaient les colis aux pauvres. Elles les leur distribuaient.
They were distributing the parcels to the poor. They were distributing them to them.

Racontez cette plaisanterie à mon mari. Racontez-la-lui.
Tell that joke to my husband. Tell it to him.

c.   In combination with other pronouns, the forms **y** and **en** are placed closest to the verb, except in affirmative imperatives.

On distribuera des vivres aux réfugiés. On leur en distribuera.
Provisions will be distributed to the refugees. They will be distributed to them.

Il a dû expédier ses dépêches au journal. Il a dû les y expédier.
He had to send his dispatches to the newspaper. He had to send them there.

Donnons du lait à la chatte. Donnons-lui-en.
Let's give some milk to the cat. Let's give her some.

Note that, in affirmative imperatives, **moi** and **toi** are replaced by **m'** and **t'** before **y** and **en.** However, such combinations tend to be avoided in favor of some other construction; the same is true of **l'en** and **l'y.**

Lis-moi des poèmes. Lis-m'en. Veux-tu m'en lire?
Read me some poems. Read me some. Will you read me some?

Conduisez-moi à la gare. Conduisez-m'y. Conduisez-moi là.
Drive me to the station. Drive me there. Drive me there.

Sortez le chien de la maison. Sortez-l'en. Vous l'en sortirez.
Take the dog out of the house. Take it out. You will take it out.

d.   No more than one direct object and one indirect object may be used conjunctively. A double direct or a double indirect object must be expressed by a reprise construction.

Il nous a aperçus, vous et moi.
He noticed you and me.

Je vous ai aperçus, toi et ton chien.
I noticed you and your dog.

Nous le leur donnerons, à lui et à elle.
We'll give it to him and to her.

e. The forms **me, te, nous, vous, se** may not be used together with one another. When two such objects must be expressed, one direct and the other indirect, the direct object occurs as a conjunctive pronoun and the indirect is given the form of **à** + disjunctive. Similarly, as direct objects, these forms may not be paired with the conjunctives **lui** and **leur;** the latter must be replaced by **à** + disjunctive pronoun.

Elle s'est présentée à nous.
She introduced herself to us.

Qui vous a envoyé à nous?
Who has sent you to us?

Fie-toi à moi.
Trust me.

Il s'est intéressé à elle.
He took an interest in her.

Elle nous présentera à eux.
She will introduce us to them.

Note that the form **y,** as an indirect object of non-human reference, does occur in combination with the direct object pronouns **me, te, nous, vous, se.**

Il s'est intéressé à cette affaire. Il s'y est intéressé.
He took an interest in this matter. He took an interest in it.

Vous pouvez vous fier à sa bonne volonté. Vous pouvez vous y fier.
You may trust his good will. You may trust it.

III. THIRD-PERSON OBJECT PRONOUN USAGE

A. The direct object pronoun **le** is used not only to refer to a masculine singular noun, but also to represent an idea expressed in a preceding phrase. The forms **y** and **en** are similarly used. Such a reference is far more usual in French than in English.

1. **Le** may represent an infinitive phrase or a clause.

Je voulais aller au Japon, mais je ne savais pas si je le pourrais.
I wanted to go to Japan, but I did not know whether I could [do it].

Vas-tu mieux aujourd'hui? Je l'espère.
Are you better today? I hope [so].

2. **Le** may represent an adjective or a participle.

Suis-je contente? Oui, je le suis.
Am I happy? Yes, I am.

Elles n'étaient pas bronzées, mais elles le sont devenues.
They were not tanned, but they have become so.

Nous ne serons pas vaincus. Nous ne le serons pas.
We will not be defeated. We will not be.

3. With a verb of being, **le** may represent a noun without definite determination.

J'étais danseuse et je ne le suis plus.
I used to be a dancer and am no longer.

C'est une véritable mégère, mais elle ne le paraît pas.
She is a real shrew, but she doesn't seem one.

Ce ne sont plus des jeunes, mais ils voudraient l'être.
They are no longer youngsters, but they would like to be.

4. **Y** is used with verbs taking an indirect object.

Toi, tu consentirais à ce que les enfants fassent de l'auto-stop? Moi,
je n'y consens pas.
You would consent to the children's hitchhiking? I don't consent.

5. **En** is used with verbs taking a **de** complement.

Qu'est-ce qu'on a bien pu lui proposer? Il refuse d'en parler.
What can they have proposed to him? He refuses to speak about it.

B. To represent indirect objects, **lui** and **leur** (or their disjunctive equivalents) are normally used for persons; **y** is normally used for nonhuman reference.

Il répond au postulant. Il lui répond.
He answers the applicant. He answers him.

Il répond à la lettre. Il y répond.
He answers the letter. He answers it.

1. The indirect object of certain verbs and verbal phrases, when it is human, is expressed by **à** + disjunctive pronoun rather than a conjunctive form. The form **y** is used as an indirect object of nonhuman reference.

accoutumer	*accustom (to)*
habituer	*accustom (to)*
penser	*think (about)*
rêver	*think (about)*
songer	*think (about)*
renoncer	*renounce*
tenir	*like; insist (on)*
toucher	*touch; bother*
avoir affaire	*have to deal (with)*
avoir recours	*have recourse (to)*
faire attention	*pay attention (to)*
prendre garde	*beware (of)*
être	*belong (to)*

Il pense à ses amis. Il pense à eux.
He thinks about his friends. He thinks about them.

Il pense à ses obligations. Il y pense.
He thinks about his obligations. He thinks about them.

Il a dû renoncer à celle qu'il aimait. Il a dû renoncer à elle.
He had to give up the woman he loved. He had to give her up.

Il a dû renoncer à son projet. Il a dû y renoncer.
He had to give up his plan. He had to give it up.

A qui sont ces gants? Ils sont à lui.
Whose gloves are these? They are his.

2. With verbs that take a conjunctive indirect object, the use of **lui**, **leur** or **y** depends upon the kind of object, human or nonhuman, normally taken.

  a. Verbs restricted to a nonhuman indirect object take **y**.

ajouter	*add*
assister	*attend*
s'attendre	*expect*
collaborer	*collaborate*
consentir	*consent*
contribuer	*contribute*
mettre fin	*put an end*
participer	*participate*
se plaire	*enjoy*
prendre part	*participate, share*
prétendre	*claim*
remédier	*remedy*
se résigner	*resign oneself*
réussir	*succeed*

On m'a offert un rôle dans cette opérette; malheureusement, je ne pourrai pas y prendre part.
I've been offered a role in that operetta; unfortunately, I won't be able to take part in it.

On fait actuellement une grande campagne en faveur du recyclage; même les enfants y collaborent.
There is a great recycling campaign now underway; even children are collaborating in it.

b. Certain verbs whose indirect object may be either human or non-human generally take **lui, leur** for either type of object.

accorder	*grant*
communiquer	*communicate*
demander	*ask for*
devoir	*owe*
donner	*give*
enlever	*remove*
fournir	*furnish*
ôter	*remove*
préférer	*prefer*
prendre	*take*
prêter	*lend*
rendre	*return*
ressembler	*resemble*
servir	*serve*

Quand vous verrez vos parents, vous serez bien gentil de leur donner mes compliments.
When you see your parents, be so kind as to give them my best regards.

Ce mur a tant de couches de peinture que je ne lui en donnerais pas encore une.
The wall has so many layers of paint that I would not give it one more.

Il est très déçu; on lui a préféré l'autre candidat.
He is very disappointed; they chose the other candidate over him.

On t'a acheté un beau costume de velours, et tu lui préfères toujours ton blue-jean.
We bought you a beautiful corduroy suit, and you still prefer your jeans.

On dit que les gens qui vivent avec un chien finissent par lui ressembler.
They say that people who live with a dog end up resembling it.

c. In the case of a few verbs, **lui** and **leur** are used instead of **y** when there is any degree of personification or animacy in the indirect object.

échapper	*escape*
obéir	*obey*
résister	*resist*
sacrifier	*sacrifice*
succéder	*succeed, follow*
survivre	*survive*

être ⎫ ⎧ fidèle ⎫   *be* ⎫ ⎧ *faithful* ⎫
rester ⎬ ⎨ dévoué ⎬   *remain* ⎬ ⎨ *devoted* ⎬
     ⎭ ⎩ attaché ⎭   ⎭ ⎩ *attached* ⎭

La tradition religieuse règle leur vie; elles ne songent même pas à lui résister.
Religious tradition rules their life; they do not even dream of resisting it.

Les odeurs de cuisine étaient si délicieuses qu'il n'a pu y résister.
The cooking aromas were so delicious that he could not resist them.

Il ne veut pas vendre la maison paternelle tellement il lui est attaché.
He is so attached to the family house that he will not sell it.

Ça ne me coûtera rien de quitter ce travail, je n'y suis pas attaché.
It won't bother me to leave this job; I am not attached to it.

3. When preceded by a preposition, the disjunctive pronouns **lui, elle, eux, elles** are used only rarely for antecedents of nonhuman reference.

a. When the preposition is, or would be, **à,** the form **y** is used. In the case of **en, dans, sur, sous,** a corresponding adverb or **y** may be used.

Elle vient de Lille mais ne veut pas y retourner.
She comes from Lille but does not want to return [there].

Si elle avait su qu'il n'y avait personne dans la maison, elle n'y serait pas entrée.
If she had known there was no one in the house, she would not have gone in.

Donne-moi l'escabeau; je monterai dessus pour changer l'ampoule.
Give me the stool; I'll get up on it and change the lightbulb.

Il a ouvert le tiroir pour ranger les chemises dedans.
He opened the drawer to put the shirts away.

b. Other prepositions, except **de,** and their nonhuman complements
are replaced by adverbs.

Il a sorti le gigot du four et a mis du persil tout autour.
He took the leg of lamb out of the oven and put parsley all around it.

Ne pouvant pas éviter l'obstacle, elle a sauté par-dessus.
Unable to avoid the obstacle, she jumped over it.

Voilà un gros arbre; mets-toi devant et je fais ta photo.
There's a big tree; stand in front of it and I'll take your picture.

c. When the preposition is, or would be, **de,** the form **en** occurs.

Devant le restaurant, j'ai rencontré mon patron qui venait d'en
sortir.
*In front of the restaurant, I met my boss, who had just come out
[of it].*

Sont-ils toujours à Marseille? —Non, ils en sont revenus.
Are they still in Marseilles? —No, they have come back.

Ces chiens sont méchants, ne vous en approchez pas.
These dogs are vicious; don't get near them.

i. When the object of **de** is a person and **de** is part of a verbal
expression, the disjunctive pronoun is used. Sometimes, however, **en** may represent groups of people.

Ton frère ne se souvient pas de ses grands-parents. Te sou-
viens-tu d'eux?
*Your brother does not remember his grandparents. Do you remember
them?*

J'avais engagé une garde-malade, mais je n'ai plus besoin d'elle.
I had hired a practical nurse, but I no longer need her.

Ce sont les pires traîtres, ces gens-là; méfiez-vous-en.
Those people are the worst traitors; beware of them.

ii. When **de** + noun denotes possession by a nonhuman entity, it
may usually be replaced by **en.** See Chapter 9, Section III.B.5.

4. **En** is used to replace any direct object noun, human or nonhuman,
introduced by a partitive or indefinite plural article.

As-tu toujours des parents en Europe? Moi, j'en ai.
Do you still have relatives in Europe? I do.

Il faut de l'engrais pour le jardin. Veux-tu aller en chercher?
We need fertilizer for the garden. Will you go get some?

5. The pronoun **soi** (or **soi-même**) is used only in reference to an indefinite subject, for example, **chacun, on, personne,** or, usually in impersonal statements, to people in general. Otherwise, **lui** and the other third-person disjunctive pronouns occur in reference to the subject.

On est toujours bien chez soi.
One is always comfortable at home.

Chacun pour soi et Dieu pour tous.
Every man for himself and God for all.

Il ne faut pas toujours penser à soi (soi-même).
We must not always think of ourselves.

Il faut penser à ceux qui sont moins fortunés que soi.
You have to think of those who are less fortunate than you.

Il a fait un geste d'impatience malgré lui.
He made a gesture of impatience in spite of himself.

Elle porte toujours son passeport sur elle.
She always carries her passport with her.

IV. ADDITIONAL USES OF THE DISJUNCTIVE PRONOUNS

A. Simple disjunctive pronouns have several functions

1. To stress conjunctives or nouns, whether as subject or object. Their position is highly variable.

Moi, je ne connais pas ces gens-là.
Je ne connais pas ces gens-là, moi.
Je ne les connais pas, moi, ces gens-là.
I don't know those people.

Lui, je ne l'ai pas vu.
Je ne l'ai pas vu, lui.
I haven't seen him.

Le magistrat, lui, n'aurait pas parlé de la sorte.
Le magistrat n'aurait pas parlé de la sorte, lui.
The judge would not have spoken like that.

2. To serve as a complement of **être** when the subject is **ce.**

Qui est-ce? —C'est moi.
Who is it? —It is I (me).

C'étaient eux qui avaient frappé à la porte.
It was they (They were the ones) who had knocked at the door.

C'est nous qui le faisons d'habitude.
It is we (We are the ones) who normally do it.

3. To express subject or object without a verb.

Qui a fait cela? —Moi.
Who did that? —I [did].

Qui avez-vous vu? —Lui.
Whom have you seen? —Him.

A qui as-tu parlé? A lui.
To whom did you speak? —To him.

Leur petit frère ira plus loin qu'eux.
Their little brother will go farther than they [will].

4. To serve as subject of an infinitive in exclamations.

Toi, faire cela! Ce n'est pas possible.
You, do that! That's not possible.

Eux, nous dire des mots pareils! Qui l'aurait cru?
They, use such words to us! Who would have thought it?

5. To replace conjunctive objects when using the restrictive **que** (*only*).

Vous lui obéirez et n'obéirez qu'à lui.
You will obey him and only him.

Dans toute la foule, elle n'a reconnu que lui.
In the whole crowd, she recognized only him.

6. The collective aspect of **nous** and **vous** may be stressed by combining the pronoun with **autres;** to this combination a defining noun may be added.

Ils vous ont enfin invités, vous autres?
Did they finally get around to inviting you?

Nous autres obsédés, nous tenons à ce que tout soit toujours parfait.
We compulsives insist that everything always be perfect.

B. Compound disjunctive pronouns usually express an intense involvement of the self or a notion of self-sufficiency in performing an action.

Il a fait tout cela pour lui-même.
He did all that for himself.

Elle ne les en blâme pas, mais elle ne l'aurait pas fait elle-même.
She does not blame them for it, but she would not have done it herself.

Connais-toi toi-même.
Know thyself.

Mon père, resté veuf, a appris à faire la cuisine lui-même.
My father, when he became a widower, learned how to do the cooking himself.

Possessive Adjectives
and Pronouns

French, like English, expresses the relation of possession by the use of adjectives (**ma maison**—*my house*) and pronouns (**la mienne**—*mine*). It expresses possession too by means of the construction noun + **de** + noun and **être à** + noun or pronoun.

I. NOUN + *DE* + NOUN

l'éprouvette du chimiste   *the chemist's test tube*
la demi-sœur de Cendrillon   *Cinderella's stepsister*
les roues de la voiture   *the wheels of the car*

II. *ÊTRE À* + NOUN OR PRONOUN

This construction is used only to identify the possessor of an object.

A qui est ce livre? —Il est à moi.★
Whose book is this? —It's mine.

Ma tante prétend que la maison de grand-père est désormais à elle et pas
   à nous.
My aunt claims that Grandfather's house is now hers and not ours.

Note that the phrase **à** + pronoun may be added to a noun to reinforce the idea of possession.

Maintenant qu'elle travaille, elle a une voiture à elle.
Now that she is working, she has a car of her own.

C'est son opinion à lui, tout le monde ne la partage pas.
That is his opinion; not everyone shares it.

★To identify creator rather than possessor, **de** is used.

De qui est ce livre? —Il est de moi.
Whose book is this (Who wrote this book)? —It's mine (I did).

De qui est cette symphonie? —[Elle est] de Schubert.
Whose symphony is this? —[It is] Schubert's.

III. POSSESSIVE ADJECTIVES

A. Forms

The possessive adjective in French changes form according to the possessor and also agrees in number and gender with the object possessed (and not with the gender of the possessor).

	MASC. SINGULAR	FEM. SINGULAR	MASC./ FEM. PLURAL	MASC./ FEM. SINGULAR	MASC./ FEM. PLURAL
FIRST PERSON	mon	ma	mes	notre	nos
SECOND PERSON	ton	ta	tes	votre	vos
THIRD PERSON	son	sa	ses	leur	leurs

Elle donnait à manger à son chat.
She was feeding her cat.

Sa mère est arrivée.
His (Her) mother has arrived.

Note that the masculine singular forms **mon, ton, son** are used before feminine words beginning with a vowel or mute h.

mon amie	*my friend*
ton ancienne élève	*your former pupil*
son utilité	*its usefulness*
son héroïne	*his (her, its) heroine*

B. Use

1. The possessive adjective is used to indicate not only real possession (**mon chien, leurs livres**) but also other relations.

Notre train part à dix heures.
Our train leaves at ten o'clock.

Son médecin lui a dit de garder le lit.
Her (His) doctor told her (him) to stay in bed.

Elle fait sa grande dame, mais elle n'impressionne personne.
She is playing the great lady, but no one is impressed.

Il sent son pédant.
It is obvious what a pedant he is.

Voilà ton revenant—rien qu'un vieux tronc d'arbre.
There's your ghost—nothing but an old tree trunk.

Note that **notre** and **nos** occur in authorial and royal use just as English *our* does.

Nos conclusions n'étonneront sûrement pas le lecteur.
Our conclusions will surely not surprise the reader.

En l'an cinq de notre règne . . . .
In the fifth year of our reign . . . .

2. The possessive adjective is customarily used in certain vocatives addressing one's superior officer in the army. Similarly, the possessive adjective occurs in addressing certain members of the Catholic clergy.

   mon lieutenant, mon capitaine, mon colonel, mon général
   mon père, mon révérend père, ma sœur, ma mère

   Note that one's own parish priest is **Monsieur le curé** or **Monsieur l'abbé;** a Protestant minister is **Monsieur le pasteur;** a rabbi is **Rabbin** or **Docteur.**

3. With parts of the body and properties of the mind, possession is felt to be so amply known that French tends to use the definite article rather than the possessive adjective.

   J'ai ouvert la bouche pour répondre.
   I opened my mouth to answer.

   Avez-vous mal à la tête?
   Does your head hurt?

   Grand-père perd la mémoire.
   Grandfather is losing his memory.

   a. When the part of the body or an item of clothing acted upon does not belong to the subject, possession is usually indicated by the use of an indirect object pronoun.

      Le médecin lui a pansé l'épaule gauche.
      The doctor bandaged his/her (the patient's) left shoulder.

      Nous lui avons coupé les cheveux.
      We cut his/her hair.

      Après leur avoir enlevé les chaussures, elle leur a mis des pantoufles.
      After removing their shoes, she put on their slippers.

   b. In statements such as **il lève la main** (*he raises his hand*), the part of the body functions with apparent autonomy. When, however, the action involves the intervention of some other part of the body or of an outside agent, the reflexive pronoun is added.

Elle s'est lavé les mains.
She washed her hands.

Brosse-toi les dents après chaque repas.
Brush your teeth after every meal.

Il se ronge les ongles.
He bites his nails.

c.   In adverbial phrases containing the name of a part of the body, the definite article is used and there is no preposition.

Les négotiateurs sont rentrés les mains vides.
The negotiators came home empty-handed.

Il n'est pas poli de parler la bouche pleine.
It is impolite to speak with your mouth full.

Elle passe de longues heures le nez dans un livre.
She spends long hours with her nose in a book.

Il est sorti le chandail noué autour du cou.
He went out with his sweater tied around his neck.

d.   When the noun for the part of the body is the direct object of **avoir,** the definite article is used when an adjective of physical characteristic follows the noun. When there is an adjective of subjective appreciation, whether it comes before the noun or after, the indefinite article is used.

Elle a les pommettes hautes.
She has high cheekbones.

Ils avaient les yeux injectés de sang.
They had bloodshot eyes.

Elle a de très beaux yeux et une tête adorable.
She has very beautiful eyes and an adorable head.

e.   When the noun for a part of the body is not the object of **avoir** and is modified by a descriptive adjective (not **droit**—*right* or **gauche**—*left*), the possessive adjective is used.

Elle s'est fait couper ses magnifiques cheveux châtains.
She had her magnificent chestnut hair cut.

Elle portait des bagues à tous ses longs doigts graciles.
She wore rings on all her long slender fingers.

Il se couchait un bonnet de nuit sur sa tête chauve.
He used to go to bed with a nightcap on his bald head.

4. **The distributive singular.** When the possessor is a group of people, each one of whom has only one of the objects in possession, French, unlike English, tends to see the thing possessed as a singular rather than a plural.

Les magistrats secouaient gravement la tête.
The judges solemnly shook their heads.

Devant le défunt, tous les hommes ont ôté le chapeau.
Before the deceased, all the men removed their hats.

5. **En** as an expression of the possessive. When two nouns linked by possession refer to nonhuman entities and occur in separate clauses, French often expresses their relationship by using the definite article and the pronoun **en** instead of the possessive adjective. The possessive, however, is used if the thing possessed is the subject of a verb that takes an object (direct or indirect).

La chapelle était fermée, mais on nous en a ouvert les portes.
The chapel was closed, but its doors were opened to us.

Des hectares de forêt ont brûlé; la perte en est incalculable.
Acres of forest land have burned; the loss is incalculable.

J'admire ce manteau; l'étoffe en est belle, mais sa coupe ne me convient pas.
I admire this coat; the (its) fabric is lovely, but the (its) cut does not suit me.

Note that the possessive adjective is used if the entity possessed is introduced by a preposition.

Examinant la cheminée, nous avons été horrifiés par la condition de son mortier.
Examining the fireplace, we were horrified by the condition of its mortar.

6. Possession with **on, chacun,** and other singular indefinite pronouns and in impersonal statements is normally expressed by the third person singular of the possessive adjective.

Même dans ces circonstances difficiles, on doit faire (il faut faire) de son mieux.
Even in these trying circumstances, one must do one's best.

Chacun a son amour-propre et s'offense quand celui-ci est blessé.
Everyone has his pride and takes offense when it is wounded.

Tiens! quelqu'un a oublié son parapluie.
Look! someone has forgotten his umbrella.

Note that, when **chacun** is a distributive referring to first or second person plural, **notre, nos** or **votre, vos** are used, except with the formula **chacun de son côté.** When the reference is to a third person plural, the possessive may be either singular or plural.

Vous allez prendre chacun votre voiture?
Are you each going to take your own car?

Nous lui avons exprimé chacun nos idées par écrit.
We each gave him (her) our ideas in writing.

Après la baignade, nous sommes allés chacun de son côté.
After the swim, we each went our separate ways.

Ils vont prendre chacun sa (or leur) voiture?
Are they each going to take their own car?

IV. POSSESSIVE PRONOUNS

A. Forms

Like the possessive adjective, the possessive pronoun changes form according to the possessor and also agrees in number and gender with the object possessed.

	SING.	PLURAL	SING.	PLURAL
FIRST PERSON	le mien la mienne	les miens les miennes	le la } nôtre	les nôtres
SECOND PERSON	le tien la tienne	les tiens les tiennes	le la } vôtre	les vôtres
THIRD PERSON	le sien la sienne	les siens les siennes	le la } leur	les leurs

B. Use

The possessive pronoun refers to a specific noun and agrees with that noun in number and gender.

J'ai mes clés; as-tu les tiennes?
I have my keys; do you have yours?

Nos photos ne sont pas mal, mais les leurs sont très réussies.
Our photos are not bad, but theirs are very successful.

1.   Without the definite article, the possessive forms sometimes occur as adjectives in literary usage.

un mien sonnet
a sonnet of mine

Il prend comme siennes les idées des autres.
He takes other people's ideas as his own.

Leurs revendications, je les fais miennes.
I am making their demands my own.

2.   There are a few idiomatic locutions in which possessive pronouns are used without explicit antecedents.

   a.   The masculine plural, used alone, refers to one's family, friends, or followers.

Il m'a demandé des nouvelles des miens.
He asked after my family.

On n'aime pas être loin des siens à Noël.
People don't like to be away from their families at Christmas.

Il est des nôtres.
He is on our side.
He is one of us (of ours).

   b.   The masculine singular is used to designate one's personal talent or effort.

Il y a mis du sien.
He made a real effort. (He contributed his share.)

   c.   **faire des siennes**

Tu fais encore des tiennes!
You're up to your old tricks again!

10

Demonstrative Adjectives and Pronouns

I. ADJECTIVES

A. Forms

	MASCULINE	FEMININE
SINGULAR	ce cet	cette
PLURAL	ces	

Note that the masculine singular form **cet** is used only before words beginning with a vowel or mute h.

cet homme	*this/that man*
cet arbre	*this/that tree*
cet abominable vice	*this/that abominable vice*

B. Use

1. The demonstrative adjective is repeated before each noun in a series.

ces carburateurs et ces bougies
these/those carburetors and spark plugs

ce phare, cet embrayage et cette roue
this/that headlight, clutch, and wheel

2. The French demonstrative adjectives do not by themselves establish a clear distinction between *this* and *that* (or *these* and *those*). When it is necessary to mark that distinction, the particle **-ci** or **-là** is added to the noun in question. In the case of compound nouns, the particle follows the second element.

Ces dinosaures-ci sont plus impressionnants que ces mammouths-là.
These dinosaurs are more impressive than those mammoths.

Cette machine à écrire-ci et cette machine-là sont de même qualité.
This typewriter and that typewriter are of the same quality.

3. With nouns designating a unit of time, the particle **-là** is used to refer to past or future, while reference to the present is usually expressed with no particle at all.

Cette année-là, la production agricole a été faible.
That year, agricultural production was meager.

En ce moment, tout est tranquille.
At this moment, everything is calm.

a. Ordinarily, the opposite of **ce jour-là** (*that day*) is **aujourd'hui** (*today*) rather than **ce jour** (*this day*).

b. *These days, nowadays* is generally rendered by **ces jours-ci**.

c. **Cette nuit** means either *last night* or *tonight*, depending upon the context.

Tu voudrais aller danser ce soir? —Non, merci, j'ai très peu dormi cette nuit.
Would you like to go dancing this evening? —No, thank you; I slept very little last night.

4. There are occasional occurrences of the demonstrative in English which are rendered by the definite article in French.

a. Instances in which the noun is modified by a restrictive clause or its equivalent.

Les jeunes gens qui connaissent le chemin mèneront les autres.
Those young people who know the way will lead the others.

Les étudiants qui ont fini l'examen peuvent partir.
Those students finished with the exam may leave.

b. The idiomatic expression **de la sorte**

Ne dis pas cela! Il ne faut pas parler de la sorte.
Don't say that! You mustn't speak that way.

II. PRONOUNS

A. Forms

	VARIABLE		INVARIABLE
	MASCULINE	FEMININE	
SINGULAR	celui	celle	ce, c' ceci
PLURAL	ceux	celles	cela, ça

Note that the form **c'** is used before **e** and **ç'** before **a**.

B.   Use of the variable pronouns

1.   When not followed by a modifier, the variable forms are reinforced by **-ci** or **-là.**

> Quelle scie préférez-vous? —Celle-ci.
> *Which saw do you prefer? —This one.*

> De tous les emplois que j'ai eus, celui-là était le plus désagréable.
> *Of all the jobs I've had, that one was the most unpleasant.*

2.   The variable forms, when not reinforced by **-ci** or **-là,** are always followed by a modifier. This is generally a relative clause or a prepositional phrase introduced by **de,** but other modifiers are possible.

> Les paysans du 9e siècle préférèrent la brouette à deux roues à celle qui n'en a qu'une.
> *The peasants of the 9th century preferred the two-wheel wheelbarrow to the one with one wheel.*

> Les peintures murales de Lascaux sont plus connues que celles de toute autre grotte.
> *The wall paintings of Lascaux are better known than those of any other cave.*

> Les rideaux légers isolent moins que ceux en tissus épais comme le velours.
> *Light curtains insulate less than those in heavy fabrics like velvet.*

> Cette expérience a confirmé celle faite par nos homologues écossais.
> *This experiment confirmed the one performed by our Scottish counterparts.*

  a.   To express *the latter* and *the former*, French uses the particles **-ci** and **-là** and arranges the contrasting statements in an order opposite from that of English.

> On a vendu récemment aux enchères des vases chinois et étrusques; ceux-ci ont suscité plus d'intérêt que ceux-là.
> *Chinese and Etruscan vases were recently sold at auction; the former aroused less interest than the latter.*

  b.   While the English construction *all those* + relative pronoun may be shortened to *all* + relative. the French equivalent **tous ceux** (**toutes celles**) + relative is never reduced.

> Ce roman plaît à tous ceux qui le lisent.
> *All [those] who read this novel like it.*

  c.   If the relative clause modifying the pronoun does not follow immediately, **-là** is required.

De tous mes parents, celui-là est arrivé que j'attendais le moins.
Of all my family, the one I expected least arrived.

C. Use of the invariable pronouns

1. **Ce.** The invariable form **ce** appears above all as subject in a number of important constructions with the verb **être** (which may be preceded by **devoir** or **pouvoir**).

   a. The construction **ce** + **être** + noun or pronoun is used to identify a person or thing. The verb is always third person singular, except when the noun or pronoun following is third person plural.

   Qui sont ces congressistes? —Ce sont des dermatologues.
   Who are these conventioneers? —They are dermatologists.

   J'entends un bruit terrible. —Ce n'est que le vent qui hurle.
   I hear a terrible noise. —It's only the wind howling.

   Quelles mesures de sécurité! Ce doit être quelqu'un de très important qui arrive.
   What security measures! It must be someone very important who's coming.

   Quelle est cette facture? —C'est celle dont je t'ai parlé.
   What is this bill? —It's the one I told you about.

   Si quelqu'un doit prendre cette responsabilité, ce sera sans doute nous.
   If someone must assume this responsibility, it will no doubt be we (us).

   b. The construction **ce** + **être** + adjective is used to characterize a phenomenon not denoted by a noun.

   Vouloir se détendre, c'est naturel.
   To want to relax is natural.

   Qu'il pleuve dans le désert, c'est extraordinaire.
   That it should rain in the desert is extraordinary.

   Ce n'est pas gentil, ce que tu dis là.
   It's not nice, what you're saying.

   J'ai regardé devant moi. Comme c'était beau!
   I looked in front of me. How beautiful it was!

      i. When the phenomenon characterized takes the form of a clause introduced by **que** or an infinitive introduced by **de** and when this construction is placed after the adjective without any pause or comma, it is normal to use **il est** (**était,** etc.). In this use, **il** is impersonal and invariable, and simply anticipates the real subject of the sentence, which is the clause or the infinitive phrase following the adjective.

Il est naturel de vouloir se détendre.
It is natural to want to relax.

Il est extraordinaire qu'il pleuve dans le désert.
It is extraordinary that it should rain in the desert.

Note that **ce** is always used in the formulas of politeness **c'est [bien] aimable à vous de** + infinitive and **c'est [bien] gentil de votre part de** + infinitive.

C'est bien aimable à vous de m'avoir invité pour jeudi.
It is very kind of you to have invited me for Thursday.

C'est gentil de ta part de nous apporter ces nouvelles.
It is good of you to bring us this news.

ii. Sometimes, in a given context, the constructions **ce** + **être** + adjective and **il(s)/elle(s)** + **être** + adjective are both possible. They are not interchangeable, however: the pronouns refer to different things.

Tu veux que je lise ce roman, mais c'est trop difficile. Je n'ai pas le temps.
You want me to read this novel, but that's too hard. I don't have the time.

Tu veux que je lise ce roman, mais il est trop difficile. L'auteur emploie trop de mots que je ne connais pas.
You want me to read this novel, but it's too hard. The author uses too many words I don't know.

L'émeraude, entourée de petits diamants, était sertie dans un chaton de vieil or. C'était très beau.
The emerald, surrounded by small diamonds, was in a setting of old gold. It was [all] very beautiful.

L'émeraude, entourée de petits diamants, était sertie dans un chaton de vieil or. Elle était très belle.
The emerald, surrounded by small diamonds, was in a setting of old gold. It (The emerald) was very beautiful.

c. The construction **ce** + **être** + . . . + **qui/que** + . . . is widely used to emphasize a particular word or phrase in a sentence. (Equivalent emphasis in English is often achieved through vocal stress alone.) The tense of **être** tends to be present whatever the tense of the verb in the following clause may be.

C'est toi qui t'es trompé, pas moi.
You made a mistake, not I.

Est-ce eux que vous avez recommandés pour les postes?
Did you recommend them (Are they the ones you recommended) for the positions?

C'est (C'était) avec véhémence qu'elle défendait les dissidents.
It was with vehemence that she defended the dissidents.

C'est précisément parce que je t'aime que je ne veux plus te voir.
It's precisely because I love you that I don't want to see you anymore.

  i. If the verb following **qui** is a form of **être,** it may be omitted along with **qui.**

C'est nous [qui sommes] vos propriétaires.
We are your landlords.

  ii. There is a similar construction used when the emphasized element is a noun characterizing another noun: **ce** + **être** + indefinite article + noun + **que** + noun.

C'est un beau garçon que ton fiancé.
Your fiancé is a handsome fellow.

  iii. There is a parallel construction used when the emphasized element is a noun or an infinitive characterizing an infinitive.

$$\textbf{ce} + \textbf{être} + \left\{ \begin{array}{c} \text{indef. art.} + \text{noun} \\ \text{infinitive} \end{array} \right\} + \textbf{que de} + \text{infinitive}$$

C'est une honte que de mentir.
It is a disgrace to lie.

  d. The construction **ce** + **être** + noun (or equivalent) is used with a few common adverbs of place and time.

C'était là son moindre défaut.
That was his (her) slightest shortcoming.

Ne cherchez pas ailleurs; c'est ici ce qu'il vous faut.
Don't look elsewhere; what you need is here.

Ce sera demain son anniversaire.
Her (His) birthday is tomorrow.

  e. **Ce** is regularly used with a predicate noun, pronoun, infinitive, or clause to repeat the subject when the latter contains a relative clause or a superlative or has the form of an infinitive or a noun clause.

Le fantôme que nous voyions tous les soirs, c'était vous!
The ghost we saw every evening was you!

Ce que nous aimons le mieux, c'est la musique classique.
What we like best is classical music.

Ce à quoi je tiens, c'est à vous voir heureux.
What I really want is to see you happy.

Ce dont elle a besoin, c'est d'un mois de repos.
What she needs is a month's rest.

Ce qu'elle veut, c'est [de] partir en vacances.
What she wants is to leave on vacation.

Le plus étonnant, c'est qu'il croit tout ce qu'il lit.
The most surprising thing is that he believes everything he reads.

Le plus petit pays du monde, c'est Saint-Marin.
The smallest country in the world is San Marino.

Qu'on veuille faire un roman sans savoir écrire, c'est une aberration.
That one should want to write a novel without knowing how to write is an aberration.

Voir c'est croire.
Seeing is believing.

Note that, in the equation of two infinitives, **ce** is usually not used if the verb is negated.

Comprendre n'est pas forcément approuver.
To understand is not necessarily to approve.

   f. The phrase **c'est que** serves to introduce an explanation of something just said.

S'il tremble, c'est qu'il a peur.
If he is trembling, it's because he is afraid.

   g. There are a few fixed expressions in which **ce** functions by itself as an object rather than subject: **sur ce, pour ce faire,** and **ce disant.**

Sur ce, je vous quitte.
With that, I leave you.

Ils voulaient se protéger et, pour ce faire, ont acheté un chien de garde.
They wanted to protect themselves and, to do so, they bought a watchdog.

Ce disant, il raccrocha violemment.
With those words, he slammed the receiver down.

2. **Ceci** and **cela** (**ça**). These invariable forms have no specific noun antecedent; they may occur as subject, object of verb, or object of preposition. Words agreeing with them always remain singular and masculine.

Ecoutez ceci: on croit avoir trouvé un remède contre le rhume.
Listen to this: they think they've found a cure for the common cold.

Cela (Ça) revient au même.
It all comes down to the same thing.

C'est pour cela (ça) qu'on s'est brouillés.
That's why they had a falling out.

Pleurer, ça console.
Crying consoles you.

a. Although these pronouns are theoretically opposite in reference, **ceci** (*this*) is often replaced by **cela** (*that*) or by the more colloquial **ça** (*that*) when no misunderstanding will result.

Prends ça et couche-toi; tu te sentiras bientôt mieux.
Take this and lie down; you will feel better soon.

b. In reference to statements, **ceci** usually points toward forthcoming information, whereas **cela** points back to information given.

Le plan du Président a ceci d'intéressant: il prévoit une hausse des impôts, un plafond de prix et de salaires, et d'autres mesures pour stopper l'inflation.
What is interesting about the President's plan is this: it provides for a tax increase, a wage and price ceiling, and other measures to curb inflation.

Ce plan devrait freiner l'inflation. Cela est bien intéressant, mais je me demande comment.
The plan is supposed to check inflation. That is very interesting, but I wonder how.

c. **Ceci** and **cela** (**ça**) as subjects of **être** are stronger demonstratives than **ce** and must be used to express contrast.

C'est vrai. Cela est vrai.
That (It) is true.

Ceci est faisable, mais cela ne l'est pas.
This is feasible, but that is not.

   i.   When **être** is preceded by a modal auxiliary, **ce** may be used with **devoir** and **pouvoir** but only **cela (ça)** may occur with **aller.**

       Cela (Ce) peut être une erreur.
       That (It) may be a mistake.

       Cela (Ce) a dû être ma faute.
       That (It) may have been my fault.

       Cela va être facile à démontrer.
       That (It) is going to be easy to show.

   ii.   In colloquial usage, **ça** may be added to **c'est** for emphasis.

       Ça, c'est beau!
       That's beautiful!

       Ça, c'est le (un) comble!
       That's the limit!

  d.   **Cela** and **ça** are sometimes used to refer to persons—with scorn, condescension, or even affection.

       Les enfants, ça fait du bruit, ça crie, ça pleure.
       Children—they're noisy, they shout, they cry.

       Ça se croit instruit et ne sait même pas qui était Charlemagne!
       That one thinks he (or she) is educated and doesn't even know who Charlemagne was!

  e.   There are some common useful expressions with **cela** and **ça.**

à cela près	*with that one exception*
à part cela (ça)	*apart from that*
Il ne manquait plus que ça!	*That's all we needed!*
Qui ça?	*Who?*
Où ça?	*Where?*
Comment cela?	*How?*
Ah, ça alors!	*Really, now!*
C'est ça (cela).	*That's right.*
Ça y est.	*That's that.*

Interrogation and Exclamation

INTERROGATION

I. YES-OR-NO QUESTIONS

Direct questions that bear on an entire sentence, asking for yes or no in reply, may be formulated in four ways in French.*

A. Intonational questions

A question may have the same word order as a declarative sentence and be distinguished only by rising intonation or, in written form, a question mark.

Ta voiture est tombée en panne?
Your car broke down?

Elle est tombée en panne, ta voiture?
Your car broke down?

Il y a un train à six heures. Vous le prenez, celui-là?
There is a train at six o'clock. You're taking that one?

B. *Est-ce que* + declarative sentence

Est-ce que ta voiture est tombée en panne?
Est-ce qu'elle est tombée en panne, ta voiture?
Did your car break down?

C. Inversion of subject and verb

1. **Simple inversion.** When the subject is a personal pronoun, **on,** or **ce,** it is placed, with a hyphen, after the verb. If the third person singular form does not end in **-t** or **-d,** a **-t-** is inserted between the verb and the inverted pronoun.

---

*Note that *yes* may be rendered as **oui** or **si. Oui** expresses neutral affirmation or agreement with the speaker; **si** is used to contradict a negative utterance.

Vous n'allez pas proposer cela? —Mais si.
You are not going to suggest that? —Yes, I am.

Avez-vous un piano?
Do you have a piano?

Est-ce un film doublé?
Is it a dubbed film?

Prend-elle ses vacances en juillet?
Is she taking her vacation in July?

Lui prête-t-il ses disques?
Does he lend her (him) his records?

N'allons-nous pas finir bientôt?
Aren't we going to finish soon?

a. In **-er** verbs, final **-e** becomes **-é** before **je**.

Rêvé-je?
Am I dreaming?

b. With the exception of nine forms, inversion is generally avoided in the first person singular present indicative.

ai-je?	*have I?*	dis-je?	*do I say?*
dois-je?	*must I?*	fais-je?	*do I do?*
puis-je?	*may I?*	sais-je?	*do I know?*
suis-je?	*am I?*	vais-je?	*do I go?*
		vois-je?	*do I see?*

2. **Complex inversion.** When the subject is a noun or a nonpersonal pronoun, it remains before the verb and is repeated as a personal pronoun after the verb.

Ta voiture est-elle tombée en panne?
Did your car break down?

Cela va-t-il réussir?
Is that going to succeed?

D. **N'est-ce pas** may be added to a declarative sentence to form a question eliciting confirmation.

C'est un film tout récent, n'est-ce pas? —Oui, il vient de sortir.
It's a very recent film, isn't it? —Yes, it has just come out.

Ces plans, tu ne les montreras à personne, n'est-ce pas? —Bien sûr que non.
You won't show these plans to anyone, will you? —Of course not.

II. PARTIAL QUESTIONS

These bear on a particular part of the sentence and involve the use of an interrogative pronoun, adjective, or adverb. They are otherwise formed in the same way as yes-or-no questions, except that **n'est-ce pas** cannot be used.

A. Interrogative pronouns

1. **Forms.** There are two sets: invariable and variable. The invariable pronouns are equivalent to *who, whom,* and *what;* the variable pronouns are equivalent to *which* or *which one(s).*

	INVARIABLE		
	SUBJECT	DIRECT OBJECT	OBJECT OF PREPOSITION
HUMAN	qui qui est-ce qui	qui qui est-ce que, qui est-ce qu'	qui qui est-ce que, qui est-ce qu'
NONHUMAN	qu'est-ce qui	que, qu' qu'est-ce que, qu'est-ce qu'	quoi quoi est-ce que, quoi est-ce qu'

	VARIABLE	
	MASCULINE	FEMININE
SINGULAR	lequel	laquelle
PLURAL	lesquels	lesquelles

Note that the variable forms contract with **à** and **de** just as definite articles do: **auquel, auxquels, auxquelles; duquel, desquels, desquelles,** but **à laquelle, de laquelle.**

2. **Use.** Invariable forms with **est-ce que (qui)** entail declarative order of subject and verb; the short forms other than subject **qui** normally require inversion. The variable forms behave similarly.

a. *Invariable subject*

Qui a composé quinze symphonies?
Qui est-ce qui a composé quinze symphonies?
Who composed fifteen symphonies?

Qu'est-ce qui te vexe?
What is irritating you?

Qu'est-ce qui se passe?
What is going on?

Note that questions involving impersonal verbs such as **se passer, arriver, rester** may be formulated with **que** and inversion.

Que se passe-t-il?
What is going on?

b. *Invariable direct object*

   i. Simple inversion

      Qui dépeint-elle dans son roman?
      Qui est-ce qu'elle dépeint dans son roman?
      Whom does she depict in her novel?

      Qu'ont-ils déterré dans le jardin?
      Qu'est-ce qu'ils ont déterré dans le jardin?
      What did they dig up in the garden?

      Que fait ce monsieur dans la vie?
      Qu'est-ce que ce monsieur fait dans la vie?
      What does this man do in life?

   ii. Complex inversion. This occurs with **qui** but not with **que**.

      Qui la nation va-t-elle élire?
      Qui est-ce que la nation va élire?
      Whom is the country going to elect?

c. *Invariable object of preposition*

   i. Simple inversion. This does not occur if both subject and direct object are nouns.

      A qui penses-tu?
      A qui est-ce que tu penses?
      Whom are you thinking about?

      Sur quoi a-t-elle fondé ses arguments?
      Sur quoi est-ce qu'elle a fondé ses arguments?
      What did she base her arguments on?

      Contre qui a tempêté l'orateur?
      Contre qui est-ce que l'orateur a tempêté?
      Whom did the speaker rage against?

      Vers quoi tend cette politique?
      Vers quoi est-ce que cette politique tend?
      What is that policy tending toward?

ii.   Complex inversion

A qui l'adolescent troublé peut-il faire confiance?
A qui est-ce que l'adolescent troublé peut faire confiance?
In whom can the troubled adolescent confide?

Sur quoi la correspondante a-t-elle besoin de renseignements?
Sur quoi est-ce que la correspondante a besoin de renseigne-
ments?
What does the correspondent need information about?

d.   *Invariable pronouns in utterances asking for identification or definition.* Such questions entail the use of **être** and the noun or pronoun to be identified.

i.   Human reference: **qui, qui est-ce que.** The verb agrees with
the noun or pronoun.

Qui suis-je? Qui est-ce que je suis?
Who am I?

Qui est cette femme? Qui est-ce que cette femme?
Who is that woman?

Note that the variable interrogative adjective **quel** may replace
qui when the subject is a noun.

Quelle est cette femme?
Who is that woman?

ii.   Nonhuman reference: **qu'est-ce que c'est que** + noun or pronoun. In literary usage two shorter forms occur: **qu'est** and
qu'est-ce que.

Qu'est-ce que c'est que l'astrophysique?
What is astrophysics?

Qu'est-ce que c'est que cela?
What is that?

Qu'est-ce que c'était que le servage médiéval?
What was medieval serfdom?

Qu'est la grammaire?
Qu'est-ce que la grammaire?
What is grammar?

Note that variable **quel est** is used when a name or other identification is sought rather than a basic definition.

Qu'est-ce que c'est que cette machine? —C'est une machine à
coudre.
What is that machine? —It's a sewing machine.

Quelle est cette machine? —C'est une marque japonaise.
What kind of machine is that? —It's a Japanese brand.

e.   *Variable pronouns.* They are used to inquire about one or more
members of a group and may occur as subject, direct object, or
object of preposition. Word order generally follows the patterns
presented above.★

Laquelle de ces revues traite de sujets scientifiques?
Which [one] of these magazines treats scientific subjects?

Ils ont fait des photos de leurs enfants. Lesquelles vous ont-ils
envoyées?
. . . Lesquelles est-ce qu'ils vous ont envoyées?
They took pictures of their children. Which [ones] did they send you?

Desquelles de ses pièces va parler la conférencière?
Desquelles de ses pièces est-ce que la conférencière va parler?
Desquelles de ses pièces la conférencière va-t-elle parler?
Which of her plays is the lecturer going to speak about?

B.   Interrogative adjectives†

Quel, quelle, quels, and **quelles** (*which, what*) normally precede the
noun they modify and always agree in number and gender. For word
order, see Section A.2.e.

Quel coureur est arrivé le premier?
Which runner came in first?

Quels robots-cuisine vendez-vous?
Quels robots-cuisine est-ce que vous vendez?
Which food processors do you sell?

★Patterns that would result in misunderstanding are avoided. Thus, *which one does the jour-nalist prefer?* cannot be rendered with simple inversion of subject and verb, and must be formulated in another way.

Lequel est-ce que le journaliste préfère?
Lequel le journaliste préfère-t-il?

†The English interrogative adjective *whose* has no adjectival counterpart in French and is rendered by preposition + **qui.**

A qui sont ces gants?   *Whose gloves are these?*
De qui êtes-vous le fils?   *Whose son are you?*

See, too, Chapter 9, Section II. footnote.

Sur quelle voie arrive le train de Venise?
Sur quelle voie est-ce que le train de Venise arrive?
Sur quelle voie le train de Venise arrive-t-il?
Which track does the Venice train come in on?

Note that, when used with **être, quel** (*what*) is separated from its noun.

Quelles sont vos intentions?   *What are your intentions?*

See, too, Section A.2.d.i. and ii. above.

C. Interrogative adverbs

combien?	*how much? how many?*
comment?	*how?*
où?	*where?*
d'où?	*whence (from where)?*
pourquoi?	*why?*
quand?	*when?*

1. These adverbs may be used freely with **est-ce que** or complex in-
    version (as well as simple inversion when the subject is a pro-
    noun).★

    Où vont-elles? D'où viennent-elles?
    Where are they going? Where are they coming from?

    Comment le chercheur a-t-il découvert ce remède?
    How did the researcher discover this remedy?

    Combien est-ce qu'on devra payer ce sofa?
    How much will we have to pay for this sofa?

    Quand allez-vous régler cette facture?
    When are you going to pay this bill?

    Pourquoi voit-on de moins en moins de papillons?
    Why are we seeing fewer and fewer butterflies?

Note that there are two common questions with adverbs fixed in inverted form and
never asked with **est-ce que.** There are a few similar expressions with **quel.**

★In colloquial usage, when the sentence begins with an interrogative adverb, questions of
the following type are frequently found.

Comment tu t'appelles?	*What's your name?*
Où il va?	*Where is he going?*
Pourquoi ton amie a fait ça?	*Why did your friend do that?*

Comment allez-vous?   *How are you?*
Comment vous appelez-vous?   *What is your name?*
Quel âge avez-vous?   *How old are you?*
Quel temps fait-il?   *What is the weather?*
Quelle heure est-il?   *What time is it?*

2. When the subject is a noun and there is no direct object, simple inversion of the subject and verb is usual with all adverbs except **pourquoi.**

D'où proviennent ces mots?
Where do these words come from?

Quand viendra le médecin?
When will the doctor come?

Pourquoi la fin arrive-t-elle si vite?
Pourquoi est-ce que la fin arrive si vite?
Why does the end come so quickly?

D. Interrogative words in phrases without a conjugated verb

1. **Quoi de** + masculine singular adjective

Quoi de neuf?   *What's new?*

Quoi de plus gracieux que cette danseuse?
What could be more graceful than this dancer?

2. **Que, quoi,** or adverb + infinitive

Que (Quoi) faire? J'ai perdu un plomb et mon dentiste est en vacances.
What should I do? I've lost a filling and my dentist is on vacation.

J'ai tout ce qu'il faut chez moi. Pourquoi chercher ailleurs?
I have everything I need at home. Why look elsewhere?

3. **A quoi bon** + infinitive

A quoi bon prêcher aux convertis?
What's the use of preaching to the converted?

III. INDIRECT QUESTIONS

A question may be asked by means of a declarative sentence. The information sought is expressed in a subordinate clause beginning with an interrogative word; there is no use of complex inversion or of **est-ce que.**

A. Yes-or-no questions

The indirect question begins with **si.**

Dis-moi
Je voudrais savoir ⎬ si ta voiture est tombée en panne.
Je me demande

Tell me
I'd like to know ⎬ *whether your car broke down.*
I wonder

B. Partial questions

The interrogative words used are the same as those in direct questions, with three exceptions. **Qu'est-ce qui** is replaced by **ce qui**; **qu'est-ce** and **que** become **ce que**; **qu'est-ce que c'est que** becomes **ce que c'est que.**

Je voudrais apprendre comment fonctionne le microscope électronique.
I would like to learn how the electron microscope works.

Nous nous demandons selon quels critères l'auteur a procédé.
We wonder according to which criteria the author proceeded.

Expliquez-moi à quoi serviront ces études démographiques.
Explain to me the purpose of these population studies.

On aimerait comprendre ce qui l'a poussé au suicide.
We would like to understand what drove him to suicide.

Toute la question est de savoir ce qu'ils avaient en vue en lançant cette campagne.
The whole question is what they had in mind when they launched that campaign.

Dites-moi ce que c'est que l'interféron.
Tell me what interferon is.

EXCLAMATION

I. Any word, phrase, or short declarative sentence may become an exclamation; an interjection may reinforce the exclamation.

Incroyable!	*Unbelievable!*
Au secours!	*Help!*
Ah, voilà une bonne idée!	*Oh, that's a good idea!*
Mais c'est impossible!	*But that's impossible!*

II. Inversion may be used when the subject is a pronoun.

Suis-je bête!	*Am I stupid!*
N'est-il pas entêté!	*Isn't he stubborn!*
Veux-tu te taire!	*Can't you be quiet!*

III. EXCLAMATORY ADVERBS

A. The forms **comme, que, ce que,** and **qu'est-ce que** (*how*) are used adverbially to qualify an adjective, adverb, or verb in exclamations. French, unlike English, maintains normal declarative word order after the exclamatory word.

Comme ce travail est fastidieux!
How tedious this work is!

Qu'elles passent vite, les heures!
How fast the hours go by!

Ce que j'ai peur dans ce tunnel!
How scared I am in this tunnel!

Qu'est-ce qu'on peut s'ennuyer au bord de la mer!
How boring it can get at the seashore!

B. **Que de** + noun forms an exclamation of quantity.

Que d'ennuis pour si peu de chose!
What a lot of trouble for so little!

Que de fard sur un si jeune visage!
How much makeup on so young a face!

IV. The adjective **quel/quelle** (*what a*), **quels/quelles** (*what*) may be used to form an exclamation.

Quel désordre!
What a mess!

Quel bruit affreux!
What an awful noise!

Quelles grandes dents tu as, grand-maman!
What big teeth you have, Grandma!

12

Relative Pronouns

Relative pronouns serve to link a noun or pronoun to a subordinate clause which modifies it like an adjective; they agree in gender, number, and grammatical person with their antecedent; and in the relative clause they may function as subject, direct object, predicate nominative, or object of preposition.

I. FORMS

	VARIABLE	INVARIABLE
SUBJECT	lequel	qui
DIRECT OBJECT, PREDICATE NOMINATIVE	lequel	que, qu'
OBJECT OF PREPOSITION	lequel	qui quoi
INVARIABLE FORMS WITH INCORPORATED PREPOSITION	dont où	

A. **Lequel** is variable: **lequel, laquelle, lesquels, lesquelles,** agreeing with the antecedent. It contracts with **à** and **de** to give **auquel, duquel,** and so on.

B. The **qu-** pronouns are invariable. They do not show agreement with the antecedent through any change of form. In the relative clause, however, they have the number, gender, and person of the antecedent.

II. USE

A. **Subject**

Both **qui** and **lequel** may have antecedents of either human or nonhuman reference.

1. **Qui** (*who, which, that*) is the usual subject relative pronoun and may introduce either a restrictive or a nonrestrictive clause.*

C'est moi qui suis la plus belle, dit la mère de Blanche-Neige.
I am the fairest of them all, said Snow-White's mother.

On prévoit des récoltes qui seront plus abondantes que jamais.
More abundant crops than ever are being predicted.

Il n'est rien d'humain qui me soit étranger.
There is nothing human which is foreign to me.

Il aime lire les grands poètes qui s'occupent des questions fonda-mentales de la condition humaine.
He likes to read those great poets who are concerned with the basic questions of human existence.

Il aime lire les grands poètes, qui s'occupent des questions fonda-mentales de la condition humaine.
He likes to read the great poets, who are concerned with the basic questions of human existence.

2. **Lequel** (*who, which*) occurs mainly in literary usage. Being variable, it often obviates ambiguity.

Elle va exposer la théorie de ce physicien, laquelle n'est pas facile à comprendre.
She is going to present the theory of that physicist, which is not easy to understand.

Elle va exposer la théorie de ce physicien, lequel n'est pas facile à comprendre.
She is going to present the theory of that physicist, who is not easy to understand.

a. The antecedent of **lequel** must be either masculine or feminine; an indefinite, such as **rien**, requires **qui**.

b. **Lequel**, unlike **qui**, may introduce only a nonrestrictive clause.

Il aime lire les grands poètes, lesquels s'occupent des questions fondamentales de la condition humaine.
He likes to read the great poets, who are concerned with the basic questions of human existence.

---

*The restrictive clause provides a necessary specification: **Mon oncle qui habite Paris est malade** (*My uncle who lives in Paris is ill*); the relative clause specifies which one of several un-cles is ill. In contrast, **Mon oncle, qui habite Paris, est malade** (*My uncle, who lives in Paris, is ill*), implies that there is only one uncle and offers parenthetically the information that he lives in Paris.

B. Direct object and predicate nominative

Both **que** and **lequel** may have antecedents of either human or nonhuman reference.

1. **Que** (*whom, which, that*) is the usual form and may introduce either a restrictive or a nonrestrictive clause. Sometimes, for stylistic reasons, there may be inversion of subject and verb in a **que** clause. Note that the relative pronoun must be expressed in French, unlike English.

   Ce sont eux que la mousson a laissés sans abri.
   They are the ones [whom] the monsoon left homeless.

   Il n'est plus le costaud qu'il était autrefois.
   He is no longer the robust fellow [that] he once was.

   Le niveau de vie qu'on connaît aujourd'hui est dû au progrès technique.
   The standard of living [which] we have today is due to technological progress.

   Il s'est passé quelque chose que tout le monde craignait.
   Something happened which everyone had feared.

   C'est là l'avis d'un sociologue que n'étonne plus la méfiance devenue générale à l'égard de l'autorité.
   That is the opinion of a sociologist who is no longer surprised by the now generalized mistrust of authority.

2. The use of **lequel** (*whom, which*) as direct object parallels its use as subject.

   Les spectateurs étaient tout occupés du jeu des personnages, lesquels ils tenaient pour véritables.
   The audience was completely absorbed in the interplay of the characters, whom they took to be real.

C. Object of preposition

The relative pronoun used depends upon the type of antecedent.

1. **Qui** (*whom*) is used in human reference and, by extension, for animals and personified entities.

   La puéricultrice à qui ils ont confié leurs enfants était très recommandée.
   The nursery-school teacher to whom they entrusted their children was highly recommended.

   Son seul compagnon était un chien avec qui il se promenait tous les soirs.
   His only companion was a dog that he took walks with every evening.

O maudite voiture, sans qui je ne saurais vivre et que j'abhorre!
O accursed car, without which I cannot live and which I abhor!

Note that **qui** is not used with the prepositions **parmi** and **entre**; see **lequel** below.

2.   Quoi (*which*) may refer only to an indefinite.

Il n'y a rien sur quoi on ait tant discouru.
There is nothing about which there has been so much discussion.

Note that **quoi** is not used with the preposition **de** after **ce, cela, rien**; see **dont** below.

3.   Lequel (*whom, which*) may have any antecedent except an indefinite.

Il n'a pas reçu les applaudissements auxquels il s'attendait.
He did not get the applause [that] he was expecting.

Le puéricultrice à laquelle ils ont confié leurs enfants était très recommandée.
The nursery-school teacher to whom they entrusted their children was highly recommended.

On a présenté tous les délégués, parmi lesquels se trouvaient plusieurs chefs d'entreprise.
They introduced all the delegates, among whom there were several heads of businesses.

Note that, in a relative clause introduced by **parmi lesquel(le)s**, a verb of existence (**être, se trouver**, and the like) need not be expressed.

On a présenté tous les délégués, parmis lesquels plusieurs chefs d'entreprise.

D.   Dont (*of whom, of which, whose*) has the same meaning as **de qui, de quoi, duquel** and may have any noun or pronoun as its antecedent. Generally, the simple form **dont** is preferred to **de** + object. **Dont** may link its noun or pronoun antecedent in the main clause to various elements in the relative clause; it follows its antecedent immediately.

1.   Link to subject

Le médecin parlait avec une femme dont le fils était atteint d'hémophilie.
The doctor was speaking with a woman whose son was suffering from hemophilia.

C'est un roman dont l'auteur est un débutant.
It is a novel whose author (the author of which) is a beginner.

Il m'a montré des tableaux dont plusieurs m'ont fort intéressé.
He showed me some paintings several of which interested me greatly.

Note that, while English *whose* requires the omission of the definite article or other determiner, **dont** requires the use of a determiner (other than possessive adjective).

une femme dont le fils était
a woman whose son was

2. Link to verb

La directrice dont ils s'étaient plaints a démissionné.
The directress whom they complained about has resigned.

C'est là la caméra dont il a parlé.
That is the movie camera that he spoke about.

Je n'ai rien fait dont j'aie à rougir.
I have done nothing to be ashamed of.

3. Link to direct object

Il possède sept villas dont il n'habite que deux.
He owns seven houses only two of which he occupies (of which he occupies only two).

Elle a évoqué des problèmes dont il était impossible de préciser les causes.
She brought up problems the causes of which it was impossible to specify.

Il m'a rapporté le médicament dont j'avais besoin.
He brought me back the medicine [that] I needed.

L'agriculteur dont nous avons visité la ferme-modèle en est très fier.
The farmer whose model farm he visited is very proud of it.

Note that French maintains normal declarative word order after **dont,** whereas English tends to place the direct object before the subject.

l'agriculteur dont nous avons visité la ferme
the farmer whose farm we visited

4. Link to predicate adjective or nominative

Il n'y a rien dont je sois plus certain.
There is nothing I am more certain of.

Voilà la maison dont il est propriétaire.
That is the house which he is the owner of.

5. Link to an adverbial complement

Il a contesté la manière dont on distribuait les rôles.
He challenged the way [in which] the parts were being assigned.

6. After an antecedent introduced by a number, **dont** may be used instead of **parmi lesquel(le)s** if the verb, a verb of existence, is not expressed.

Il avait huit enfants, dont six filles.
Il avait huit enfants, parmi lesquels [étaient] six filles.
He had eight children, six of whom were daughters.

7. **Dont** is replaced by **de qui** or **duquel** in two cases.

a. When the antecedent is the object of a preposition.

Elle a épousé celui pour le frère de qui (duquel) elle travaillait.
She married the man for whose brother she was working.

b. When the **de** incorporated into **dont** would be the final element of a compound preposition, such as **à côté de** (*beside*), **près de** (*near*), **à cause de** (*because of*).

Il est tombé dans le puits auprès duquel il creusait pour le trésor.
He fell into the well beside which he was digging for the treasure.

E. **Où** (*where, when*) is used in reference to nouns of place (or nouns which may be so regarded) and of time.

1. Without preposition, **où** is the equivalent of **à** or **dans + lequel**, expressing location (*in which*), destination (*to which*), or time (*when*). (Note that the word **quand**, unlike English *when* is never used as a relative.)

Bien des Américains se rendent en Europe pour visiter les lieux où vivaient leurs aïeux.
Many Americans go to Europe to visit the places where their ancestors once lived.

Dans l'état où elle est, elle ne sait que faire.
In the state she is in, she does not know what to do.

La station de ski où ils aiment aller est devenue trop chère.
The ski resort they like to go to (where they like to go) has become too expensive.

Le tiroir où je voulais mettre les microfilms était déjà rempli.
The drawer I wanted to put the microfilms in was already full.

Le jour où nous l'avons rencontré, il avait très mauvaise mine.
The day [when] we met him, he looked awful.

2. With preposition

a. **D'où,** like English *whence, from which,* expresses source or origin.

Le village d'où venaient leurs ancêtres n'existe plus.
The village their ancestors came from no longer exists.

Il y a eu des grèves d'où résultera sans doute une hausse des prix.
There have been strikes which will no doubt give rise to price increases.

b. **Où** preceded by other prepositions, such as **par, vers, jusque**

On lui a montré le chemin par où il fallait passer.
He was shown the path he had to take.

Jusqu'où le mèneront ses excès de jalousie?
How far will his excessive jealousy take him?

F. **Relative pronouns with antecedent** *ce*

The relative pronouns other than **lequel** may refer to an idea rather than a given noun or pronoun. Generally, the demonstrative pronoun **ce** assumes the role of antecedent. In certain cases, the relative pronoun is used with no explicit antecedent at all.

1. When the reference is to something nonhuman, **ce** is followed by the relative pronoun required by a particular function within the relative clause.

a. *Subject:* **ce qui** (*what, that which, which*). **Tout** (*all, everything*) may precede **ce qui.**

Ce qui la passionne, c'est l'archéologie.
What fascinates her is archeology.

Il n'hésite pas à dire tout ce qui lui passe par la tête.
He does not hesitate to say everything (anything) that occurs to him.

L'épidémiologie historique nous parle, par exemple, de ce qui se passait dans les villes médiévales frappées par la peste.
Historical epidemiology tells us, for example, about what happened in the medieval cities struck by the plague.

Il a demandé notre adresse, ce qui nous a étonnés.
He asked for our address, which surprised us.

Note that, after **voici** and **voilà, qui** may be used without **ce.**

Voilà [ce] qui est fait.
There, that's done.

b. *Direct object:* **ce que** (*what, that which, which*). **Tout** may precede **ce que.**

Ce qu'elle aime surtout, c'est l'archéologie.
What she likes best is archeology.

Il fera tout ce qu'on lui demande.
He will do everything (anything) you ask him.

C'est un article sur ce qui se passait dans les villes frappées par la peste.
It is an article on what happened in the cities struck by the plague.

Il a demandé notre adresse, ce que nous avons trouvé étonnant.
He asked for our address, which we found surprising.

c. *Object of preposition:* **ce dont, ce à quoi, ce par quoi,** etc. When there is any degree of indirect questioning involved, **ce** is omitted and **de quoi, à quoi, par quoi,** etc., are used instead, if the relative clause itself is the direct object of the verb in the main clause.

Ce dont ils se plaignent surtout, c'est [de] leur logement.
What they complain about most is their housing.

Il nous a demandé de quoi nous aurions besoin.
He asked us what we would be needing.

Il nous a promis tout ce dont nous aurions besoin.
He promised us everything we would need.

Elle écrira un livre sur ce dont elle a été témoin pendant les émeutes.
She will write a book about what she observed during the riots.

Il était un peu sourd, ce dont je ne m'étais pas aperçu plus tôt.
He was a little deaf, which I had not noticed earlier.

Ce à quoi il aspire, c'est le (au) succès politique.
What he aspires to is political success.

Il nous a demandé sur quoi se fondaient nos arguments.
He asked us what our arguments were based on.

Il a bien voulu nous accorder ce sur quoi nous comptions.
He consented to grant us what we had been counting on.

Elle doit renoncer à ce à quoi elle tient le plus.
She must give up what she holds dearest.

Note that there are several instances where **ce** may be omitted, although there is no indirect question: after **voici** and **voilà,** and in reference to the entire preceding clause.

Voilà de quoi il s'agit dans ce livre.
That's what the book is about.

Voici à quoi tu devrais réfléchir.
Here's what you should think about.

Il a fini par remporter la victoire, [ce] à quoi nous ne nous étions pas attendus.
He finally won the victory, which we had not expected.

    d. **Où.** The antecedent equivalent to **ce** is **là,** or sometimes **ici,** and it must be expressed.

        Les mauvaises herbes poussent là où l'on ne cultive pas intensément.
        Weeds grow where cultivation is not intensive.

Note that **d'où** without explicit antecedent is used in certain formulas expressing a conclusion.

    Le prix du pétrole augmente sans cesse, d'où je conclus (d'où il résulte) qu'il faut accélérer la recherche de nouvelles sources d'énergie.
    The price of oil keeps rising, whence I conclude that (as a result of which) it is necessary to speed up the search for new sources of energy.

  2. When the reference is to human beings, **qui** alone is used, whatever the function of the pronoun may be in the relative clause.

    Qui vivra verra.
    Whoever (He who) lives will see.

    Aimez qui vous aime.
    Love whoever (the person who) loves you.

    Il le dit à qui veut bien l'entendre.
    He tells it to anyone who (to whoever) is willing to hear it.

    Pour qui sait réfléchir, cet événement est instructif.
    To anyone who can think, this event is instructive.

    Choisis qui tu voudras.
    Choose whomever (anyone) you wish.

    Cette lettre a été envoyée par qui vous savez.
    This letter was sent by you-know-who.

    Voilà de qui je parle.
    That's whom I am speaking about.

Indefinite Adjectives and Pronouns

Indefinite adjectives (including articles) and indefinite pronouns indicate an unspecified quantity, quality, identity, similarity, or difference. These include **un, l'un l'autre, autre, autrui, certain, chaque, chacun, différent, divers, même, on, plusieurs, quelconque, quiconque, quelque, quelqu'un, quelque chose, tel, tout,** and others.*

A. *Un*

For the use of **un, une, des** as indefinite articles, see Chapter 3. As a pronoun **un(e)** (*one*) is used only in the singular and agrees in gender with its antecedent. It is complemented by **de** + noun or pronoun or by the conjunctive pronoun **en.** With **en,** there is no **l'** before **un;** elsewhere, it is optional, but usually omitted. Note that when **un** is modified by an adjective or participle, the modifier is usually introduced by **de.**

Un (L'un) de nos consuls se trouve séquestré par des personnes encore inconnues.
One of our consuls is being held by persons yet unknown.

Connaissez-vous un claveciniste? —Oui, j'en connais un, et de très doué.
Do you know a harpsichordist? —Yes, I know one, a very talented one.

Il s'est plongé dans une (l'une) de ces rêveries qui le consolaient.
He sank into one of those daydreams that used to console him.

Le vendeur nous a proposé une belle bague, mais nous en cherchions une de moins chère.
The clerk showed us a beautiful ring, but we were looking for one less expensive.

B. *L'un l'autre*

1. **L'un l'autre** and **l'un à l'autre** are used with pronominal verbs to reinforce the idea of reciprocity. Both **l'un** and **l'autre** are variable.

---

*For certain of these adjectives, see Chapter 5 as well.

Ces deux divas, ce qui peut paraître exceptionnel, s'estiment l'une l'autre.
These two opera stars—and this may seem unusual—respect each other.

Les astronautes et les cosmonautes doivent se comprendre profondément les uns les autres.
The astronauts and the cosmonauts must deeply understand one another.

Souvent, grâce à la mode, des personnes très différentes se ressemblent les unes aux autres.
Often, thanks to fashion, people who are very different resemble one another.

2. **L'un** + preposition + *l'autre*

J'ai épinglé les deux coupures au tableau d'affichage l'une à côté de l'autre.
I pinned the two clippings beside each other on the bulletin board.

Nous avons regardé les poussins sortir les uns après les autres de leurs coquilles.
We watched the chicks hatching one after the other.

3. **L'un** may be conjoined with **l'autre** by **et, ou,** or **ni . . . ni . . . .**

Pour désosser le poulet, l'un ou l'autre de ces deux couteaux fera l'affaire. —Non, ni l'un ni l'autre n'est suffisamment aiguisé.
To bone the chicken, either one of these knives will do. —No, neither of them is sharp enough.

Nous venons d'embaucher deux mécaniciens; l'un et l'autre sont tout ce qu'il y a de plus prometteur.
We have just hired two mechanics; they are both as promising as can be.

L'ambassadeur avait l'habitude d'inviter les uns et les autres pour fêter le 4 juillet.
The ambassador customarily invited everyone to celebrate the Fourth of July.

Malgré des mois de discussions entre enseignants et parents d'élèves, ni les uns ni les autres n'ont voulu céder en rien.
Despite months of discussion between teachers and parents, neither side was willing to give in on anything.

4. **L'un** and **l'autre** may be used in different clauses or the equivalent.

Les uns voulaient jouer aux cartes, les autres préféraient regarder la télé.
Some wanted to play cards; the others preferred to watch TV.

En parlant aux uns, il faut se garder d'offenser les autres.
When speaking to some (to one group), one must take care not to offend the others (the other group).

On invitait les uns pour pouvoir parler des autres.
They invited some in order to speak about the others.

5. **Les uns** and **d'autres** may be used in different clauses. (**D'autres** (*others*) denotes some of the others, while **les autres** denotes all of them.)

Les uns sont droitiers, d'autres sont gauchers, et d'autres encore sont ambidextres.
Some are right-handed, others are left-handed, and still others ambidextrous.

C. *Autre*

1. As an adjective, **autre** (*other*) behaves like any other adjective. It is normally preposed; separated from its noun, it has the sense of *different*.

Vous trouverez ce mot peut-être dans un autre dictionnaire.
Perhaps you'll find that word in another dictionary.

J'ai enfin décidé; je prendrai cette autre couverture.
I've made up my mind at last; I'll take that other blanket.

Il est revenu de la guerre tout autre.
He came back from the war completely changed.

Note that the indefinite plural article used with **autres** is always **d'**, whether a noun follows or is understood.

Certains voyages sont des rêves réalisés, d'autres voyages sont réussis, et d'autres sont infernaux.
Certain trips are dreams come true; other trips are less successful and others are hellish.

2. As a pronoun, **autre** is preceded by an indefinite article (*un, une, d'*). When it is the direct object of a verb, it requires the complement **en.**

C'est là ton avis. D'autres diront le contraire.
That's your opinion. Others (Other people) will say the opposite.

La machine à laver est en panne. Nous espérons ne pas avoir à en acheter une autre.
The washing machine's broken down. We hope we won't have to buy another.

3.   There are numerous common expressions with **autre**.

autre chose	*something else*
autre part	*somewhere else, elsewhere*
qui d'autre?	*who else?*
quoi d'autre?	*what else?*
quelqu'un d'autre	*someone else*
personne d'autre	*no one (anyone) else*
rien d'autre	*nothing (anything) else*
comme un(e) autre	*ordinary, good enough*
d'un jour à l'autre	*from one day to the next, any day now*
entre autres	*among other things*
d'une part . . . d'autre part	*on the one hand . . . on the other*

Il n'a pas été nommé à ce poste, entre autres, à cause de sa désin-
volture.
*He wasn't named to that position, among other reasons, because of his
nonchalance.*

C'est un immeuble comme un autre, malgré son prix.
It's just an ordinary building, despite its cost.

D.   **Autrui** (*other people, another person*) is an invariable pronoun, used
only as the object of a preposition or the direct object of a verb. In
either case it is rare.

Tu ne convoiteras pas la femme d'autrui.
Thou shalt not covet thy neighbor's wife.

E.   *Certain* (*certain, some*)

1.   As a preposed indefinite adjective, **certain** is used without an article
in the plural and with **un(e)** in the singular.

Depuis son accident, il a une certaine difficulté à marcher.
Since his accident, he has had a certain difficulty [in] walking.

Certains pays ont créé des réseaux d'auberges destinées surtout aux
touristes étrangers.
*Certain (Some) countries have created networks of inns meant mainly for
foreign tourists.*

2.   As a pronoun, only plural **certain(e)s** is used, and with no determiner. **Certains** may take a complement introduced by **de** or, in the
case of a personal pronoun, by **d'entre**.

Certains prétendent, encore aujourd'hui, que la terre est plate.
Some people claim, even today, that the earth is flat.

Certaines d'entre elles, figurez-vous, ont l'intention de rester
femmes d'intérieur.
Some of them, just imagine, intend to remain housewives.

Les restaurants d'ici n'ont pas bonne réputation, mais nous [en] connaissons certains qui sont tout à fait honnêtes.
The restaurants here don't have a good reputation, but we know a few which are perfectly all right.

F. *Chaque, chacun*

1. The adjective **chaque** (*each, every*) is used only in the singular and without any determiner.

   A chaque nouveau feu d'artifice, la foule poussa des cris de joie.
   At each new burst of fireworks, shouts of joy rose from the crowd.

2. The pronoun **chacun(e)** (*each one, everyone*) is used only in the singular.

   a. Used without reference to any particular noun, **chacun** is always masculine and means *everyone*.

   Dans une petite ville, chacun sait tout sur ses voisins.
   In a small town, everyone knows everything about his neighbors.

   b. **Chacun(e)** may be followed by **de** + noun or pronoun or may be used in apposition to a noun or pronoun. In the first case, agreement is made between **chacun** and the other words in the sentence which depend upon it: adjective, pronoun, and so forth. When **chacun** is in apposition to a noun or pronoun, agreement of following adjectives, pronouns or the like is made with the noun or pronoun rather than with **chacun**. (See Chapter 9, Section III.B.6.)

   Chacune des planètes, à l'exception de la nôtre, porte le nom d'un dieu ou d'une déesse.
   Each of the planets, except for ours, bears the name of a god or goddess.

   Chacun d'[entre] eux a refusé de prendre la responsabilité de ce vaste projet.
   Every one of them refused to accept the responsibility for that huge project.

   Le juge d'instruction nous a écoutés chacun à notre tour.
   The examining magistrate listened to each of us in turn.

   Les billets coûtent quarante francs cinquante chacun (chacun quarante francs cinquante).
   The tickets cost forty francs fifty each.

G. **Différent** and **divers** (*various, different*) may be used as indefinite preposed adjectives, always in the plural, without any determiner.

Différentes (Diverses) victimes ont pu identifier l'agresseur.
Various victims were able to identify the mugger.

H.   *Même*

In addition to its use as an adverb (*even*), **même** serves as an indefinite adjective and pronoun.

1.   As an adjective, **même(s)** means *same* before the noun it modifies, *very* after the noun; see Chapter 5. Note that the article may be omitted after **de** before preposed **même**.

   Le concombre et la courgette sont des plantes de même espèce.
   The cucumber and the zucchini are plants of the same species.

2.   As a pronoun, **même(s)** (*same one(s)*) is always preceded by the definite article.

   Les règles du rugby ne sont pas les mêmes que celles du football américain.
   The rules of rugby are not the same as those of American football.

3.   There are various common expressions with **même**.

à même de	*in a position to, able to*
boire à même la bouteille	*drink straight from the bottle*
se coucher (s'asseoir, etc.) à même le sol	*lie down (sit down, etc.) right on the ground*
tout de même	*anyway, even so*
tout de même!	*really, now!*
quand même	*anyway, all the same, in spite of everything*
quand même!	*really, now!*
de même	*in the same way, similarly*
il en va de même pour + noun or pronoun	*the same applies to . . .*

I. N'importe combines with certain interrogative adjectives, pronouns, and adverbs to form indefinite locutions expressing *any . . . at all, no matter . . . , -ever,* and the like.

1.   Adjectival: **n'importe + quel. Quel** agrees in number and gender with the noun it modifies.

   Il ne s'agit que d'une petite réparation; n'importe quel maçon pourrait te la faire.
   It's just a small repair; any mason could do it for you.

Il est si crédule qu'il autorisera n'importe quelles depenses.
He is so credulous that he will authorize any expenditures at all.

C'est un article courant que vous trouverez dans n'importe quelle quincaillerie.
It's an everyday item which you'll find in any hardware store.

2. Pronominal

  a. **n'importe + lequel. Lequel** agrees in number and gender with the noun which it represents.

  Etant donné les dimensions de la pièce, n'importe laquelle de ces lampes nous donnera un éclairage satisfaisant.
  Given the size of the room, any one of these lamps will give us satisfactory lighting.

  Dans quel ordre veux-tu que j'inscrive les noms? —Dans n'importe lequel.
  In what order do you want me to write down the names? —In any order whatever.

  b. **n'importe + qui** and **n'importe + quoi.** These expressions may not be used with a **de** + noun complement or with a relative clause;* they may be modified by **de** + invariable adjective.

  C'est un ambitieux qui ferait n'importe quoi pour réussir.
  He is an ambitious type who would do anything to succeed.

  N'importe qui d'un peu sensible aurait su que ces propos la blesseraient.
  Anyone who was a little bit sensitive would have known that those words would wound her.

  Il faut la recevoir avec une certain cérémonie; elle n'est pas n'importe qui.
  We have to entertain her with a certain formality; she is not just anyone.

---

*Note that *anyone who(m)* and *anything that* require a construction other than **n'importe . . .** if a relative clause is to be expressed in French.

He says anything at all.
Il dit n'importe quoi.

He says anything that occurs to him.
Il dit tout ce qui lui passe par la tête.

See, too, Section R.5. below.

3. Adverbial: **n'importe + où, comment, quand**

C'est un travail délicat, on ne peut pas le faire n'importe comment.
It is a delicate task and cannot be done just any old way.

La science-fiction pourrait avoir pour devise: N'importe où hors de
   ce monde.
The motto of science fiction could be: Anywhere out of this world.

Venez nous voir n'importe quand, vous serez toujours le bienvenu.
Come see us whenever (any time) you like; you will always be welcome.

J. **On** is exclusively a subject pronoun, taking a third person singular
verb. It may represent not only *one, someone* but an indefinite *you,
people* and, depending upon the context, any person. Its corresponding nonsubject forms are normally the possessives **son (sa, ses), le
sien (la sienne, les siens, les siennes),** the reflexive **se,** and the dis-
junctives **soi** and **soi-même.**

On se souvient des détails de son enfance quand on est vieux.
People remember the details of their childhood when they are old.

On ne saurait vivre uniquement pour soi.
One cannot live only for oneself.

On lit dans les vitrines de toutes ces boutiques: Ici on parle français.
There are signs in the windows of all these shops: French is spoken here.

On s'entend bien, toi et moi, n'est-ce pas?
We get along well, you and I, don't we?

1. To express an indefinite object, French has recourse to **nous, vous,
les gens,** and similar expressions or may omit the object altogether
if it is the object of a verb.

On aime souvent le mieux ses parents quand ils sont loin de vous
   (nous).
One often loves one's relatives best when they are far away from one.

Quand on souffre de la paranoïa, on a l'impression que tout le
   monde vous déteste.
*When people suffer from paranoia, they have the impression that every-
one hates them.*

C'est une explication quasi-convaincante mais qui laisse à désirer.
*That explanation is almost convincing, but it leaves something to be de-
sired.*

2. To avoid ambiguity, **son (le sien)** is replaced by **notre, votre, ton
(le nôtre,** etc.).

On trouve difficile de se préoccuper des problèmes d'un autre
  lorsque votre (notre) vie est agitée.
*It is hard to be concerned with another's problems when your life is trou-
  bled.*

3.   **On** often designates one or more specific persons. In this case, an
     adjective, participle, or predicate noun usually agrees in number
     and gender with the real referent; the verb, however, remains in the
     third person singular.

     Que je suis content de te revoir! On ne s'est pas vus depuis une
       éternité.
     How glad I am to see you again! We haven't seen each other in ages.

     Eh bien, chérie, on est un peu distraite ce matin?
     Well, dear, a little distracted this morning, are we?

4.   In literary language, **l'on** often occurs at the beginning of a sentence or
     after such words as **et, ou, où, qui, que, si, aussi, déjà, comme.**

     L'on (On) reste toujours un peu enfant.
     A little bit of the child always remains in us.

     Je ne sais plus où l'on va.
     I no longer know where we are going.

Note that **l'on** is not used after **dont** or before a word beginning with **l**.

  Ce dont on parlait ne m'intéressait pas.
  What was being spoken of did not interest me.

  Il demandait qu'on le laisse tranquille.
  He asked that he be left in peace.

K.   **Plusieurs** (*several*) is always plural and shows no distinction between
     masculine and feminine

1.   As an adjective, **plusieurs** is not preceded by a determiner.

     Plusieurs vieilles bouteilles de vin ont été découvertes au fond de la
       cave.
     Several old bottles of wine were discovered in the back of the cellar.

2.   As a pronoun, **plusieurs** may be used with or without a comple-
     ment, generally introduced by **de**. When the complement is a per-
     sonal pronoun, **d'entre** replaces **de**.

     Plusieurs des maladies qu'on craignait il y a quarante ans n'existent
       presque plus.
     Several of the diseases feared forty years ago hardly exist anymore.

     Vous cherchez un taxi? Mais j'en ai vu plusieurs tout à l'heure.
     You're looking for a taxi? Why, I saw several just a little while ago.

Plusieurs d'entre vous lui ont déconseillé ce mariage. Pourquoi?
Several of you advised him (her) against this marriage. Why?

L. *Quelconque, quiconque*

1. The adjective **quelconque** (*any . . . at all, whatever, some sort of*) usually follows the noun it modifies. It shows agreement in number only.

Le truc dans ces examens, c'est de ne jamais laisser un blanc; il faut donner une réponse quelconque.
The trick in these exams is never to leave a blank; you've got to give some sort of answer.

C'est un juge très sévère et qui ne tolère pas des raisonnements quelconques.
He is a very strict judge, who does not tolerate just any kind of argument.

Note that **quelconque** may also mean *mediocre, commonplace.*

C'est un architecte trop quelconque pour que je lui confie ce travail.
He is too mediocre an architect for me to entrust this work to him.

2. The pronoun **quiconque** is invariable and refers only to persons.

a. Functioning within one clause, **quiconque** means *anyone at all, just anyone, anyone else.*

Cette nouvelle, il faut la traiter avec discrétion et ne pas la révéler à quiconque.
This news has to be handled discreetly and not revealed to just anyone at all.

Avec son expérience, il a compris mieux que quiconque les possibilités de vente de ce produit.
With his experience, he understood better than anyone else the sales possibilities of this product.

b. Functioning within two clauses, **quiconque** means *whoever, whomever, anyone who(m)*. Like *who(m)ever*, **quiconque** is not followed by a relative pronoun.

Quiconque trouvera le moyen de nettoyer la Méditerranée aura la reconnaissance de deux continents.
Whoever finds a way to clean up the Mediterranean will have the gratitude of two continents.

A cette époque-là, on embauchait quiconque se présentait.
At that time, they hired anyone who (whoever) came along.

Le prix sera décerné à quiconque le donateur désignera.
The prize will be awarded to whomever the donor designates.

M. *Quelque, quelqu'un*

1. As an adjective, **quelque(s)** (*some, any, a few*) precedes the noun, generally without a determiner. It may, however, be preceded by a definite article, a demonstrative, or a possessive.

   Vous avez sûrement quelques idées là-dessus?
   You surely have some (a few) ideas about it?

   Il a appris le rôle en moins d'un jour, non sans quelque difficulté.
   He learned the part in less than a day, not without some difficulty.

   Ils se sont brouillés pour les quelques hectares de vignobles de leur père.
   They had a falling out over their father's few acres of vineyards.

Note that **quelque** may function as an indefinite adverb modifying **peu** or numbers. (For another use of adverbial use of **quelque,** see Section **R.** below.)

Pour un homme raisonnable, il se montre quelque peu entêté sur ce chapitre.
For a reasonable man, he appears somewhat stubborn on this matter.

Les quelque dix mille francs qu'elle a gagnés à la loterie disparaîtront bien vite.
The some ten thousand francs that she won in the lottery will disappear very quickly.

2. The pronoun forms **quelqu'un(e)** (*someone, anyone*) and **quelques-un(e)s** (*some, a few*) may be used with or without a complement. The singular always refers to persons.

   a. With no explicit referent, only the masculine forms occur.

      Il porte un brassard noir; il a sûrement perdu quelqu'un de sa famille.
      He is wearing a black armband; he has no doubt lost someone in his family.

      A la suite du scrutin, quelqu'un qui était particulièrement content c'était la mère de la gagnante.
      Once the vote was counted, someone who was particularly happy was the mother of the woman who had won.

      Quelques-uns prétendent que les cartes de crédit remplaceront bientôt les chèques.
      Some [people] claim that credit cards will soon replace checks.

Note that **quelqu'un** may express importance.

A le voir, on dirait un zéro, mais dans son milieu il est quelqu'un.
To see him, you'd say he was a nonentity, but in his world he is somebody.

b. With an explicit referent, **quelqu'un** may occur in any of its forms; the feminine singular is normally replaced by **une,** however. A personal pronoun serving as complement is introduced by **d'entre.**

Cette chanteuse des années 20 a fait bon nombre de disques mais quelques-uns seulement sont parvenus jusqu'à nous.
This 1920s singer made quite a number of records, but only a few have come down to us.

Quelques-unes de ses découvertes lui vaudront un jour une renommée mondiale.
Some of her (his) discoveries will bring her (him) world fame one day.

C'est sans doute une (quelqu'une) d'entre elles qui est responsable de ce compte-rendu non signé.
It is no doubt one of them who is responsible for that unsigned review.

c. For adjectives modifying **quelqu'un,** see Chapter 5, Section II.B.8.

3. There are a few common expressions with **quelque.**

quelque part	*somewhere*
quelque peu	*somewhat, a bit*
en quelque sorte	*in a way*

Cette mort, après tant de souffrances, fut en quelque sorte un soulagement.
The death, after so much suffering, was a relief, in a way.

N. **Quelque chose** (*something*), though written as two words, is a single indefinite pronoun always treated as a masculine singular. A modifying adjective is introduced by **de.**

Il y a chez elle quelque chose qui déplaît.
There is something disagreeable about her.

Quelque chose d'inattendu s'est produit à la clôture de la séance.
Something unexpected happened at the conclusion of the session.

Note that there are a few other indefinite locutions incorporating **chose.**

autre chose	*something else, anything else*
peu de chose	*little, not much*
(pas) grand-chose	*(not) much*

Si cette démarche n'aboutit à rien, essaie autre chose.
If this approach doesn't produce any results, try something else.

Il ne faut pas se tracasser pour si peu de chose.
You must not get upset for so little.

Cette montre ne vaut pas grand-chose, mais j'y tiens.
This watch is not worth much, but I'm attached to it.

O.   **Tel** serves as an adjective or pronoun agreeing in number and gender
with its noun. It denotes similarity with or without an explicit term of
comparison; in this use, it often expresses intensity as well. **Tel** is also
used to mark indeterminateness.

1.   Adjective **tel** (*such, such a*) may precede or follow a noun introduced
by an indefinite article* or may occur as a predicate adjective; in the
latter case, the noun modified may be introduced by a determiner
other than an indefinite article. When there is an explicit term of
comparison, that term is preceded by **que** (*as, than*).

Avec un tel métro
Avec un métro tel que celui-là ⎫, j'aime mieux me déplacer à pied.

With such a subway system
With a subway system like ⎬*, I prefer to get around on foot.*
(such as) that one

On ne voyait pas autrefois une telle insertion des handicapés dans la
vie normale.
*Such integration of the handicapped into normal life was not to be seen
in the past.*

Je ne peux même pas songer à de telles vacances; c'est bien au-dessus de mes moyens.
I cannot even consider such a vacation; it is well beyond my means.

Sa dépression était telle qu'on craignait pour sa vie.
Her (His) depression was such that we feared for her (his) life.

Mon emploi du temps n'est pas tel que je ne puisse déjeuner avec
vous lundi prochain.
*My schedule is not such that I cannot have lunch with you next Mon-
day.*

---

*Note that **tel** bears upon a noun: **une telle maison** (*such a house*); intensification of an
adjective, as in *such a beautiful house*, is accomplished through si or **tellement: une si belle maison, une réaction tellement spontanée** (*such a spontaneous reaction*).

a. **Tel que** may introduce an enumeration or a specifying example.

Plusieurs sports développent la coordination entre l'œil et la
main, tels que le tennis, le volleyball et le golf.
*Several sports develop hand-eye coordination, such as tennis, volley-
ball, and golf.*

Le candidat désirait prononcer un discours devant un groupe de
scientifiques, tel que l'Académie des Sciences.
*The candidate wished to address a group of scientists, such as the
Academy of Sciences.*

b. **Tel** may replace **comme** in a literary simile.

Le roc surplombait l'eau glacée, tel une figure de proue.
The rock hung over the icy water like a ship's figurehead.

c. Marking indeterminateness, **tel** (*whatever, certain*) is used before a
noun with no article or equivalent. It tends to be doubled to **tel
et tel** or **tel ou tel.**

Moi j'apporte le vin, toi tu apportes un camembert ou tel autre
fromage qu'il te plaira.
*I'm bringing the wine; you bring a camembert or whatever other
cheese you like.*

La révélation de tels ou (et) tels plagiats ferait esclandre dans le
monde de l'édition.
*The disclosure of certain instances of plagiarism would create a scan-
dal in the world of publishing.*

2. As a pronoun, **tel** represents a nonspecified person or nonspecified
persons. It is usually singular and not preceded by a determiner; in
this function, **tel** is limited to literary or proverbial style. It may be
expanded to **tel et tel** or **tel ou tel.**

Tel sautait à la corde, tel faisait courir un cerceau.
Some were jumping rope; some were rolling hoops.

Ce cheval gagnera à coup sûr telle ou telle course importante.
*This horse will surely win one or another important race (some important
race or other).*

Note that **un tel** may stand for the name of a person.

Monsieur un tel (Untel)	*Mr. So-and-so*
Madame une telle (Untel)	*Mrs. What's-her-name*

3. There are a few common locutions with **tel.**

tel quel	*as is*
rien de tel que	*nothing like*

Oseriez-vous envoyer cette lettre telle quelle?
Would you dare send this letter as is?

P. **Tout** may be an adjective, pronoun, noun, or adverb. As a noun, **le tout** (*the whole, the main thing*) is always singular. For **tout** as an adverb, see Chapter 6, Section I.B.

1. As an adjective, **tout** may immediately precede a noun or pronoun or be separated from it by a determiner.

   a. When there is a pronoun or a noun with determiner, singular **tout(e)** means *whole* or *all* and plural **tous** (**toutes**) means *every* or *all*.

   Tout un quartier de la ville a été inondé il y a dix ans.
   A whole section of the city was flooded ten years ago.

   Le yogi maîtrise les fonctions du corps en concentrant toute son énergie.
   The yogi controls the body functions by concentrating all his energy.

   Tous vos efforts pour me convaincre échoueront.
   All your efforts to convince me will fail.

   Pour être vraiment utile, cet exercice doit se faire tous les jours sans exception.
   To be really useful, this exercise must be done every day with no exception.

   Je suis profondément reconnaissant envers tous ceux et toutes celles qui m'ont aidé.
   I am deeply grateful to all those who have helped me.

   b. When **tout** is used without a determiner, the singular may mean *each, any, entire,* and the like; the plural means *all*.

   Il y en a qui croient que tout homme a son prix.
   There are those who believe that every man has his price.

   Tout soliste vous dira que le trac est universel.
   Any soloist will tell you that stagefright is universal.

   Un rêve persistant des citadins est de vivre à la campagne en toute simplicité.
   A persistent dream of city dwellers is to live in the country in utter simplicity.

   Pour se protéger contre l'ennemi, les vaisseaux avancèrent tous feux éteints.
   To protect themselves from the enemy, the vessels moved forward no lights showing (with all lights out).

2. As a pronoun, **tout** may be used in an absolute sense or in apposition to a noun or pronoun.

    a. In its absolute use, the singular **tout** (*all, everything, anything*) refers only to things. The plural forms **tous, toutes** (*everyone*) refer normally to people.

        Il faut se méfier d'eux; ce sont des gens capables de tout.
        You have to watch out for them; they are people capable of anything.

        Reviens, et tu verras que tout a changé.
        Come back, and you will see that everything (all) has changed.

        Tous au village ont reconnu l'utilité de l'électricité.
        Everyone in the village acknowledged the usefulness of electrification.

    b. **Tout** generally refers to one or more nouns or pronouns expressed in a preceding clause or in the same clause.

        On entend exprimer beaucoup d'opinions; toutes ne sont pas de valeur égale.
        One can hear many opinions expressed; not all are of equal value.

        Elle travaillait sur des théorèmes qui n'étaient pas tous démontrables.
        She was working on some theorems which were not all demonstrable.

        Il nous a divulgué à tous des détails de sa vie qu'on aurait préféré ne pas savoir.
        He divulged to all of us details of his life we would rather not have known.

3. **Tout** occurs in the indefinite concessive construction **tout** + adjective or noun + **que** + indicative clause (*however . . . , as . . . as . . .* and the like. **Tout** shows its normal patterns of agreement.

    Tout charlatan qu'il est, il a ses fidèles.
    As much of a charlatan as he is, he has his followers.

    Toute simple et tout illettrée qu'elle était, elle avait beaucoup de bon sens.
    However simple and uneducated she was, she had a great deal of common sense.

4. There are numerous common expressions with **tout.**

une [bonne] fois pour toutes	*once and for all*
tout à fait	*perfectly, completely*
tout de suite	*right away, immediately*
tout à coup	*suddenly*
tout d'un coup	*all at once*
pas du tout	*not at all*
tout le monde	*everyone*

Q. For the negative indefinites **aucun, nul, personne,** and **rien,** see Chapter 2.

R. The concessive, indeterminative constructions equivalent to English *-ever*

1. Adjective **quelque** + noun + $\left\{ \begin{array}{l} \textbf{qui} \\ \textbf{que} \end{array} \right\}$ + subjunctive clause (*whatever . . .*); **quelque** agrees with the noun.

    Quelques raisons que vous donniez, vous ne convaincrez personne.
    Whatever reasons you [may] give, you will not convince anyone.

    Quelque émotion qui puisse l'ébranler, elle aura l'air tout à fait calme.
    Whatever emotion may upset her, she will look perfectly calm.

2. Adverb **quelque** or **si** or **aussi** or **pour** + adjective or adverb + **que** + subjunctive clause (*however . . .*); **quelque** is invariable.

    Quelque (Si, Aussi, Pour) lents que soient vos progrès, ne vous découragez pas.
    However slow your progress may be, do not be discouraged.

    Si (Quelque, Aussi, Pour) vite qu'on puisse courir, on ne l'attrapera pas.
    No matter how fast we can run, we won't catch him (her).

3. Adjective **quel** + **que** + clause with **être** (or equivalent) in the subjunctive (*whatever . . .*); **quel** agrees with the noun or pronoun it modifies.

    Il affronte tous les dangers, quels qu'ils soient.
    He faces all dangers, whatever they are (may be).

    Quel que soit le cadeau, il faudra le refuser.
    Whatever the gift may be, it must be refused.

4. **Qui que** (*who(m)ever*) and **quoi que** (*whatever*) are not used as subjects.

    A qui que vous parliez, faites-lui savoir la vérité.
    Whomever you speak to, let him know the truth.

    Qui qu'elle soit et quoi qu'elle ait fait, elle sera la bienvenue parmi nous.
    Whoever she is (may be) and whatever she has (may have) done, she will be welcome among us.

5. **Qui que ce soit** (*anyone, who(m)ever*) and **quoi que ce soit** (*anything, whatever*), despite their appearance, function as unitary pro-

nouns, occurring as either subjects or objects. For their use in negative utterances, see Chapter 2.

Qui que ce soit qui vous fasse de telles propositions ne mériterait
   pas votre respect.
*Whoever (Anyone who) made such proposals to you would not deserve
   your respect.*

Quand tu verras qui que ce soit de nos anciens collègues, tu lui
   diras bien des choses de ma part.
When you see any of our old colleagues, do give my best regards.

Il s'est remis à l'enquête sans savoir s'il y trouverait quoi que ce soit
   de probant.
*He resumed the inquiry not knowing whether he would turn up anything
   at all conclusive.*

6. **Où que** (*wherever*) + subjunctive is usually replaced by **partout où**
   + indicative.

Ou que tu ailles ⎱ cet été, tu trouveras des prix nettement plus
Partout où tu iras ⎰   élevés que ceux de l'année passée.

*Wherever you go this summer, you will find prices sharply higher than
   last year's.*

Numbers

I. CARDINAL NUMBERS

A. Forms

0	*zéro*	50	*cinquante*
1	*un(e)*	51	*cinquante et un(e)*
2	*deux*	60	*soixante*
3	*trois*	61	*soixante et un(e)*
4	*quatre*	70	*soixante-dix*
5	*cinq*	71	*soixante et onze*
6	*six*	72	*soixante-douze*
7	*sept*	80	*quatre-vingts*
8	*huit*	81	*quatre-vingt-un(e)*
9	*neuf*	82	*quatre-vingt-deux*
10	*dix*	90	*quatre-vingt-dix*
11	*onze*	91	*quatre-vingt-onze*
12	*douze*	99	*quatre-vingt-dix-neuf*
13	*treize*	100	*cent*
14	*quatorze*	101	*cent un(e)*
15	*quinze*	200	*deux cents*
16	*seize*	201	*deux cent un(e)*
17	*dix-sept*	250	*deux cent cinquante*
18	*dix-huit*	500	*cinq cents*
19	*dix-neuf*	1000	*mille*
20	*vingt*	1001	*mille un(e)*
21	*vingt et un(e)*	1100	*mille cent/onze cents*
22	*vingt-deux*	1200	*mille deux cents/douze cents*
23	*vingt-trois*	2000	*deux mille*
30	*trente*	1,000,000	*un million*
31	*trente et un(e)*	1,000,000,000	*un milliard*
32	*trente-deux*		
40	*quarante*		
41	*quarante et un(e)*		

B. Remarks

1. The alternate forms **septante** (70), **huitante** (80), and **nonante** (90) are widely used in Belgium, Switzerland, and various other French-speaking areas.

2.   The numbers 100 and 1,000 are expressed simply by **cent** and **mille: cent disques** (*one hundred records*).

3.   While the specific number 1,001 is **mille un(e)**, the indeterminate *a thousand and one* is **mille et un(e)**.

J'ai mille et une choses à te dire.
I've a thousand and one things to tell you.

4.   Cardinal numbers are generally invariable.

J'ai un numéro de téléphone avec trois quatre.
I have a telephone number with three fours [in it].

Cette cinémathèque compte plus de trois mille films.
This film library contains more than 3,000 movies.

a.   **Un** by itself or in a compound agrees in gender with the noun it modifies, unless the noun immediately precedes.

Il a trente et une chemises, dont une de soie.
He has 31 shirts, including one silk one.

«Reprenons à la mesure cent un,» dit le chef d'orchestre.
"Let's take it from measure 101," said the conductor.

b.   While **quatre-vingts** (80) has a final **s,** its compounds contain **vingt: quatre-vingt-trois** (83). Moreover, when it follows the noun to which it applies, there is no **s: la page quatre-vingt** (*page 80*).

c.   While multiples of **cent** have a final **s,** there is no **s** in compounds: **deux cents** (200), but **deux cent trois** (203). Moreover, when a multiple of **cent** follows its noun, there is no **s: l'an huit cent** (*the year 800*).

5.   As a noun, *thousand* is **un millier.** As nouns of quantity, **millier, million,** and **milliard** are constructed with **de** + noun: **des milliers de pages** (*thousands of pages*), **trois millions de barils de pétrole** (*three million barrels of oil*), **cinq milliards de dollars** (*five billion dollars*).

6.   Where English uses a period, French uses a comma, and vice versa.

English:	*French:*
1,000	1.000
2,300,000	2.300.000
3.2 percent	3,2 pour cent
15.8	15,8

7.   Between 1,100 and 1,999 (or the dates 1100 and 1999), French tends to count by hundreds instead of thousands. If *thousand* is ex-

pressed in dates, **mil** generally replaces **mille**, except in **l'an mille** (*the year 1000*).

quinze cents mètres carrés
1,500 square metres

né en dix-neuf cent trente-six
born in 1936

l'an de grâce mil sept cent soixante-seize
the year of Our Lord 1776

Note that, while English may omit *hundred* from a date, French never deletes **cent.** Also note that, while English may use *and* in expressing a date, French never uses **et:** 1806 (*eighteen-o-six, eighteen-six, eighteen hundred* [*and*] *six*)—**dix-huit cent six.**

8. Cardinal numbers are used in dates and in dynastic designations, except in the case of *first* (**premier [première].**)*

le 30 (trente) mai	*May 30th (30 May)*
le 2 (deux) février	*February 2nd (2 February)*
Louis XIV (Quatorze)	*Louis XIV (the Fourteenth)*
Henri IV (Quatre)	*Henry IV (the Fourth)*
le 1er (premier) août	*August 1st (1 August)*
Elisabeth Ière (Première)	*Elizabeth I (the First)*
François Ier (Premier)	*Francis I (the First)*

9. Unlike English, French places cardinal numbers before **premiers** (*first*) and **derniers** (*last*).

les trois premiers coureurs	*the first three runners*
les cinq dernières heures	*the last five hours*

II. ORDINAL NUMBERS

A. Forms

1st	*premier, première*
2nd	*deuxième*
3rd	*troisième*
4th	*quatrième*
5th	*cinquième*
6th	*sixième*
7th	*septième*
8th	*huitième*
9th	*neuvième*

*Note that Emperor Charles V is known as **Charles-Quint.**

10th	*dixième*
11th	*onzième*
17th	*dix-septième*
20th	*vingtième*
21st	*vingt et unième*
22nd	*vingt-deuxième*
30th	*trentième*
31st	*trente et unième*
40th	*quarantième*
50th	*cinquantième*
60th	*soixantième*
70th	*soixante-dixième*
71st	*soixante et onzième*
72nd	*soixante-douzième*
80th	*quatre-vingtième*
81st	*quatre-vingt-unième*
90th	*quatre-vingt-dixième*
91st	*quatre-vingt-onzième*
100th	*centième*
101st	*cent unième*
500th	*cinq centième*
867th	*huit cent soixante-septième*
1000th	*millième*
1001st	*mille unième*
5003rd	*cinq mille troisième*
1,000,000th	*millionième*

B. Remarks

1. The alternate form **second(e)** (*second*) implies that the series does not extend beyond two. Like **premier,** it is not used in any compound numbers.

2. The alternate forms **tiers (tierce)** (*third*), **quart(e)** (*fourth*), and **quint(e)** (*fifth*) occur only in a few fixed terms.

le Tiers monde	*the Third World*
un tiers } une tierce personne }	*a third party, an outsider*
en main tierce	*in the hands of a third party*
Le Quart Livre de Rabelais	*Rabelais' Fourth Book*
la fièvre quarte	*quartan fever*
Charles-Quint	*Emperor Charles V*

3. Ordinal numbers agree in gender and number with the nouns they modify, and they are normally preposed. In a dynastic designation, **premier** always follows the name to which it applies.

François Ier fut le neuvième roi de la dynastie des Valois.
Francis I was the ninth king of the Valois dynasty.

Ce pianiste a eu l'idée saugrenue de ne présenter à son récital que des cinquièmes sonates.
That pianist had the preposterous idea of presenting only fifth sonatas at his recital.

When two ordinals are joined by **et** or **ou,** the first may be replaced by a cardinal number: **la sept ou huitième fois** (*the seventh or eighth time*).

III. FRACTIONS

A. Forms

The forms **demi(s)** (*half*), **tiers** (*third*), **quart(s)** (*quarter, fourth*) serve as denominators; from *fifth* on, the ordinal forms in **-ième(s)** are used.

B. Remarks

1. A fraction may be expressed as, for example, **trois cinquièmes** (*three fifths*) or **trois sur cinq** (*three over five, three out of five*).

2. While **demi** is used as a noun in mathematical calculations, *half* is elsewhere expressed by **la moitié.**

   Quatre demis font deux.
   Four halves equal two.

   Il n'a peint que la moitié inférieure du mur.
   He painted only the lower half of the wall.

3. When **demi** is used with a noun, it is invariable if it precedes the noun and variable if it follows.

une demi-heure	*a half-hour*
une heure et demie	*an hour and a half*
deux kilos et demi	*two and a half kilos*

4. Fractions are usually preceded by the definite article.

   Elle a laissé à diverses œuvres de bienfaisance les deux tiers de sa fortune.
   She left two-thirds of her fortune to various charities.

IV. MULTIPLICATIVES

The common forms are: **double** (*double*), **triple** (*triple*), **quadruple** (*quad-*

ruple), **quintuple** (*fivefold*), **sextuple** (*sixfold*), **décuple** (*tenfold*), **centuple** (*hundredfold*). They function as both adjectives and (masculine) nouns.

C'était un cauchemar de documents à faire en triple exemplaire.
It was a nightmare of documents to be filled out in triplicate.

J'en connais qui gagnent le quadruple de ce que je gagne mais qui paient moins d'impôts que moi.
I know people who earn four times what (four times as much as) I earn but who pay less in taxes than I.

V. OTHER QUANTITATIVE FORMS

A. Forms in **-aine**

With numerals from 5 to 60 and 100, **-aine** is used to form (feminine) nouns denoting approximate quantities.

une dizaine de personnes
about ten people

Passé la trentaine, on commence à se soigner mieux.
After thirty (In their thirties), people begin to take better care of themselves.

Il a passé la cinquantaine.
He's past fifty.

Note that **la douzaine** (*dozen*) and **la quinzaine** (*two-week period, fortnight*) denote specific quantities.

B. Forms in **-génaire** are used as adjectives or nouns expressing the decades of a human life: **quadragénaire, quinquagénaire, sexagénaire, septuagénaire, octogénaire, nonagénaire.**

Il a l'air si jeune qu'on croit difficilement qu'il est septuagénaire.
He looks so young that you have difficulty believing that he is in his seventies.

Note that **centenaire** may, and **millénaire** must, have nonhuman reference.

La route fait un coude ici pour protéger un arbre centenaire.
The road makes a bend here to protect a hundred-year-old tree.

Le deuxième centenaire s'appelle le bicentenaire.
The two-hundredth anniversary is called the bicentennial.

C. There are many words designating a group composed of a specified number of persons or things, such as the following:

le duo	*duet*
les triplé(e)s	*triplets (babies)*
le triolet	*triplet (music)*
le quatuor	*quartet (music)*
le quintal	*100 kilograms*
le sizain	*six-line stanza*
le septennat	*seven-year term*
un octosyllabe	*eight-syllable line (poetry)*

15

Prepositions

I. FORMS

Prepositions may be simple, participial, or compound.

A. Simple prepositions

à	*to, at, in*	envers	*toward*
après	*after*	hormis	*except*
avant	*before (with noun or pronoun)*	hors	*outside*
avec	*with*	malgré	*despite*
chez	*at . . .'s place, in*	outre	*beyond*
contre	*against*	par	*by, through*
dans	*in, into*	parmi	*among*
de	*of, from, by*	pendant	*during, for*
depuis	*since, for*	pour	*for*
derrière	*behind*	sans	*without*
dès	*from . . . on*	sauf	*except*
devant	*in front of*	selon	*according to*
durant	*during*	sous	*under*
en	*in, into, as*	sur	*on, upon, onto*
entre	*between, among*	vers	*toward*

1. The prepositions **à**, **de**, and **en** are normally repeated before each of the words they govern.

    Il répugna aux mensonges et aux compromissions qui auraient assuré son succès.
    He was repelled by the lies and the compromises that would have ensured his success.

2. In certain expressions, **durant** may be placed after its object.

des heures (années) durant	*for hours (years) on end*
sa vie durant	*throughout his life*

B. Participial prepositions

concernant	*concerning*
moyennant	*in return for*
suivant	*according to*

touchant	concerning
étant donné	given
attendu	considering
y compris	including
excepté	except
passé	beyond
vu	given, in view of

1. Like all prepositions, the participials are invariable.

Tout nous plaît ici excepté la chaleur.
We like everything here except the heat.

2. Unlike other prepositions, the participials may never govern a personal pronoun. With such an object, another turn of phrase must be used.

Cette lettre concernant notre nièce nous apprend des choses surprenantes à son sujet.
This letter concerning our niece tells us surprising things about her.

C. Compound prepositions

à cause de	because of
à côté de	beside, next to
à défaut de	for lack of
afin de	in order to
à force de	by dint of
à la faveur de	thanks to
à la suite de	following
à l'égard de	with regard to
à l'insu de	unbeknownst to
à l'intention de	for
à moins de	without, barring
à part	aside from
à partir de	beginning with
à propos de	about, regarding
à raison de	at the rate of
à titre de	as
à travers	through, across
au-dedans de	within
au-dehors de	outside
au-delà de	beyond
au dépens de	at the expense of
au-dessous de	beneath, below
au-dessus de	above, over
au lieu de	instead of
auprès de	next to, beside

au sujet de	*about, concerning*
autour de	*around*
avant de	*before (with infinitive)*
d'après	*according to*
d'avec	*from*
de chez	*from the house of*
de derrière	*from behind*
de dessous	*from below*
de dessus	*from above*
de devant	*from in front of*
d'entre	*among, of*
de par	*by, in the name of*
du côté de	*in the direction of, toward*
en deçà de	*on this side of*
en dehors de	*outside of*
en dépit de	*in spite of*
en face de	*across from, opposite*
en raison de	*because of*
faute de	*for lack of*
grâce à	*thanks to*
hors de	*out of*
jusqu'à	*up to, until*
jusque dans	*up to*
le long de	*along*
loin de	*far from*
lors de	*at the time of*
par-dessous	*under, underneath*
par-dessus	*above, over*
par rapport à	*in relation to*
par suite de	*as a consequence of*
près de	*near*
quant à	*as for*
vis-à-vis [de]	*opposite, next to, toward*

1. The final element **à** or **de** of a compound preposition is always repeated before each of the words governed.

   grâce à son talent et à son enthousiasme
   thanks to her (his) talent and enthusiasm

   faute de moyens et de temps
   for lack of means and time

2. Certain compound prepositions never govern a personal pronoun, but incorporate a possessive adjective instead.

   à l'insu du douanier/à son insu
   unbeknownst to the customs officer/unbeknownst to him

à l'égard des contribuables/à leur égard
with regard to the taxpayers/with regard to them

à l'intention de ma belle-mère/à son intention
for my mother-in-law (stepmother)/for her

à mon sujet
about me

Note that **à côté de** allows both constructions.

à côté de toi/à ton côté
beside you

II. REPLACEMENT OF PREPOSITIONAL PHRASES BY ADVERBS

Instead of the combination preposition + personal pronoun of inanimate reference, French generally uses an adverb.

A.   The conjunctive adverb **en** replaces **de** + object; the conjunctive **y** replaces **à** (**en, dans, sur,** etc.) + object.

Il est sorti de sa cachette./Il en est sorti.
He came out of his hiding place./He came out of it.

Elle est rentrée à sa ville natale./Elle y est rentrée.
She went back to the city of her birth./She went back there (to it).

J'aime me promener dans ce quartier historique; j'y passe volontiers
  des après-midi entiers.
*I like to walk around in this historic neighborhood; I gladly spend whole
  afternoons in it (there).*

B.   **Other substitutions**

Note that in some cases the form of the adverb is the same as that of the preposition or clearly related to it.

J'ai écouté son discours avec stupéfaction; il n'y avait rien dedans.
I listened to his (her) speech with amazement; there was nothing in it.

Au son de la musique, il s'est précipité vers la scène et a sauté dessus.
At the sound of the music, he rushed to the stage and jumped up on it.

Au premier signe d'une tornade, je vais au piano pour me cacher dessous.
At the first sign of a tornado, I go hide under the piano.

Il est si vaniteux que, chaque fois qu'il voit un miroir, il s'arrête devant.
He is so vain that, every time he sees a mirror, he stops in front of it.

Qu'on mette cet adjectif avant le nom ou après, peu importe, le sens reste le même.
Whether you put this adjective before the noun or after it doesn't matter; the meaning stays the same.

Vous connaissez la boulangerie du coin? Eh bien, la papeterie se trouve à côté.
You know the corner bakery? Well, the stationery store is next to it.

La ville a beaucoup changé; il y a maintenant une zone industrielle tout autour.
The city has changed a lot; there is an industrial zone all around it now.

Note that **avec** also occurs as an adverb, but only in colloquial usage.

Le chien a saisi mon pantoufle et a joué avec.
The dog seized my slipper and played with it.

III. REMARKS ON PARTICULAR FRENCH PREPOSITIONS

A.   **A, de,** and **en** are widely used to form adjectival phrases.

1.   **A**

a.   **A** may introduce a phrase expressing a salient trait of the noun modified.

un clown au visage triste	*sad-faced clown*
une femme aux yeux bleus	*blue-eyed woman*
un appartement à trois chambres	*three-bedroom apartment*
une chambre à deux lits	*room with two beds*
des rideaux à franges	*curtains with fringes*
une omelette au fromage	*cheese omelette*
un mot à initiale vocalique	*word beginning with a vowel*
un avion à réaction	*jet plane*

b.   The **à**-phrase may express the use or function of the noun modified.

une tasse à thé	*teacup*
une brosse à dents	*toothbrush*
une boîte aux lettres	*mailbox*
un bateau à vapeur	*steamboat*
une salle à manger	*dining room*
une machine à coudre	*sewing machine*

c.   An **à**-phrase containing the infinitive of a transitive verb may denote an action that the noun must undergo.

une course à faire	*errand to do*
un livre à ne pas lire	*book not to be read*
un monument à visiter	*monument to visit*
une langue à apprendre	*language to be learned*

2. ***De***

a. **De** may introduce a phrase expressing a salient characteristic of the noun modified, its components or content, or the substance of which it is made.

un homme de bonne volonté	*man of good will*
une femme de tête	*strong-minded woman*
un troupeau de moutons	*flock of sheep*
une bouteille d'eau minérale	*bottle of mineral water*
une statue de bronze	*bronze statue*
du sulfate de fer	*iron sulfate*

b. The **de**-phrase may express the whole to which the modified noun belongs or its habitat or location.

un agent de police	*police officer*
des côtelettes de porc	*pork chops*
une lame de couteau	*knife blade*
un poisson d'eau douce	*fresh-water fish*
un pin de montagne	*mountain pine*
une maison de campagne	*country house*

c. The **de**-phrase may express the source of the noun modified.

du lait de chèvre	*goat's milk*
de l'huile d'arachide	*peanut oil*
du gaz de houille	*coal gas*

d. The **de**-phrase may express the goal of the noun modified: its purpose or function, the person using it, the place or occasion of its use, or the object of the action it implies.

des outils de jardinage	*gardening tools*
une serviette de bain	*bath towel*
une voiture d'enfant	*baby carriage*
des ciseaux de brodeuse	*embroidery scissors*
un couteau de table	*table knife*
des vêtements d'hiver	*winter clothes*

un dompteur de lions	*lion tamer*
un compteur d'eau	*water meter*

3. **En.** The **en**-phrase may express the state of the noun modified, its shape, or the material (even nonconcrete) of which it is made.

une femme en deuil	*woman in mourning*
un touriste en vacances	*tourist on vacation*
un toit en réparation	*roof under repair*
des arbres en fleur	*trees in bloom*
un escalier en spirale	*spiral staircase*
des yeux en amande	*almond-shaped eyes*
une maison en briques	*brick house*
une montre en or	*gold watch*
une tragédie en vers	*tragedy in verse*

B. *Dans* and *en*

1. The noun governed by **dans** is always introduced by a determiner while the object of **en** almost always occurs without one and represents a higher level of abstraction.★

Nous sommes venus en voiture.
We came by car.

Nous sommes venus dans la nouvelle voiture.
We came in the new car.

A cette heure-ci, elle doit être en classe.
At this time, she must be in class.

A cette heure-ci, elle doit être dans sa classe de botanique.
At this time, she must be in her botany class.

2. With units of time, **en** indicates the period needed to accomplish an action, and **dans** indicates the period at the end of which an action will take place.

Vers 1930, on a construit des paquebots pouvant traverser l'Atlantique en huit jours.
Around 1930, liners were built that could cross the Atlantic in one week.

★The same level of abstraction found in such expressions as **en prison, en ville, en province** recurs in such expressions as **à la maison, à l'école, à l'université, à l'église.** This convergence of the values of **en** + no article and **à** + definite article is particularly striking in connection with the names of countries, as in **en France, au Pérou,** and the seasons of the year: **en été, en automne, en hiver, au printemps.** For **en** + definite article, see Chapter 3, Section II.B.4.

Dépêchons-nous! L'avion part dans quelques minutes.
Let's hurry! The plane is leaving in a few minutes.

3. **En** may denote the result of a division or other change.

un livre divisé en chapitres
a book divided into chapters

briser une glace en mille morceaux
to break a mirror into a thousand pieces

un mur peint en blanc
a wall painted white

se déguiser en clown
to disguise oneself as a clown

changer du fer en acier
to change iron into steel

C. **Avant** and **devant** both mean *before.*

The first refers essentially to time, while the second refers to space.

Cela est arrivé avant ma naissance.
That happened before I was born.

Le régisseur se mit devant le rideau pour annoncer un changement
dans la distribution.
*The stage manager stepped before the curtain to announce a change in the
cast.*

D. **Chez** is basically a synonym of **à la maison de** (*in/to the house of*) and,
by extension, may refer to a shop or office. It may also mean *among,
in, in the works of*. Note that **chez** in its first sense may be preceded
by such prepositions as **devant, de,** and **jusque.**

L'enfant prodigue retourna chez son père.
The prodigal son returned to his father's house.

En rentrant de chez le médecin, je passerai chez le pharmacien.
On the way back from the doctor's [office], I'll stop at the pharmacy.

Ce qui me touche chez lui, c'est la sympathie qu'il a pour les enfants.
What I find touching about (in) him is the feeling he has for children.

Chez certains peuples, le suicide n'est pas forcément un acte négatif.
Among certain peoples, suicide is not necessarily a negative act.

On trouve toute l'histoire de l'art moderne chez Picasso.
The whole history of modern art is found in Picasso.

E. **D'entre** (*of, among*) governs a plural disjunctive pronoun after an expression of quantity, or a negative, interrogative, or demonstrative pronoun.

peu d'entre nous	*few of us*
la plupart d'entre eux	*most of them*
trois d'entre nous	*three of us*
personne d'entre vous	*no one among you*
laquelle d'entre elles?	*which one of them?*
ceux d'entre vous	*those of you*

Note that the English idiomatic construction *There are three of us* (*five of you, etc.*) is rendered in French by **Nous sommes trois** (**On est six, Ils sont deux,** etc.).

F. **Depuis** usually occurs in the sense of *since* or *for* referring to time. (See Chapter 1, Section I.J.2) It is also used, often in combination with **jusqu'à,** in the sense of *from*, sometimes with reference to space.

Nous attendons depuis mardi qu'on nous livre du charbon.
We have been waiting since Tuesday for coal to be delivered.

Ils étaient mariés depuis dix ans avant d'avoir un enfant.
They had been married for ten years before having a child.

depuis le matin jusqu'au soir
from morning to evening

depuis les pieds jusqu'à la tête
from head to foot (toe)

La fusée sera téléguidée depuis le sol.
The rocket will be guided by remote control from the ground.

G. **Dès** [*from (. . . on), as early as*] stresses the fact that a given action occurs at a certain moment and no later.

Ce champion a appris à nager dès l'âge de trois ans.
This champion learned to swim when he was only three.

Dès les premiers signes d'une grossesse, il est prudent d'éviter le tabac et l'alcool.
From the earliest signs of pregnancy, it is wise to avoid smoking and drinking.

Note that temporality is still stressed when the object of **dès** is a noun of place.

Dès la grille du jardin, ils annoncèrent la nouvelle que nous attendions tous.
As soon as they had reached the garden gate, they announced the news we had all been waiting for.

H. **A partir de** (*from . . . onward, beginning with*) refers primarily to time, marking the inception of a state or repeated action. It may also be used with a nontemporal meaning.

Ce film sera projeté en permanence tous les jours à partir de midi.
There will be a continuous showing of this film every day from noon on.

A partir de l'âge de 18 ans, on est responsable devant la loi de tous ses actes.
Beginning with the age of 18, one is legally responsible for all of one's actions.

Ce magasin vend des robes à partir de 1500 francs.
This store sells dresses from 1500 francs [up].

En quelques années, ils ont créé un musée splendide à partir de rien du tout.
In a few years, they created a splendid museum out of nothing at all.

I.   **Vers** and **envers** both mean *toward*. The first is used in reference to space or time, while the second, a synonym of **à l'égard de,** has a psychological sense.

Le malade se dirigea d'un pas chancelant vers la porte.
The sick man walked unsteadily toward the door.

Ils se sont connus vers le début de leur carrière.
They met near the beginning of their career.

Leur attitude envers les minorités a beaucoup changé depuis quelques années.
Their attitude toward minorities has changed considerably in the last few years.

J.   **Miscellanea**

   1.   The adverbs of quantity **assez** and **trop** are joined to an infinitive by the preposition **pour.**

Nous ne sommes pas assez riches pour nous permettre de telles dépenses.
We are not rich enough to allow ourselves such expenses.

Tu as trop d'intelligence pour ne pas comprendre.
You are too intelligent not to understand.

   2.   With the points of the compass, **à** is used for orientation and **dans** designates the interior of a region.

Strasbourg se trouve à l'est de Paris.
Strasbourg is [to the] east of Paris.

Strasbourg se trouve dans l'Est de la France.
Strasbourg is in the East of France.

   3.   Prepositions denoting *on*, *in* with kinds of streets: **dans** + **rue, dans** or **sur** + **avenue, sur** + **boulevard, sur** + **place.**

L'accident a eu lieu dans une avenue très fréquentée.
The accident took place on a very busy avenue.

Note various ways of stating an address, complete or partial.

habiter $\begin{Bmatrix} \text{rue} \\ \text{dans la rue} \end{Bmatrix}$ Amélie

habiter $\begin{Bmatrix} 11, \\ \text{au } 11, \end{Bmatrix}$ avenue de l'Opéra

Je dois aller 6, rue Bonaparte; pourriez-vous m'y conduire?
I have to go to 6 rue Bonaparte; could you drive me there?

4. Prepositions with **droite** (*right*) and **gauche** (*left*).

tourner à droite/gauche
turn [to the] right/left

se diriger vers la droite/gauche
go toward (to) the right/left

être assis à la droite/gauche de quelqu'un
sit on someone's right/left

$\begin{Bmatrix} \text{à} \\ \text{sur} \end{Bmatrix}$ + possessive adjective + **droite/gauche**

$\begin{Bmatrix} to \\ on \end{Bmatrix}$ + possessive adjective + *right/left*

Le pilote a annoncé que sur notre droite nous verrions bientôt la baie.
The pilot announced that on our right we would soon see the bay.

IV. REMARKS ON PARTICULAR ENGLISH PREPOSITIONS

A. *About*

1. **Approximation. A peu près** and **environ** are used with expressions of measurement; **vers** is used with expressions of time.

    There were about (around) two hundred of us taking that course.
    Nous étions environ (à peu près) deux cents à suivre ce cours.

    For a long time, we went to bed at about (around) midnight.
    Longtemps, nous nous sommes couchés vers minuit.

    He spent about twenty years in exile.
    Il a passé une vingtaine d'années en exil.

2. **Subject**

    We spoke about one thing and another.
    Nous avons parlé de choses et d'autres.

    I am going to have a word with my neighbor about his dog which barks all night.
    Je vais toucher un mot à mon voisin au sujet de (à propos de) son chien qui aboie toute la nuit.

The speaker will talk about (on) UFOs.
Le conférencier parlera sur les (au sujet des) Ovni.★

She asked us questions about our future.
Elle nous a posé des questions sur (touchant, concernant) notre avenir.

What is that film about?
De quoi s'agit-il dans ce film?

3. **Imminence**

We were about to leave when it began to rain.
On était sur le point de partir quand il a commencé à pleuvoir.

B. *Above*

I don't like a picture hanging above my bed.
Je n'aime pas avoir un tableau au-dessus de mon lit.

He behaved like a man above all suspicion.
Il se comportait comme un homme au-dessus de tout soupçon.

This morning, the temperature is above normal.
Ce matin, la température est supérieure à (au-dessus de) la normale.

You must above all avoid mentioning that name in front of her.
Il faut surtout (avant tout) éviter de prononcer ce nom devant elle.

C. *According to*

According to the old jurists, polygamy was a hanging offense.
D'après (Selon) les légistes anciens, la polygamie était un cas pendable.

He is trying to conduct his investigation according to the law.
Il essaie de mener son enquête conformément à (suivant, selon) la loi.

D. *After*

You become a butcher only after a lengthy apprenticeship.
On ne devient boucher qu'après de longues années d'apprentissage.

I shall be free after three o'clock.
Je serai libre à partir de trois heures.

★Objets volants non identifiés.

It is after (past) two o'clock.

Il est $\begin{cases} \textbf{plus de deux heures.} \\ \textbf{deux heures passées.} \end{cases}$

It is surprising to what an extent he takes after his father.
C'est étonnant à quel point il tient de son père.

My neighbor is going to look after the cats while I'm gone.
La voisine va s'occuper de mes chats pendant mon absence.

E. *Against*

He spent his life in the struggle against illiteracy.
Il a passé sa vie dans la lutte contre l'analphabétisme.

The steeple of the church stands out against the sky lit up by fireworks.
La flèche de l'église se profile sur le ciel éclairé par des feux d'artifice.

Why of course, go ahead; it's not against the law.
Mais bien sûr, vas-y; ce n'est pas contraire à la loi.

What do you have against him?
Que lui reprochez-vous?

F. *Among*

Some remarkable poems were found among his writings.
Parmi ses écrits, on a trouvé quelques poèmes remarquables.

The thieves quarreled among (amongst) themselves.
Les voleurs se sont querellés entre eux.

There you will be among friends.
Là vous serez entre amis.

See, too, Section III.D. above.

G. *At* is expressed not only with **à** but in other ways as well.

look at	**regarder**
aim at	**viser**
shoot at	**tirer sur**
rush at	**se précipiter sur, se jeter sur**
laugh at	**rire de**
laugh at (make fun of)	**se moquer de**
blush at	**rougir de**
take offense at	**s'offenser de**
be surprised at	**être surpris (étonné) de, s'étonner de**

Don't take offense at what I am saying; I'm not laughing at you.
Ne t'offense pas de ce que je dis; je ne me moque pas de toi.

at issue (in question)	**en question**
at hand (handy)	**sous la main**
at the request of	**sur la demande de**
at sea	**en mer**
at war	**en guerre**
at peace	**en paix**
at the same time	**en même temps**
at home	**chez soi**

We take full responsibility for it; they acted at our request.
Nous en prenons l'entière responsabilité; ils ont agi sur notre demande.

H. *By*

Apart from being expressed by **par** and **de** in the passive (Chapter 1, Section IV.B.4.), by **par, à,** and **de** in the causative constructions (Chapter 1, Section IX.F., G., and H.), and by **en** with **-ant** forms (Chapter 1, Section XI.B.2.), *by* is rendered in various ways.

1. Means

by bus	**en autobus, en car**
by car	**en voiture, en auto**
by taxi	**en taxi**
by boat	**en (par) bateau**
by plane	**en (par) avion**
by train	**par le train**
by subway	**par le métro**
by bicycle	**à bicyclette, à (en) vélo**
by motorcycle	**à (en) moto**

know someone by sight, by name, by reputation
connaître quelqu'un de vue, de nom, de réputation

recognize someone by his voice, by his walk, by his scar
reconnaître quelqu'un à sa voix, à sa démarche, à sa cicatrice

by hand	**à la main**
by force	**de force**
by chance	**par hasard**
by oneself	**tout seul**

2. Authorship is expressed with **de.**

a novel by Balzac	**un roman de Balzac**
an opera by Bizet	**un opéra de Bizet**
a suit by Chanel	**un tailleur de Chanel**
a building by Le Corbusier	**un bâtiment de Le Corbusier**

3. **Time**

by now	déjà, maintenant
by tomorrow	avant demain
by + noun	d'ici + noun

I shall send him my answer by Friday.
Je lui enverrai ma réponse d'ici vendredi.

We must move by the end of the month.
Nous devons déménager avant la fin du mois.

4. Rate is expressed with **à.**

by the dozen	à la douzaine
by the box (can)	à la boîte
by the kilo	au kilo
by the liter	au litre
by the meter	au mètre
by the piece	à la pièce
by the hour	à l'heure
by the day	à la journée
by the month	au mois

*Here and there in the United States, gasoline is now being sold by the
    liter.*
Ici et là aux Etats-Unis, l'essence se vend maintenant au litre.

Cars are normally rented by the day.
La location des voitures se fait normalement à la journée.

5. Numerical difference is expressed with **de.**

She is older than her husband by two years.
Elle est plus âgée que son mari de deux ans.

The meter is longer than the yard by about eight centimeters.
Le mètre est plus long que le yard d'environ huit centimètres.

6. Dimensions are expressed with **sur.**

It is a large living room, measuring ten meters by twelve.
C'est une grande salle de séjour qui fait dix mètres sur douze.

7. **Distributive phrases**

one by one	un à un
step by step	pas à pas
little by little	peu à peu
side by side	côte à côte

I. *For*

1. Time

    a. **Pour** expresses time intended rather than time elapsed.

       She went to France for a year but stayed only six months.
       Elle est allée en France pour un an mais y est restée six mois seulement.

    b. **Pendant** expresses time seen as a single block.

       Our entomologist friend studied ant colonies in Africa for three years.
       Notre ami entomologiste a étudié pendant trois ans les colonies de fourmis en Afrique.

    c. **Ne . . . pas avant** expresses the time that must go by before an action can take place.

       He will not be able to go out for two days (before two days have passed).
       Il ne pourra pas sortir avant deux jours.

    d. Durative *for* is expressed by **depuis;** see Chapter 1, Section I.J.2., as well as Section III.F. above.

2. Cause is expressed by **pour.**

    He was indicted for embezzlement.
    Il fut inculpé pour détournement de fonds.

    She was dismissed for neglecting her work.
    Elle a été renvoyée pour avoir négligé son travail.

3. Goal is usually expressed by **pour.**

    There is a letter for you on the table.
    Il y a une lettre pour toi sur la table.

    He writes poems for his own pleasure.
    Il écrit des poèmes pour son plaisir.

    We took up a collection for the orphans.
    On a fait une collecte à l'intention des orphelins.

4. Remedies. **Pour** is used with the name of a part of the body; **contre** is used with the name of an illness.

    He took a pill for his heart every three hours.
    Il prenait une pilule pour le cœur toutes les trois heures.

    Do you have anything for a cold?
    Avez-vous quelque chose contre le rhume?

5. **Miscellanea**

look for	**chercher**
ask for	**demander**
pay for	**payer**
apologize for	**s'excuser de**
thank for	**remercier de (pour)**
substitute X for Y	**substituer X à Y**
translate word for word	**traduire mot à mot**
good for nothing	**bon à rien**
good-for-nothing	**un vaurien**
the reason for	**la raison de**
for example	**par exemple**
for rent	**à louer**
for sale	**à vendre**

J. *From* is expressed not only with **de** but in other ways as well.

1. **Verbs of separation.** The French equivalents of *take, borrow, steal, hide, buy, remove from someone* take **à**. **Séparer** and **divorcer** take **de** or **d'avec**.

> *In order to buy the house, we had to borrow a large amount from our parents.*
> **Pour acheter la maison, nous avons dû emprunter une grosse somme à nos parents.**

Note that removal from a container is expressed with **dans** and removal from a flat surface with **sur**. Removal by eating or drinking is expressed similarly.

> *Take a handkerchief from my drawer.*
> **Prends un mouchoir dans mon tiroir.**

> *He took the photograph from the desk and put it into the suitcase.*
> **Il prit la photo sur le bureau et la mit dans la valise.**

eat from a plate	**manger dans une assiette**
drink from a glass	**boire dans un verre**
drink right from the bottle	**boire à même la bouteille**

2. **Origin or source. De** alone is often insufficient to convey the sense of movement expressed by *from* and requires amplification.

> *The planes from Montreal had to be diverted because of the snow.*
> **A cause de la neige, il a fallu détourner tous les avions en provenance de (venant de) Montréal.**

> *I've just had a phone call from you-know-who.*
> **Je viens d'avoir un coup de fil de la part de qui tu sais.**

> *There were people from all countries at the meeting.*
> **Il y avait au congrès des gens venus de tous les pays.**

This sculptor is from Nigeria but he has made his home here.
Ce sculpteur est originaire du Nigeria mais il a fixé sa résidence chez nous.

3. **Time**

Twenty years from now, this will all seem inconsequential.
Dans (D'ici) vingt ans, tout cela semblera sans importance.

She watches over her patients from morning till night.
Elle veille sur ses malades du (depuis le) matin au (jusqu'au) soir.

We'll see each other a week from Thursday.
On se reverra [de] jeudi en huit.

4. Distance from a given place is expressed with **à**.

We are still 30 kilometers from our destination.
Nous sommes encore à 30 kilomètres de notre destination.

5. *From = according to.*

From what I've heard, the killer will soon be caught.

D'après
Selon } **ce que j'ai entendu dire, l'assassin sera bientôt pris.**
A

For other equivalents of *from*, see Section III.F., G., and H.

K. *In*

In addition to the instances of **à, dans,** and **en** treated elsewhere, there are numerous common locutions.

in the future	**à l'avenir**
in the past	**dans (par) le passé**
in January	**en (au mois de) janvier**
in 1936	**en 1936**
in the twentieth century	**au vingtième siècle**
in the distance	**au loin**
in my (your, etc.) place	**à ma (ta, etc.) place**
in my (your, etc.) opinion	**à mon (ton, etc.) avis**
one in (out of) three	**un sur trois**
in a sense	**en (dans) un sens**
in the {*literal* / *figurative*} *sense*	**au sens** {**propre** / **figuré**}
in the Turkish (French, etc.) style	**à la turque (française, etc.)**
in the style of	**à la mode (manière) de**
in a + adjective + way	**d'une façon (manière) + adjective**

in any case	**de toute façon (manière), en tout cas**
in all likelihood	**selon toute probabilité**
in writing	**par écrit**
in ink	**à l'encre**
in pencil	**au crayon**
in time	**à temps**

L. *Of*

There are some instances where the French equivalent is not **de**.

She is thinking of her friend.
Elle pense (songe) à son ami.

It is very kind of you to invite me.
C'est bien aimable de votre part (à vous) de m'inviter.

What has become of him?
Qu'est-il devenu?

M. *On*

Apart from the frequent use of **sur** and of **en** (+ **-ant**), *on* is rendered in various ways.

1. Time

We expect to arrive on Saturday.
Nous comptons arriver samedi.

Most bakeries are closed on Mondays.
La plupart des boulangeries sont fermées le lundi.

They signed the contract on May 20.
Ils ont signé le contrat le 20 mai.

On a day like this, I am not going to set foot out of doors.
Par une journée pareille, je ne mets pas le nez dehors.

on the day of	**le jour de**
on the occasion of	**à, à l'occasion de, lors de**

2. Direction

on this side (in this direction)	**de ce côté**
on the other side of the street	**de l'autre côté de la rue**
on the north (east, etc.) side	**du côté nord (est, etc.)**
on the one hand	**d'une part**
on the other hand	**d'autre part, par contre**

For *right* and *left,* see Section III.J.4. above.

3.   Miscellanea

depend on (upon)	**dépendre de**
wait on	**servir**
work on (at)	**travailler à (sur)**
live on	**vivre de**
have pity on	**avoir pitié de, plaindre**
on purpose	**exprès**
on a trip	**en voyage**
on leave	**en congé**
on vacation	**en vacances**
on the telephone	**au téléphone**
on the radio	**à la radio**
on (the) television	**à la télévision**
on the way	**en chemin, en route, chemin faisant**
on the ceiling	**au plafond**
on the wall	**au mur**
on the contrary	**au contraire**
on time	**à l'heure**

N.   *Out of*

1.   Cause: *par* + abstract noun

He gave in out of weakness.
Il a cédé par faiblesse.

2.   Exhaustion

out of stock (print)	**épuisé**
out of date	**périmé**
out of patience	**à bout de patience**
out of breath	**à bout de souffle, hors d'haleine**
out of order (not working)	**en panne**
out of gas[oline]	**en panne sèche**
out of tune	**faux**

3.   Externality

out of bounds	*hors des limites, hors du jeu* (sports)
out of sight	*hors de vue*
out of danger	*hors de danger, à l'abri du danger*
out of season	*hors de saison*
out of style (fashion)	*démodé*
be out of one's mind (senses)	*avoir perdu la raison (la tête)*

O. *Per*

per year	**par an**
per month	**par mois**
per day	**par jour**
per minute	**par minute**
per hour	**[de] l'heure**
kilometers (miles) per hour	**kilomètres (miles) à l'heure**

P. *To* is expressed not only with **à** (and **en** with countries) but in other ways as well.

The road to glory is long and difficult.
Le chemin de la gloire est long et ardu.

It was announced that the train to Geneva would not leave until midnight.
On a annoncé que le train [à destination] de Genève ne partirait qu'à (ne partirait pas avant) minuit.

He was elected president by a vote of six to three.
Il a été élu président par six voix contre trois.

count to + number	**compter jusqu'à + number**
see s.o. to the door	**accompagner qqn. jusqu'à la porte**
accompany s.o. to his house	**accompagner qqn. jusque chez lui**
defend to the death	**défendre jusqu'à la mort**
be moved to tears	**être ému jusqu'aux larmes**
to the best of my knowledge	**autant que je sache**
to the best of my memory	**autant que je m'en souvienne**

See, too, Section III.D., I., and J.

Q. *Until*

The constructions **ne . . . pas avant** and **ne . . . que** serve to mark the beginning of an action or state: **ne . . . pas jusqu'à** denies that an action or state will last until a certain time.

Where we come from, young people cannot get a driver's license until (before) the age of sixteen.
Chez nous, les jeunes gens ne peuvent pas avoir le permis de conduire avant l'âge de seize ans.

This year, as an exception, courses will not begin until October 1.
Cette année, exceptionnellement, les cours ne reprendront que le Ier octobre.

I've got very little to do today; I don't need to stay at the office until five o'clock.
J'ai très peu à faire aujourd'hui; je n'ai pas besoin de rester au bureau jusqu'à cinq heures.

R. *With* is expressed not only with **avec** but in other ways as well.

1. Characteristic feature. **A** is normal.

a man with black hair	**un homme aux cheveux noirs**
a knife with a silver handle	**un couteau à manche d'argent**

2. **Manner.** No preposition is used in French.

He walked in with a parcel under his arm.
Il est entré un paquet sous le bras.

She was speaking with a cigarette in her mouth and with her head down.
Elle parlait la cigarette à la bouche et la tête baissée.

3. **Instrumentality.** When the instrument of the action is a part or aspect of the person, it is introduced by **de;** when it is a concrete object, other prepositions are used.

He stared at her with a strange look.
Il la fixait d'un air bizarre.

She answered with a trembling voice.
Elle a répondu d'une voix tremblante.

They were struggling with all their might.
Ils luttaient de toutes leurs forces.

An ambidextrous person writes as easily with the left hand as with the right.
L'ambidextre écrit aussi facilement de la main gauche que de la main droite.

How do you expect me to write with this old pen?
Comment voulez-vous que j'écrive avec cette vieille plume?

He was finding it hard to hit the ball back with his new racket.
Il trouvait difficile de renvoyer la balle avec sa nouvelle raquette.

The victim was killed with a hammer.
La victime a été tuée à coups de marteau.

He entered the apartment with a ladder.
Il a pénétré dans l'appartement à l'aide d'une échelle.

4. **Cause**

weep with joy	**pleurer de joie**
tremble with fear	**trembler de peur**
blush with shame	**rougir de honte**

5. Miscellanea

with open arms	**à bras ouverts**
with regret	**à regret**
with a few exceptions	**à part quelques exceptions, à quelques exceptions près**
cover with, be covered with	**couvrir de, être couvert de**
fill with, be filled with	**remplir de, être rempli de**
happy with	**content de**
satisfied with	**satisfait de**
interfere with	**se mêler de**
be angry with	**se fâcher contre**
cope with	**faire face à**
begin with	**commencer par**

I'll be with you in a moment.
Je suis (serai) à vous dans un instant.

V. PREPOSITIONS LINKING ADJECTIVES WITH INFINITIVES

The following list shows the construction with following infinitive of a number of common adjectives and past participles used to describe human beings.

aptc à	*apt to*	habile à	*skillful in*
attentif à	*attentive to*	heureux de	*happy to*
bon à	*good for*	honteux de	*ashamed to*
capable de	*capable of*	impatient de	*impatient to*
certain de	*certain to*	impropre à	*ill-suited to*
confus de	*embarrassed to*	impuissant à	*powerless to*
conscient de	*aware of*	incapable de	*incapable of*
content de	*glad to*	indigne de	*unworthy of*
coupable de	*guilty of*	inquiet de	*worried about*
curieux de	*curious to*	las de	*weary of*
dernier à	*the last to*	lent à	*slow to*
désireux de	*desirous of*	libre de	*free to*
digne de	*worthy to*	long à	*slow to*
disposé à	*disposed to*	mécontent de	*displeased to*
embarrassé de	*hard put to*	obligé de	*obliged to*
enchanté de	*delighted to*	oblieux de	*forgetful of*
enclin à	*inclined to*	premier à	*the first to*
étonné de	*surprised to*	préparé à	*prepared to*
exempt de	*exempt from*	prêt à	*ready to*
expert à	*skilled in*	prompt à	*prompt to*
fâché de	*vexed to*	propre à	*suitable for*
fatigué de	*tired of*	ravi de	*delighted to*
fier de	*proud to*	reconnaissant de	*grateful to*
forcé de	*forced to*	résolu à	*resolved to*

satisfait de	*satisfied to*	surpris de	*surprised to*
seul à	*the only one to*	susceptible de	*apt to*
soucieux de	*concerned to*	tenu de	*obliged to*
stupéfait de	*staggered to*		
sûr de	*sure to*		

VI. PREPOSITIONS LINKING VERBS WITH INFINITIVES

This list also includes verbs which do not require a preposition.

s'abstenir de faire qqch.	*abstain from doing sth.*
accepter de faire qqch.	*accept (agree) to do sth.*
s'accorder (*plural subject*) de/pour faire qqch.	*agree to do sth.*
s'accoutumer à faire qqch.	*get used to doing sth.*
accuser qqn. de faire/d'avoir fait qqch.	*accuse s.o. of doing (having done) sth.*
s'acharner à faire qqch.	*work unceasingly at (persist in) doing sth.*
achever de faire qqch.	*finish doing sth.*
aider qqn. à faire qqch.	*help s.o. to do sth.*
aimer (à) faire qqch.	*like to do sth.*
aimer mieux faire qqch. que de faire autre chose	*prefer doing sth. to doing sth. else*
aller faire qqch.	*go [and] do sth.*
amener qqn. à faire qqch.	*lead s.o. to do sth.*
s'amuser à faire qqch.	*have a good time doing sth.*
s'appliquer à faire qqch.	*apply oneself to doing sth.*
apprendre à faire qqch.	*learn to do sth.*
apprendre à qqn. à faire qqch.	*teach s.o. to do sth.*
(s') arrêter de faire qqch.*	*stop doing sth.*
arriver à faire qqch.	*succeed in doing sth.*
aspirer à faire qqch.	*aspire to do sth.*
s'attacher à faire qqch.	*pay particular attention to (be fussy about) doing sth.*
s'attarder à faire qqch.	*stay late doing sth.*
s'attendre à faire qqch.	*expect to do sth.*
autoriser qqn. à faire qqch.	*authorize s.o. to do sth.*
s'aviser de faire qqch.	*take into one's head to do sth.*
avoir à faire qqch.	*have to do sth.*
avoir beau faire qqch.	*do sth. in vain*

---

*S'arrêter is followed by **pour** when the meaning is *to stop (in order) to do* and by **de** when the meaning is *to stop doing*.

blâmer qqn. de faire/d'avoir fait qqch.	blame s.o. for doing (having done) sth.
se borner à faire qqch.	limit oneself to doing sth.
brûler de faire qqch.	be eager to do sth.
cesser de faire qqch.	stop doing sth.
charger qqn. de faire qqch.	entrust (charge) s.o. with doing sth.
se charger de faire qqch.	take upon oneself (undertake) to do sth.
chercher à faire qqch.	try (seek) to do sth.
choisir de faire qqch.	choose to do sth.
commander à qqn. de faire qqch.	order s.o. to do sth.
commencer à/de faire qqch.★	begin to do sth.
compter faire qqch.	count on doing (intend to do) sth.
conseiller à qqn. de faire qqch.	advise s.o. to do sth.
consentir à faire qqch.	consent to do sth.
consister à faire qqch.	consist in doing sth.
se contenter de faire qqch.	be satisfied with doing sth.
continuer à/de faire qqch.	continue to do sth.
contribuer à faire qqch.	contribute in doing sth.
convenir de faire qqch.	agree upon doing sth.
courir faire qqch.	run and do sth.
craindre de faire qqch.	fear to do (doing) sth.
croire faire qqch.	believe that one is doing sth.
daigner faire qqch.	condescend to do sth.
décider de faire qqch.	decide to do sth.
décider qqn. à faire qqch.	persuade (prevail upon) s.o. to do sth.
se décider à faire qqch.	make up one's mind to do sth.
décourager qqn. de faire qqch.	discourage s.o. from doing sth.
dédaigner de faire qqch.	not deign (not condescend) to do sth.
défendre à qqn. de faire qqch.	forbid s.o. to do sth.
demander à qqn. de faire qqch.	ask s.o. to do sth.
demander à qqn. à faire qqch.	ask s.o. permission to do sth.
se dépêcher de faire qqch.	hurry to do sth.
déplaire (impersonal) à qqn. de faire qqch.	be displeasing to s.o. to do sth.
descendre faire qqch.	go down and do sth.
désespérer de faire qqch.	despair of doing sth.
désirer faire qqch.	want to do sth.
détester de faire qqch.	hate doing sth.
devoir faire qqch.	be obliged to do sth.
se devoir de faire qqch.	owe it to oneself to do sth.
dire à qqn. de faire qqch.	tell s.o. to do sth.

★**Commencer** and **finir** are followed by **par** when the meaning is *to begin/finish by doing.*

dire faire/avoir fait qqch.
say that one does (has done) sth.

dissuader qqn. de faire qqch.
dissuade s.o. from doing sth.

écrire à qqn. de faire qqch.
write to s.o. to do sth.

s'efforcer de faire qqch.
strive (do one's utmost) to do sth.

empêcher qqn. de faire qqch.
prevent s.o. from doing sth.

s'empresser à faire qqch.
show eagerness in doing sth.

s'empresser de faire qqch.
hasten to do sth.

encourager qqn. à faire qqch.
encourage s.o. to do sth.

engager qqn. à faire qqch
hire (enlist, recruit) s.o. to do sth.

s'engager à faire qqch.
undertake (commit oneself) to do sth.

s'ennuyer à/de faire qqch.
be bored doing sth.

enseigner à qqn. à faire qqch.
teach s.o. to do sth.

entendre qqn. faire qqch.
hear s.o. doing sth.

entreprendre de faire qqch.
undertake to do sth.

envoyer qqn. faire qqch.
send s.o. to do sth.

espérer faire qqch.
hope to do sth.

essayer de faire qqch.
try to do sth.

estimer faire qqch.
consider that one is doing sth.

s'étonner de faire qqch.
be surprised to do (at doing) sth.

éviter de faire qqch.
avoid doing sth.

excuser qqn. de faire/d'avoir fait qqch.
excuse s.o. for [from] doing sth.

s'exercer à faire qqch.
practice doing sth.

exhorter qqn. à faire qqch.
exhort (urge) s.o. to do sth.

faillir faire qqch.
just miss doing (almost to do) sth.

faire bien/mieux de faire qqch.
do well (better) to do sth.

falloir (impersonal) faire qqch.
be necessary to do sth.

se fatiguer à faire qqch.
tire oneself out doing sth.

feindre de faire qqch.
pretend to do sth.

féliciter qqn. de faire/d'avoir fait qqch.
congratulate s.o. on doing (having done) sth.

finir de faire qqch.*
finish doing sth.

forcer qqn. à faire qqch.
force s.o. to do sth.

frémir de faire qqch.
tremble (shudder) to do (at doing) sth.

se garder de faire qqch.
take care not to do sth.

s'habituer à faire qqch.
get used to doing sth.

se hâter de faire qqch.
hasten to do sth.

hésiter à faire qqch.
hesitate to do sth.

imaginer de faire qqch.
think (of a way to do sth.)

inciter qqn. à faire qqch.
incite (prompt) s.o. to do sth.

insister pour faire qqch.
insist on doing sth.

interdire à qqn. de faire qqch.
forbid s.o. to do sth.

---

*See note to **commencer**.

inviter qqn. à faire qqch.	*invite s.o. to do sth.*
jurer de faire qqch.	*swear to do sth.*
laisser qqn. faire qqch.	*allow s.o. to do sth.*
manquer à faire qqch.	*fail to do sth.*
manquer [de] faire qqch.	*almost do sth.*
ne pas manquer de faire qqch.	*not fail to do sth.*
méditer de faire qqch.	*be thinking of doing sth.*
se mêler de faire qqch.	*take into one's head to do sth.*
menacer qqn. de faire qqch.	*threaten s.o. with doing sth.*
mériter de faire qqch.	*deserve to do sth.*
se mettre à faire qqch.	*begin to do sth.*
monter faire qqch.	*go up to do sth.*
négliger de faire qqch.	*neglect to do sth.*
nier [de] faire/[d']avoir fait qqch.	*deny doing (having done) sth.*
obliger qqn. à faire qqch.	*oblige s.o. to do sth.*
s'obstiner à faire qqch.	*persist in doing sth.*
obtenir de faire qqch.	*manage (get) to do sth.*
s'occuper à faire qqch.	*be busy doing sth.*
s'occuper de faire qqch.	*be in charge of (concerned with) doing sth.*
s'offrir à faire qqch.	*volunteer to do sth.*
omettre de faire qqch.	*omit doing sth.*
ordonner à qqn. de faire qqch.	*order s.o. to do sth.*
oser faire qqch.	*dare to do sth.*
oublier de faire qqch.	*forget to do sth.*
paraître faire qqch.	*appear to do sth.*
pardonner à qqn. d'avoir fait qqch.	*forgive s.o. for having done sth.*
parler de faire qqch.	*speak about doing sth.*
partir faire qqch.	*to go off [in order] to do sth.*
parvenir à faire qqch.	*succeed in doing sth.*
passer (*time*) à faire qqch.	*spend (time) doing sth.*
penser (à) faire qqch.	*think of doing sth.*
permettre à qqn. de faire qqch.	*allow s.o. to do sth.*
se permettre de faire qqch.	*take the liberty to do sth.*
persévérer à faire qqch.	*persevere in doing sth.*
persister à faire qqch.	*persist in doing sth.*
persuader à qqn. de faire qqch.	*persuade s.o. to do sth.*
se plaindre de faire qqch.	*complain of doing sth.*
plaire (impersonal) à qqn. de faire qqch.	*be agreeable to s.o. to do sth.*
se plaire à faire qqch.	*take pleasure in doing sth.*
pousser qqn. à faire qqch.	*urge s.o. to do sth.*
pouvoir faire qqch.	*be able to do sth.*
préférer faire qqch. que de faire autre chose	*prefer to do sth. rather than to do sth. else*

se préparer à faire qqch.	*prepare to do sth.*
prétendre faire qqch.	*claim to do sth.*
prier qqn. de faire qqch.	*ask s.o. to do sth.*
projeter de faire qqch.	*plan to do sth.*
promettre à qqn. de faire qqch.	*promise s.o. to do sth.*
proposer à qqn. de faire qqch.	*propose (suggest) to s.o. to do sth.*
se proposer de faire qqch.	*intend to do sth.*
provoquer qqn. à faire qqch.	*incite s.o. to do sth.*
se rappeler de faire qqch.	*remember to do sth.*
se rappeler avoir fait qqch.	*recall having done (doing) sth.*
recommander à qqn. de faire qqch.	*advise s.o. to do sth.*
redouter de faire qqch.	*dread (fear) doing sth.*
réduire qqn. à faire qqch.	*compel (reduce) s.o. to do sth.*
refuser de faire qqch.	*refuse to do sth.*
se refuser à faire qqch.	*decline (refuse) to do sth.*
regarder qqn. faire qqch.	*look at s.o. doing sth.*
regretter de faire/d'avoir fait qqch.	*regret doing (having done) sth.*
se réjouir de faire qqch.	*rejoice (be glad) at doing sth.*
remercier qqn. de faire/d'avoir fait qqch.	*thank s.o. for doing (having done) sth.*
se remettre à faire qqch.	*start doing sth. again*
renoncer à faire qqch.	*give up doing sth.*
rentrer faire qqch.	*go back [home] to do sth.*
se repentir d'avoir fait qqch.	*repent (rue) having done sth.*
reprocher à qqn. de faire/d'avoir fait qqch.	*reproach s.o. for doing (having done) sth.*
répugner à faire qqch.	*feel repugnance at doing sth.*
se résigner à faire qqch.	*resign oneself to doing sth.*
résoudre de faire qqch.	*decide to (resolve on) doing sth.*
se résoudre à faire qqch.	*make up one's mind to do sth.*
rester [à] faire qqch.	*remain [in order] to do sth.*
rester (impersonal) à qqn. à faire qqch.	*remain to s.o. to do sth.*
retourner faire qqch.	*go back [in order] to do sth.*
réussir à faire qqch.	*succeed in doing sth.*
revenir faire qqch.	*come back to do sth.*
rêver de faire qqch.	*dream of doing sth.*
rire de faire qqch.	*laugh at doing sth.*
risquer de faire qqch.	*risk doing sth.*
rougir de faire qqch.	*blush at doing sth.*
savoir faire qqch.	*know how to do sth.*
sentir qqn. faire qqch.	*be aware of s.o. doing sth.*
servir à faire qqch.	*be useful for doing sth.*
songer à faire qqch.	*think of doing sth.*

sortir faire qqch.	*go out to do sth.*
souhaiter [de] faire qqch.	*want (wish) to do sth.*
soupçonner qqn. de faire/d'avoir fait qqch.	*suspect s.o. of doing (having done) sth.*
se souvenir d'avoir fait qqch.	*remember having done sth.*
suffire à/pour faire qqch.	*be enough to do sth.*
suffire (impersonal) à qqn. de faire qqch.	*be sufficient for s.o. to do sth.*
suggérer à qqn. de faire qqch.	*suggest to s.o. to do sth.*
supplier qqn. de faire qqch.	*beg s.o. to do sth.*
supporter de faire qqch.	*stand to do (doing) sth.*
surprendre qqn. à faire qqch.	*surprise s.o. doing (at doing) sth.*
tâcher de faire qqch.	*try to do sth.*
tarder à faire qqch.	*put off (be slow in) doing sth.*
tarder (impersonal) à qqn. de faire qqch.	*long to do sth.*
téléphoner à qqn. de faire qqch.	*telephone s.o. to do sth.*
tenir à faire qqch.	*be bent on doing sth.*
travailler à faire qqch.	*work to do sth.*
trembler de faire qqch.	*tremble at doing sth.*
trouver + adjective + de faire qqch.★	*find it + adjective + to do sth.*
valoir mieux faire qqch. que de faire autre chose	*be better to do sth. than) do sth. else*
se vanter de faire qqch.	*boast of doing sth.*
veiller à faire qqch.	*be careful to do sth.*
venir faire qqch.	*come to do sth.*
venir à faire qqch.	*happen to do sth.*
venir de faire qqch.	*have just done sth.*
viser à faire qqch.	*aspire to do (aim at doing) sth.*
voir qqn. faire qqch.	*see s.o. doing sth.*
vouloir faire qqch.	*want to do sth.*

★**Trouver possible**, etc., **de faire** is an abbreviated form of **trouver qu'il est possible**, etc., **de faire**; it is a means of combining in a single clause a verb of opinion and an impersonal expression. Note that in the English translation of this infinitive construction the pronoun *it* is necessarily used to anticipate the infinitive: *to find/think it possible to* . . . . Other verbs used in the same way: **croire, estimer, juger, considérer (comme)**.

Appendix

1

Regular Verbs

This table provides a complete conjugation of the active voice of a typical verb from each of the regular groups whose infinitives end in **-er** (Section I.A.), **-ir** (**-iss-**) (Section II.), or **-re** (Section III.). For the **-er** verb there is also a conjugation of the passive voice (Section I.B.) and of a pronominal verb (Section I.C.).

I. **-er** verbs: *flatter*

A. Active voice

Infinitives

Present: flatter   *Past:* avoir flatté

Participles

Present: flattant   *Perfect:* ayant flatté
Past: flatté

Indicative

Present	Passé composé
je flatte	j' ai flatté
tu flattes	tu as flatté
elle flatte	elle a flatté
nous flattons	nous avons flatté
vous flattez	vous avez flatté
elles flattent	elles ont flatté

Imperfect	Pluperfect
je flattais	j' avais flatté
tu flattais	tu avais flatté
il flattait	il avait flatté
nous flattions	nous avions flatté
vous flattiez	vous aviez flatté
ils flattaient	ils avaient flatté

Passé simple   *Passé antérieur*

   je flattai   j' eus flatté
   tu flattas   tu eus flatté
   on flatta   on eut flatté
nous flattâmes   nous eûmes flatté
vous flattâtes   vous eûtes flatté
elles flattèrent   ils eurent flatté

Future   *Future perfect*

   je flatterai   j' aurai flatté
   tu flatteras   tu auras flatté
   il flattera   elle aura flatté
nous flatterons   nous aurons flatté
vous flatterez   vous aurez flatté
elles flatteront   ils auront flatté

Imperative

flatte   flattons   flattez

Conditional

Present   *Past*

   je flatterais   j' aurais flatté
   tu flatterais   tu aurais flatté
elle flatterait   on aurait flatté
nous flatterions   nous aurions flatté
vous flatteriez   vous auriez flatté
   ils flatteraient   elles auraient flatté

Subjunctive

Present   *Past*

   je flatte   j' aie flatté
   tu flattes   tu aies flatté
   il flatte   elle ait flatté
nous flattions   nous ayons flatté
vous flattiez   vous ayez flatté
elles flattent   ils aient flatté

Imperfect   *Pluperfect*

   je flattasse   j' eusse flatte
   tu flattasses   tu eusses flatté
   on flattât   il eût flatté
nous flattassions   nous eussions flatté
vous flattassiez   vous eussiez flatté
   ils flattassent   elles eussent flatté

B. Passive voice

Infinitives

Present: être flatté(e)(s)   *Past:* avoir été flatté(e)(s)

Participles

Present: étant flatté(e)(s)   *Perfect:* ayant été flatté(e)(s)
Past: été flatté(e)(s)

Indicative

Present	*Passé composé*
je suis flatté(e)	j' ai été flatté(e)
tu es flatté(e)	tu as été flatté(e)
il est flatté	elle a été flattée
nous sommes flatté(e)s	nous avons été flatté(e)s
vous êtes flatté(e)(s)	vous avez été flatté(e)(s)
elles sont flattées	ils ont été flattés

Imperfect	*Pluperfect*
j' étais flatté(e)	j' avais été flatté(e)
tu étais flatté(e)	tu avais été flatté(e)
elle était flattée	on avait été flatté
nous étions flatté(e)s	nous avions été flatté(e)s
vous étiez flatté(e)(s)	vous aviez été flatté(e)(s)
ils étaient flattés	elles avaient été flattées

Passé simple	*Passé antérieur*
je fus flatté(e)	j' eus été flatté(e)
tu fus flatté(e)	tu eus été flatté(e)
elle fut flattée	il eut été flatté
nous fûmes flatté(e)s	nous eûmes été flatté(e)s
vous fûtes flatté(e)(s)	vous eûtes été flatté(e)(s)
elles furent flattées	ils eurent été flattés

Future	*Future perfect*
je serai flatté(e)	j' aurai été flatté(e)
tu seras flatté(e)	tu auras été flatté(e)
on sera flatté	elle aura été flattée
nous serons flatté(e)s	nous aurons été flatté(e)s
vous serez flatté(e)(s)	vous aurez été flatté(e)(s)
ils seront flattés	elles auront été flattées

Imperative

sois flatté(e)   soyons flatté(e)s   soyez flatté(e)(s)

Conditional

Present	*Past*
je serais flatté(e)	j' aurais été flatté(e)
tu serais flatté(e)	tu aurais été flatté(e)
il serait flatté	elle aurait été flattée
nous serions flatté(e)s	nous aurions été flatté(e)s
vous seriez flatté(e)(s)	vous auriez été flatté(e)(s)
elles seraient flattées	ils auraient été flattés

Subjunctive

Present	*Past*
je sois flatté(e)	j' aie été flatté(e)
tu sois flatté(e)	tu aies été flatté(e)
on soit flatté	elle ait été flattée
nous soyons flatté(e)s	nous ayons été flatté(e)s
vous soyez flatté(e)(s)	vous ayez été flatté(e)(s)
elles soient flattées	ils aient été flattés

Imperfect	*Pluperfect*
je fusse flatté(e)	j' eusse été flatté(e)
tu fusses flatté(e)	tu eusses été flatté(e)
elle fût flattée	il eût été flatté
nous fussions flatté(e)s	nous eussions été flatté(e)s
vous fussiez flatté(e)(s)	vous eussiez été flatté(e)(s)
ils fussent flattées	elles eussent été flattées

C.   Pronominal verb: **se flatter**

Infinitives

Present: se flatter   *Past:* s'être flatté(e)(s)

Participles

Present: se flattant   *Perfect:* s'étant flatté(e)(s)
Past: flatté

Indicative

Present	*Passé composé*
je me flatte	je me suis flatté(e)
tu te flattes	tu t'es flatté(e)
on se flatte	elle s'est flattée
nous nous flattons	nous nous sommes flatté(e)s
vous vous flattez	vous vous êtes flatté(e)(s)
elles se flattent	ils se sont flattés

Imperfect	*Pluperfect*
je me flattais	je m'étais flatté(e)
tu te flattais	tu t'étais flatté(e)
elle se flattait	il s'était flatté
nous nous flattions	nous nous étions flatté(e)s
vous vous flattiez	vous vous étiez flatté(e)(s)
ils se flattaient	elles s'étaient flattées

Passé simple	*Passé antérieur*
je me flattai	je me fus flatté(e)
tu te flattas	tu te fus flatté(e)
il se flatta	elle se fut flattée
nous nous flattâmes	nous nous fûmes flatté(e)s
vous vous flattâtes	vous vous fûtes flatté(e)(s)
ils se flattèrent	elles se furent flattées

Future	*Future perfect*
je me flatterai	je me serai flatté(e)
tu te flatteras	tu te seras flatté(e)
on se flattera	elle se sera flattée
nous nous flatterons	nous nous serons flatté(e)s
vous vous flatterez	vous vous serez flatté(e)(s)
elles se flatteront	ils se seront flattés

Imperative

flatte-toi   flattons-nous   flattez-vous

Conditional

Present	*Past*
je me flatterais	je me serais flatté(e)
tu te flatterais	tu te serais flatté(e)
elle se flatterait	il se serait flatté
nous nous flatterions	nous nous serions flatté(e)s
vous vous flatteriez	vous vous seriez flatté(e)(s)
ils se flatteraient	elles se seraient flattées

Subjunctive

Present	*Past*
je me flatte	je me sois flatté(e)
tu te flattes	tu te sois flatté(e)
il se flatte	elle se soit flattée
nous nous flattions	nous nous soyons flatté(e)s
vous vous flattiez	vous vous soyez flatté(e)(s)
elles se flattent	ils se soient flattés

Imperfect	*Pluperfect*
je me flattasse	je me fusse flatté(e)
tu te flattasses	tu te fusses flatté(e)
il se flattât	elle se fût flattée
nous nous flattassions	nous nous fussions flatté(e)s
vous vous flattassiez	vous vous fussiez flatté(e)(s)
elles se flattassent	ils se fussent flattés

II. *-ir (-iss-)* verbs: *finir*

Infinitives

Present: finir   *Past:* avoir fini

Participles

Present: finissant   *Perfect:* ayant fini
Past: fini

Indicative

Present	*Passé composé*
je finis	j' ai fini
tu finis	tu as fini
elle finit	on a fini
nous finissons	nous avons fini
vous finissez	vous avez fini
ils finissent	elles ont fini

Imperfect	*Pluperfect*
je finissais	j' avais fini
tu finissais	tu avais fini
il finissait	elle avait fini
nous finissions	nous avions fini
vous finissiez	vous aviez fini
elles finissaient	ils avaient fini

Passé simple	*Passé antérieur*
je finis	j' eus fini
tu finis	tu eus fini
elle finit	il eut fini
nous finîmes	nous eûmes fini
vous finîtes	vous eûtes fini
ils finirent	elles eurent fini

Future   *Future perfect*

    je finirai   j' aurai fini
    tu finiras   tu auras fini
    il finira   elle aura fini
  nous finirons   nous aurons fini
  vous finirez   vous aurez fini
  elles finiront   ils auront fini

Imperative

finis   finissons   finissez

Conditional

Present   *Past*

    je finirais   j' aurais fini
    tu finirais   tu aurais fini
  elle finirait   on aurait fini
  nous finirions   nous aurions fini
  vous finiriez   vous auriez fini
    ils finiraient   elles auraient fini

Subjunctive

Present   *Past*

    je finisse   j' aie fini
    tu finisses   tu aies fini
    il finisse   elle ait fini
  nous finissions   nous ayons fini
  vous finissiez   vous ayez fini
  elles finissent   ils aient fini

Imperfect   *Pluperfect*

    je finisse   j' eusse fini
    tu finisses   tu eusses fini
  elle finît   il eût fini
  nous finissions   nous eussions fini
  vous finissiez   vous eussiez fini
    ils finissent   elles eussent fini

III. *-re* **verbs:** *rendre*

Infinitives

Present: rendre   *Past:* avoir rendu

Participles

Present: rendant   *Perfect:* ayant rendu
Past: rendu

Indicative

Present	*Passé composé*
je rends	j' ai rendu
tu rends	tu as rendu
elle rend	il a rendu
nous rendons	nous avons rendu
vous rendez	vous avez rendu
ils rendent	elles ont rendu

Imperfect	*Pluperfect*
je rendais	j' avais rendu
tu rendais	tu avais rendu
on rendait	elle avait rendu
nous rendions	nous avions rendu
vous rendiez	vous aviez rendu
elles rendaient	ils avaient rendu

Passé simple	*Passé antérieur*
je rendis	j' eus rendu
tu rendis	tu eus rendu
elle rendit	il eut rendu
nous rendîmes	nous eûmes rendu
vous rendîtes	vous eûtes rendu
ils rendirent	elles eurent rendu

Future	*Future perfect*
je rendrai	j' aurai rendu
tu rendras	tu auras rendu
il rendra	elle aura rendu
nous rendrons	nous aurons rendu
vous rendrez	vous aurez rendu
elles rendront	ils auront rendu

Imperative

rends   rendons   rendez

Conditional

Present	*Past*
je rendrais	j' aurais rendu
tu rendrais	tu aurais rendu
elle rendrait	on aurait rendu
nous rendrions	nous aurions rendu
vous rendriez	vous auriez rendu
ils rendraient	elles auraient rendu

Subjunctive

Present   Past

    je rende   j' aie rendu
    tu rendes   tu aies rendu
    il rende   elle ait rendu
 nous rendions   nous ayons rendu
 vous rendiez   vous ayez rendu
 elles rendent   ils aient rendu

Imperfect   Pluperfect

    je rendisse   j' eusse rendu
    tu rendisses   tu eusses rendu
   elle rendît   on eût rendu
 nous rendissions   nous eussions rendu
 vous rendissiez   vous eussiez rendu
  ils rendissent   elles eussent rendu

Appendix

2

Orthographically Changing Verbs

Verbs exhibiting orthographical changes fall into the following groups.

1. Verbs in -é + consonant(s) + -er

Verbs whose stem ends in é followed by one or more consonants change that é to è in the singular and third person plural of the present indicative and the present subjunctive, as well as in the singular imperative.

espérer—j'espère, tu espères, il espère, elles espèrent, etc.
régler—je règle, tu règles, elle règle, ils règlent, etc.

Note that verbs that end in **-éer** maintain é throughout all persons and tenses.

créer—je crée, tu crées, il crée, etc.

2. Verbs in -e + consonant + -er

a. Verbs whose infinitive ends in **-eler** or **-eter** normally double the **-l-** or the **-t-** before a mute **e,** that is, in the singular and third person plural of the present indicative and present subjunctive, the singular imperative, and all persons and numbers of the future and conditional.

appeler—j'appelle, tu appelles, nous appellerons, on appellerait, etc.
jeter—je jette, tu jettes, vous jetterez, ils jetteraient, etc.

Contrast: nous appelons, ils appelaient, etc.
vous jetez, elle jetait, etc.

Some verbs in **-eler** and **-eter** change the final **-e-** of the stem to è instead of doubling the l or t.

acheter—j'achète, tu achètes, nous achèterons, on achèterait, etc.
peler—je pèle, tu pèles, vous pèlerez, ils pèleraient, etc.

In addition to **acheter** and **peler,** some other verbs which show this change are: **celer, ciseler, congeler, crocheter, dégeler, démanteler, geler, haleter, harceler, modeler.**

b.   All other verbs ending in **-e** + consonant + **er** change the final **-e-** of the stem to **è** in the same instances as above.

peser—je pèse, tu pèses, on pèsera, elle pèserait, etc.
lever—on lève, tu lèves, je lèverai, on lèverait, etc.

3. Verbs in *-yer*

a.   Verbs whose infinitive ends in **-oyer** or **-uyer** change **y** to **i** before mute **e**. This occurs in the singular and third person plural of the present indicative and present subjunctive, the singular imperative, and all persons and numbers of the conditional and future.

nettoyer—je nettoie, il nettoiera, on nettoierait, etc.
essuyer—tu essuies, on essuiera, nous essuierons, etc.

b.   Verbs in **-ayer** may retain the **y** or change **y** to **i** before mute **e**.

essayer—j'essaie *or* j'essaye, nous essaierons *or* nous essayerons, etc.

4. Verbs in *-cer* or *-ger*

Verbs whose infinitive ends in **-cer** or **-ger** change **c** to **ç** or **g** to **ge** before endings that begin with **-a** or **-o**.

placer—je place/je plaçais, vous placez/nous plaçons, tu places/tu plaças, etc.
manger—je mange/je mangeais, vous mangez/nous mangeons, tu manges/tu mangeas, etc.

Note, too, that verbs in **-cevoir** change **c** to **ç** before endings which begin with **-o** or **-u**.

recevoir—nous recevons/je reçois, tu recevais/tu reçus, etc.

Appendix
3

Irregular Verbs

For **avoir** and **être,** complete conjugations are provided. For other verbs, the infinitive, the present and past participles, and the first person singular of the future and the **passé simple** are given. It is assumed that the present subjunctive and imperfect indicative are derived from the present participle, the imperative from the present indicative, and the imperfect subjunctive from the **passé simple.** When this is not the case, the irregular forms are listed. For defective verbs, the missing forms are indicated.

1. avoir

Infinitives

Present: avoir   *Past:* avoir eu

Participles

Present: ayant   *Perfect:* ayant eu
Past: eu

Indicative

Present		*Passé composé*	
j'	ai	j'	ai eu
tu	as	tu	as eu
elle	a	on	a eu
nous	avons	nous	avons eu
vous	avez	vous	avez eu
ils	ont	elles	ont eu

Imperfect		*Pluperfect*	
j'	avais	j'	avais eu
tu	avais	tu	avais eu
on	avait	il	avait eu
nous	avions	nous	avions eu
vous	aviez	vous	aviez eu
elles	avaient	elles	avaient eu

Passé simple	*Passé antérieur*
j' eus	j' eus eu
tu eus	tu eus eu
elle eut	il eut eu
nous eûmes	nous eûmes eu
vous eûtes	vous eûtes eu
ils eurent	elles eurent eu

Future	*Future perfect*
j' aurai	j' aurai eu
tu auras	tu auras eu
il aura	elle aura eu
nous aurons	nous aurons eu
vous aurez	vous aurez eu
elles auront	ils auront eu

Imperative

aie   ayons   ayez

Conditional

Present	*Past*
j' aurais	j' aurais eu
tu aurais	tu aurais eu
elle aurait	on aurait eu
nous aurions	nous aurions eu
vous auriez	vous auriez eu
elles auraient	ils auraient eu

Subjunctive

Present	*Past*
j' aie	j' aie eu
tu aies	tu aies eu
elle ait	il ait eu
nous ayons	nous ayons eu
vous ayez	vous ayez eu
ils aient	elles aient eu

Imperfect	*Pluperfect*
j' eusse	j' eusse eu
tu eusses	tu eusses eu
il eût	elle eût eu
nous eussions	nous eussions eu
vous eussiez	vous eussiez eu
elles eussent	ils eussent eu

2. **être**

Infinitives

Present: être   *Past:* avoir été

Participles

Present: étant   *Perfect:* ayant été
Past: été

Indicative

Present		*Passé composé*	
je	suis	j'	ai été
tu	es	tu	as été
elle	est	il	a été
nous	sommes	nous	avons été
vous	êtes	vous	avez été
elles	sont	ils	ont été

Imperfect		*Pluperfect*	
j'	étais	j'	avais été
tu	étais	tu	avais été
il	était	elle	avait été
nous	étions	nous	avions été
vous	étiez	vous	aviez été
elles	étaient	ils	avaient été

Passé simple		*Passé antérieur*	
je	fus	j'	eus été
tu	fus	tu	eus été
elle	fut	on	eut été
nous	fûmes	nous	eûmes été
vous	fûtes	vous	eûtes été
ils	furent	elles	eurent été

Future		*Future perfect*	
je	serai	j'	aurai été
tu	seras	tu	auras été
elle	sera	on	aura été
nous	serons	nous	aurons été
vous	serez	vous	aurez été
ils	seront	elles	auront été

Imperative

sois   soyons   soyez

Conditional

Present		*Past*	
je	serais	j'	aurais été
tu	serais	tu	aurais été
il	serait	elle	aurait été
nous	serions	nous	aurions été
vous	seriez	vous	auriez été
elles	seraient	ils	auraient été

Subjunctive

Present		*Past*	
je	sois	j'	aie été
tu	sois	tu	aies été
elle	soit	il	ait été
nous	soyons	nous	ayons été
vous	soyez	vous	ayez été
ils	soient	elles	aient été

Imperfect		*Pluperfect*	
je	fusse	j'	eusse été
tu	fusses	tu	eusses été
il	fût	elle	eût été
nous	fussions	nous	eussions été
vous	fussiez	vous	eussiez été
elles	fussent	ils	eussent été

3. **absoudre**

> *pr.part.:* absolvant
> *pt.part.:* absous, absoute
> *fut.:* absoudrai
> *pr.ind.:* absous, absous, absout, absolvons, absolvez, absolvent

Note: no **passé simple,** no imperfect subjunctive.

4. **accueillir.** See **cueillir** (Section 35).

5. **acquérir**

> *pr.part.:* acquérant
> *pt.part.:* acquis
> *fut.:* acquerrai
> *p.s.:* acquis
> *pr.ind.:* acquiers, acquiers, acquiert, acquérons, acquérez, acquièrent
> *pr.subj.:* acquière, acquières, acquière, acquérions, acquériez, acquièrent

6. **admettre.** See **mettre** (Section 67).

7. **aller**

   pr.part.: allant
   pt.part.: allé
   fut.: irai
   p.s.: allai
   pr.ind.: vais, vas, va, allons, allez, vont
   pr.subj.: aille, ailles, aille, allions, alliez, aillent

8. **apparaître.** See **connaître** (Section 22).

9. **appartenir.** See **tenir** (Section 114).

10. **apprendre.** See **prendre** (Section 87).

11. **assaillir.** Like **couvrir** (Section 31) except: *pt.part.* = **assailli.**

12. **asseoir**

   pr.part.: asseyant
   pt.part.: assis
   fut.: assiérai *or* assoirai
   p.s.: assis
   pr.ind.: assieds, assieds, assied, asseyons, asseyez, asseyent *or* assois, as-
      sois, assoit, assoyons, assoyez, assoient
   pr.subj.: asseye, asseyes, asseye, asseyions, asseyiez, asseyent *or* assoie,
      assoies, assoie, assoyions, assoyiez, assoient
   impf.: asseyais, asseyais, asseyait, asseyions, asseyiez, asseyaient *or* as-
      soyais, assoyais, assoyait, assoyions, assoyiez, assoyaient

13. **battre**

   pr.part.: battant
   pt.part.: battu
   fut.: battrai
   p.s.: battis
   pr.ind.: bats, bats, bat, battons, battez, battent

14. **boire**

   pr.part.: buvant
   pt.part.: bu
   fut.: boirai
   p.s.: bus
   pr.ind.: bois, bois, boit, buvons, buvez, boivent
   pr.subj.: boive, boives, boive, buvions, buviez, boivent

15. **bouillir**

   pr.part.: bouillant
   pt.part.: bouilli
   fut.: bouillirai

p.s.: bouillis
pr.ind.: bous, bous, bout, bouillons, bouillez, bouillent

16. **choir.** Like **déchoir** (Section 37) except that there are no present indicative plural forms.

17. **commettre.** See **mettre** (Section 67).

18. **comprendre.** See **prendre** (Section 87).

19. **conclure**

pr.part.: concluant
pt.part.: conclu
fut.: conclurai
p.s.: conclus
pr.ind.: conclus, conclus, conclut, concluons, concluez, concluent

20. **conduire**

pr.part.: conduisant
pt.part.: conduit
fut.: conduirai
p.s.: conduisis
pr.ind.: conduis, conduis, conduit, conduisons, conduisez, conduisent

21. **confire.** Like **conduire** (Section 20) except: *p.s.* = **confis.**

22. **connaître**

pr.part.: connaissant
pt.part.: connu
fut.: connaîtrai
p.s.: connus
pr.ind.: connais, connais, connaît, connaissons, connaissez, connaissent

23. **conquérir.** See **acquérir** (Section 5).

24. **construire.** See **conduire** (Section 20).

25. **contenir.** See **tenir** (Section 114).

26. **contredire.** Like **dire** (Section 44) except: *pr. ind. 2nd pl.* = **vous contredisez.**

27. **convenir.** See **tenir** (Section 114).

28. **convaincre.** See **vaincre** (Section 116).

29. **coudre**

pr.part.: cousant
pt.part.: cousu
fut.: coudrai

p.s.: cousis
pr.ind.: couds, couds, coud, cousons, cousez, cousent

30. **courir**

pr.part.: courant
pt.part.: couru
fut.: courrai
p.s.: courus
pr.ind.: cours, cours, court, courons, courez, courent

31. **couvrir**

pr.part.: couvrant
pt.part.: couvert
fut.: couvrirai
p.s.: couvris
pr.ind.: couvre, couvres, couvre, couvrons, couvrez, couvrent

32. **craindre**

pr.part.: craignant
pt.part.: craint
fut.: craindrai
p.s.: craignis
pr.ind.: crains, crains, craint, craignons, craignez, craignent

33. **croire**

pr.part.: croyant
pt.part.: cru
fut.: croirai
p.s.: crus
pr.ind.: crois, crois, croit, croyons, croyez, croient
pr.subj.: croie, croies, croie, croyions, croyiez, croient

34. **croître**

pr.part.: croissant
pt.part.: crû
fut.: croîtrai
p.s.: crûs
pr.ind.: croîs, croîs, croît, croissons, croissez, croissent

35. **cueillir.** Like **couvrir** (Section 31) except: *pt.part.* = **cueilli** and *fut.* = **cueillerai.**

36. **cuire.** See **conduire** (Section 20).

37. **déchoir**

pr.part.: none

pt.part.: déchu
fut.: déchoirai *or* décherrai
pr.ind.: déchois, déchois, déchoit *or* déchet, déchoyons, déchoyez, dé-
  choient

Note: no imperfect indicative.

38. **découvrir.** See **couvrir** (Section 31).

39. **décrire.** See **écrire** (Section 47).

40. **déplaire.** See **plaire** (Section 82).

41. **détruire.** See **conduire** (Section 20).

42. **devenir.** See **venir** (Section 118).

43. **devoir**

  pr.part.: devant
  pt.part.: dû, due, dus, dues
  fut.: devrai
  p.s.: dus
  pr.ind.: dois, dois, doit, devons, devez, doivent
  pr.subj.: doive, doives, doive, devions, deviez, doivent

44. **dire**

  pr.part.: disant
  pt.part.: dit
  fut.: dirai
  p.s.: dis
  pr.ind.: dis, dis, dit, disons, dites, disent

45. **disparaître.** See **connaître** (Section 22).

46. **dormir**

  pr.part.: dormant
  pt.part.: dormi
  fut.: dormirai
  p.s.: dormis
  pr.ind.: dors, dors, dort, dormons, dormez, dorment

47. **écrire**

  pr.part.: écrivant
  pt.part.: écrit
  fut.: écrirai
  p.s.: écrivis
  pr.ind.: écris, écris, écrit, écrivons, écrivez, écrivent

48. **s'endormir.** See **dormir** (Section 46).

49. élire. See **lire** (Section 62).

50. s'enfuir. See **fuir** (Section 56).

51. envoyer

> *pr.part.:* envoyant
> *pt.part.:* envoyé
> *fut.:* enverrai
> *p.s.:* envoyai
> *pr.ind.:* envoie, envoies, envoie, envoyons, envoyez, envoient
> *pr.subj.:* envoie, envoies, envoie, envoyions, envoyiez, envoient

52. éteindre. See **craindre** (Section 32).

53. faillir

> *pr.part.:* faillant
> *pt.part.:* failli
> *fut.:* faudrai *or* faillirai
> *p.s.:* faillis
> *pr.ind.:* faux, faux, faut, faillons, faillez, faillent

54. faire

> *pr.part.:* faisant
> *pt.part.:* fait
> *fut.:* ferai
> *p.s.:* fis
> *pr.ind.:* fais, fais, fait, faisons, faites, font
> *pr.subj.:* fasse, fasses, fasse, fassions, fassiez, fassent

55. falloir

> *pr.part.: none*
> *pt.part.:* fallu
> *fut.:* faudra
> *p.s.:* fallut
> *pr.ind.:* il faut
> *pr.subj.:* il faille

Note: used only in third person singular.

56. fuir

> *pr.part.:* fuyant
> *pt.part.:* fui
> *fut.:* fuirai
> *p.s.:* fuis
> *pr.ind.:* fuis, fuis, fuit, fuyons, fuyez, fuient
> *pr.subj.:* fuie, fuies, fuie, fuyions, fuyiez, fuient

57. **haïr**

   pr.part.: haïssant
   pt.part.: haï
   fut.: haïrai
   p.s.: haïs, haïs, haït, haïmes, haïtes, haïrent
   pr.ind.: hais, hais, hait, haïssons, haïssez, haïssent

58. **inscrire.** See **écrire** (Section 47).

59. **instruire.** See **conduire** (Section 20).

60. **interdire.** See **contredire** (Section 26).

61. **joindre.** See **craindre** (Section 32).

62. **lire**

   pr.part.: lisant
   pt.part.: lu
   fut.: lirai
   p.s.: lus
   pr.ind.: lis, lis, lit, lisons, lisez, lisent

63. **maintenir.** See **tenir** (Section 114).

64. **maudire**

   pr.part.: maudissant
   pt.part.: maudit
   fut.: maudirai
   p.s.: maudis
   pr.ind.: maudis, maudis, maudit, maudissons, maudissez, maudissent

65. **médire.** See **contredire** (Section 26).

66. **mentir.** See **dormir** (Section 46).

67. **mettre**

   pr.part.: mettant
   pt.part.: mis
   fut.: mettrai
   p.s.: mis
   pr.ind.: mets, mets, met, mettons, mettez, mettent

68. **moudre**

   pr.part.: moulant
   pt.part.: moulu
   fut.: moudrai
   p.s.: moulus
   pr.ind.: mouds, mouds, moud, moulons, moulez, moulent

69. **mourir**

   pr.part.: mourant
   pt.part.: mort
   fut.: mourrai
   p.s.: mourus
   pr.ind.: meurs, meurs, meurt, mourons, mourez, meurent
   pr.subj.: meure, meures, meure, mourions, mouriez, meurent

70. **mouvoir**

   pr.part.: mouvant
   pt.part.: mû, mue, mus, mues
   fut.: mouvrai
   p.s.: mus
   pr.ind.: meus, meus, meut, mouvons, mouvez, meuvent
   pr.subj.: meuve, meuves, meuve, mouvions, mouviez, meuvent

71. **naître**

   pr.part.: naissant
   pt.part.: né
   fut.: naîtrai
   p.s.: naquis
   pr.ind.: nais, nais, naît, naissons, naissez, naissent

72. **nuire.** Like **conduire** (Section 20) except: *pt.part.* = **nui**

73. **offrir.** See **couvrir** (Section 31).

74. **omettre.** See **mettre** (Section 67).

75. **ouvrir.** See **couvrir** (Section 31).

76. **paraître.** See **connaître** (Section 22).

77. **parcourir.** See **courir** (Section 30).

78. **partir.** See **dormir** (Section 46).

79. **parvenir.** See **venir** (Section 118).

80. **peindre.** See **craindre** (Section 32).

81. **permettre.** See **mettre** (Section 67).

82. **plaire**

   pr.part.: plaisant
   pt.part.: plu
   fut.: plairai
   p.s.: plus
   pr.ind.: plais, plais, plaît, plaisons, plaisez, plaisent

83. **pleuvoir**

pr.part.: pleuvant
pt.part.: plu
fut.: pleuvra
p.s.: plut
pr.ind.: il pleut

Note: used only in the third person singular.

84. **pourvoir**

pr.part.: pourvoyant
pt.part.: pourvu
fut.: pourvoirai
p.s.: pourvus
pr.ind.: pourvois, pourvois, pourvoit, pourvoyons, pourvoyez, pour-
   voient
pr.subj.: pourvoie, pourvoies, pourvoie, pourvoyions, pourvoyiez, pour-
   voient

85. **pouvoir**

pr.part.: pouvant
pt.part.: pu
fut.: pourrai
p.s.: pus
pr.ind.: peux, peux, peut, pouvons, pouvez, peuvent
pr.subj.: puisse, puisses, puisse, puissions, puissiez, puissent

Note: no imperative.

86. **prédire.** See **contredire** (Section 26).

87. **prendre**

pr.part.: prenant
pt.part.: pris
fut.: prendrai
p.s.: pris
pr.ind.: prends, prends, prend, prenons, prenez, prennent
pr.subj.: prenne, prennes, prenne, prenions, preniez, prennent

88. **préscrire.** See **écrire** (Section 47).

89. **prévenir.** See **tenir** (Section 114).

90. **prévoir.** Like **voir** (Section 121) except: *fut.* = **prevoirai.**

91. **promettre.** See **mettre** (Section 67).

92. **recevoir**

> *pr.part.:* recevant
> *pt.part.:* reçu
> *fut.:* recevrai
> *p.s.:* reçus
> *pr.ind.:* reçois, reçois, reçoit, recevons, recevez, reçoivent
> *pr.subj.:* reçoive, reçoives, reçoive, recevions, receviez, reçoivent

93. **reconnaître.** See **connaître** (Section 22).

94. **recouvrir.** See **couvrir** (Section 31).

95. **réduire.** See **conduire** (Section 20).

96. **rejoindre.** See **craindre** (Section 32).

97. **remettre.** See **mettre** (Section 67).

98. **résoudre.** Like **absoudre** (3) except: *pt.part.* = **résolu** and *p.s.* = **résolus.**

99. **se repentir.** See **dormir** (Section 46).

100. **rire**

> *pr.part.:* riant
> *pt.part.:* ri
> *fut.:* rirai
> *p.s.:* ris
> *pr.ind.:* ris, ris, rit, rions, riez, rient

101. **satisfaire.** See **faire** (Section 54).

102. **savoir**

> *pr.part.:* sachant
> *pt.part.:* su
> *fut.:* saurai
> *p.s.:* sus
> *pr.ind.:* sais, sais, sait, savons, savez, savent
> *impera.:* sache, sachons, sachez
> *pr.subj.:* sache, saches, sache, sachions, sachiez, sachent

103. **sentir.** See **dormir** (Section 46).

104. **servir.** See **dormir** (Section 46).

105. **sortir.** See **dormir** (Section 46).

106. **souffrir.** See **couvrir** (Section 31).

107. **soumettre.** See **mettre** (Section 67).

108. **sourire.** See **rire** (Section 100).

109. **soutenir.** See **tenir** (Section 114).

110. **suffire**. See **confire** (Section 21).

111. **suivre**

>   *pr.part.:* suivant
>   *pt.part.:* suivi
>   *fut.:* suivrai
>   *p.s.:* suivis
>   *pr.ind.:* suis, suis, suit, suivons, suivez, suivent

112. **surprendre**. See **prendre** (Section 87).

113. **se taire**. Like **plaire** (Section 82) except: *pr. ind. 3rd sg.* = **se tait**.

114. **tenir**

>   *pr.part.:* tenant
>   *pt.part.:* tenu
>   *fut.:* tiendrai
>   *p.s.:* tins, tins, tint, tînmes, tîntes, tinrent
>   *pr.ind.:* tiens, tiens, tient, tenons, tenez, tiennent
>   *pr.subj.:* tienne, tiennes, tienne, tenions, teniez, tiennent
>   *imp.subj.:* tinsse, tinsses, tînt, tinssions, tinssiez, tinssent

115. **traduire**. See **conduire** (Section 20).

116. **vaincre**

>   *pr.part.:* vainquant
>   *pt.part.:* vaincu
>   *fut.:* vaincrai
>   *p.s.:* vainquis
>   *pr.ind.:* vaincs, vaincs, vainc, vainquons, vainquez, vainquent

117. **valoir**

>   *pr.part.:* valant
>   *pt.part.:* valu
>   *fut.:* vaudrai
>   *p.s.:* valus
>   *pr.ind.:* vaux, vaux, vaut, valons, valez, valent
>   *pr.subj.:* vaille, vailles, vaille, valions, valiez, vaillent

118. **venir**. See **tenir** (Section 114).

119. **vêtir**

>   *pr.part.:* vêtant
>   *pt.part.:* vêtu
>   *fut.:* vêtirai
>   *p.s.:* vêtis
>   *pr.ind.:* vêts, vêts, vêt, vêtons, vêtez, vêtent

120. **vivre**

> *pr.part.:* vivant
> *pt.part.:* vécu
> *fut.:* vivrai
> *p.s.:* vécus
> *pr.ind.:* vis, vis, vit, vivons, vivez, vivent

121. **voir**

> *pr.part.:* voyant
> *pt.part.:* vu
> *fut.:* verrai
> *p.s.:* vis
> *pr.ind.:* vois, vois, voit, voyons, voyez, voient
> *pr.subj.:* voie, voies, voie, voyions, voyiez, voient

122. **vouloir**

> *pr.part.:* voulant
> *pt.part.:* voulu
> *fut.:* voudrai
> *p.s.:* voulus
> *pr.ind.:* veux, veux, veut, voulons, voulez, veulent
> *impera.:* veux *or* veuille, voulons, voulez *or* veuillez
> *pr.subj.:* veuille, veuilles, veuille, voulions, vouliez, veuillent

Index

85 86 9 8 7 6 5 4